CHRISTIAN IDENTITY CHARACTERISTICS
IN PAUL'S LETTER TO THE MEMBERS
OF THE JESUS MOVEMENT IN GALATIANS

CHRISTIAN IDENTITY CHARACTERISTICS IN PAUL'S LETTER TO THE MEMBERS OF THE JESUS MOVEMENT IN GALATIANS

CREATING DIASTRATIC UNITY IN A DIASTRATIC DIVERGENT SOUTH AFRICAN SOCIETY

JENNIFER SLATER O.P.

authorHOUSE®

AuthorHouse™
1663 Liberty Drive
Bloomington, IN 47403
www.authorhouse.com
Phone: 1-800-839-8640

Published by AuthorHouse   08/27/2012

ISBN: 978-1-4772-2694-0 (sc)
ISBN: 978-1-4772-2695-7 (e)

Emil Schönenberger and Family

CONTENTS

SECTION TWO
THE FORMATION OF A DIASTRATIC SOCIETY BASED ON GALATIANS CHRISTIAN IDENTITY CHARACTERISTICS

CHAPTER FIVE: "Inclusiveness" As A Basic Christian
Identity Characteristic Of Galatian Christianity

CHAPTER SIX: Paul's Ethics As An Established Christian

FOREWORD

This research determines the ground to distinguish the identity markers of ancient Christianity as set out in Paul's letter to the members of the Jesus-Movement in Galatia. The study recognizes that Paul's Christian identity indicators were not only a redefinition of the identity markers of Judaism in the light of faith in Jesus as the Messiah, but they served as an occasion to determine the identity characteristics of early Christianity detectable in Paul's teaching. It is apparent from the study that alongside many other identity markers such as *inclusivity, equality, freedom* and *unity in diversity* it is in reality faith in Jesus, as the Christ, that prevailed as the principal Christian identity characteristic. The latter characteristic rendered new meanings to old Jewish concepts. Since the Jewish identity markers stood at the center of the Galatian dispute, they also provided the essential framework to define and redefine the identity characteristics of Christianity in successive eras. This research sets out to establish whether the Christian identity characteristics, as identified in Paul's letter to the Galatians, have the potential to illumine the effectiveness of the eternal truths of Christianity in revolutionary environments such as the post-apartheid era in South Africa.

The thesis measures the spiritual and moral energy of the identifiable Christian identity markers against the concerned life situations in post-apartheid South Africa. These include the contrasting issues such as *exclusiveness, xenophobia, homophobia, gender violence, corrupt leadership and abuse of freedom*. The study discerns whether the primordial Christian features hold the potential to contribute towards creating *diastratic unity* in a *diastratic divergent* society where cultural, racial, gender and social alterity renders individuals to the periphery of the South African society. While "sameness" appears to be the primary force that consolidates a cohesive national identity, this research proposes that "alterity" within diastratic unity appears to be comprehensively more inclusive than the idea of unity in diversity. The study proposes that the work towards national unity in South Africa needs to consider all the ingredients of the plurifactorial dimensions of social, cultural, economic, gender, political, religious and class variations. This research is thus of opinion that the plurality of Christian identity markers possesses the potential and the eternal truth to embrace alterity and diversity in all its forms and even to hold it in balance.

ACKNOWLEDGEMENTS

I wish to acknowledge a number of people who supported, challenged and encouraged me in researching and writing of this study.

My sincere gratitude goes to Prof Benedict T. Viviano who served as a highly proficient and skilled promoter of this research. His crucial guidance, critical assessments, insightful and challenging questioning assisted and guided the unfolding of this work. My only regret is that I had to do the research from a distance as I am of opinion that regular face-to-face interaction with him would have been of greater benefit to me as well as to the value of this study. He displayed amazing scholarly insight, charity, encouragement and concern throughout the entire venture.

I also thank my friends in Switzerland, in particular Emil Schönenberger, his son Chris Schönenberger, Dorothy and Hans Brunner who assisted me with hospitality and accommodation on route to my visits to the University of Fribourg. I thank them for providing me with serene space for reading and reflection. I thank the authorities of the University of Fribourg, in particular the Faculty of Theology, who granted me the opportunity to do this research from afar.

INTRODUCTION

STATEMENT OF THE PROBLEM

The desire to ascertain some understanding of the continuity and maintenance of nascent Christian identity and expressions of being Christian in modern and post-modern times, categorically invites some analysis of Christian identity in antiquity, given that identity is connected with experienced continuity amidst the constant progression of change. Identity, no doubt, in its earliest definition is embodied and came to life in concrete situations and found expression in new realities. The identity of nascent Christianity was both embedded within the multiplicity of identity constructions of the ancient world, yet in some ways remained distinctive from them, and thus carried with it the seeds of the creation of a socially different world.

Christianity, however, always clamoured to be seen as implicated in, as well as having contributed to, the dynamics of the world in which it established itself. Thus in determining nascent Christian identity tenets, it is anticipated that one ought to look for continuities as well as discontinuities between Greek, Roman, Jewish, and Christian efforts to construct and maintain identity-continuities by means of interaction with the past and interfacing with various world-views. Another important factor that needs constant consideration is the relationship between local self-styled Christian communities with their respective modes of expression and inculturation, as well as with Christianity *per se*. The question is: what is Christianity *per se* today? This relationship in both the modern and post-modern periods had become an urgent theological, historiographical and ecclesio-political problem: the varieties of senses of identity among Christians still await to be unraveled, while partisans of the atypical manifestations of

Christian-identity-interpretations may not be desirous of any collective agreements and articulations.

As suggested by Judith Lieu (2004:2), one way of discerning how an awareness of being Christian emerged can be done by tracing the development of distinctive structures, namely the forms of ministry, membership and discipline, of collective decision-making, of worship and ritual, of distinctive patterns of belief, particularly articulated, but not limited to, creeds, a dynamic relationship to Hebrew Scriptures, and authority accorded to the growing new body of text and tradition.

Early Christianity was to some extent a de-ethnicizing movement, as suggested by Gal. 3:28 " . . . *and there are no more distinctions between Jew and Greek, slave and free, male and female, but all of you are one in Christ Jesus"*. This movement occurred concurrently with the expansion of the Church. Since early Christianity did not form a culture of its own, and neither did it claim to represent an ethnic entity of any kind; the challenge was that Christians had to invent new parameters according to which they could fashion their own identity. To this end Christian mission played a creative role in articulating the local identities, and even fostered group identities in terms of their specific Christian allegiance.

The Christian rhetoric of identity, even in making universalist claims, is articulated in terms also used in Graeco-Roman ethnography and identity formulation. This study sets out to ascertain whether the identity characteristics of Christianity, as articulated in and extrapolated from Paul's letter to the Galatians, still possess the moral strength of eternal truths to make a significant contribution towards resonant nation and identity building in post-traumatized societies such as South Africa.

IMPORTANCE OF THE STUDY

Once the identity characteristics of Christianity according to the letter of Paul to the Galatians are established, the study sets out to ascertain whether the identified characteristics possess the potential to make a constructive Christian contribution towards nation building in a post-apartheid South African that is riddled with diversity and alterity on the various stratum of society. It determines whether the eternal truths of Christianity possess the spiritual and moral energy to contribute towards the creation of *diastratic unity* in a *diastratic divergent society* where cultural, racial, gender and social complexities render some sectors of the people to the fringe of society. While "sameness" may appear to be an ingredient to consolidate a national identity, the study determines how sufficient the plurality of Christian identity features is to embrace the South African social alterity in all its diverse forms?

METHOD

The first part of the dissertation researches and evaluates the formation of the Christian identity characteristics since they were shaped within the environmental setting of the initial stages of the growth of Christianity in antiquity. Since the identity formation of Christianity occurred within the interface of Hellenism, Judaism and their respective academic climate and cultures, the thesis deals with material that is overwhelmingly prescriptive, theoretical, cultural and biblical by nature. The philosophical and biblical determination of Section One paves the way for Section Two.

The second section focuses on the specific exploration of the Christian identity characteristics as stipulated by the Letter of Paul to the Galatians. The study focuses on and how these respective characteristics relate to the contemporary society of South Africa and the feasible contribution they could render towards the construction of a united nation moving from the aftermath of division and oppression to mature liberation and democracy. The closing section draws conclusions and makes suggestions how Galatian Christian characteristics can make towards the formation of a diastratically united South Africa society.

PROCEDURE

The research consists of two sections each comprising of four chapters and a concluding chapter that presents concrete suggestions. The literature reflects the background scenario in which the Jesus-Movement and consequently Christianity took its roots. The exploration facilitates the intellectual and cultural complexity of the development of Christianity from a Jewish sect to an independent religious discipline with its own characteristics. However, the cross-cultural, multi-religious, philosophical and social contexts and systems of the Jewish-Greco-Roman world did not necessarily simplify the task of Paul in the world of nascent Christianity.

This foundational chapter deals with the formation of the New Testament identity characteristics. The chapter explores the idea of identity and identity-construction with particular reference to Christianity. It delineates the distinctive characteristics of identity formation and how identity is formed, discovered, preserved and how it can go astray. It also deals with mechanisms of maintaining and managing changes while claiming continuity of identity.

Chapter two places specific emphasis on how identity is formed in the interaction of various cultures, religious beliefs and practices such as Hellenism, Judaism and emerging Christianity. The central objective here is to identify some of the diverse factors that influenced and shaped nascent Christian identity characteristics in the Jewish-Greco-Roman world. The amalgam of religious practices and beliefs, together with cross-cultural practices and philosophical arrangements constituted a wide range of world-views that confronted Christianity in establishing its own identity tenets.

Chapter three focuses in particular on the Jewish-Messianic-Universalistic movement which constituted the rudiments of nascent Christianity. Christian identity structures would have relied on this background and it would have been most influential and instrumental in early Christian consciousness. The same conditions would have been operative in Paul's task towards orientating Christianity's sense of self-understanding.

Chapter four reflects on how Christian identity characteristics were fashioned by the content of Paul's letters to the Galatians. In Paul's effort to address the disputes and divisions between the Jewish and Greek members of the Jesus-Movement, he in fact clarified some of the fundamental Christian characteristics that were emerging in the process. This chapter also provides a detailed outline of Paul's letter to the Galatians and how certain issues that he addressed resulted in very specific characteristics of Christianity in antiquity.

Chapter five deals with the concept "inclusiviness" as a basic characteristic preached to the Galatian Christians. The inclusive nature of an emerging Christianity revealed itself by Paul stating that in *Christ there is no Jew or Greek*. This chapter explores how inclusivity was even a struggle in the larger Jewish-Greco-Roman world, but pointed out how the new-found faith in Christ envisioned a society that eliminates all kinds of divisions and differences based on race and nationality, religion and culture. It shows that egalitarian theology and ideology can be a reality despite differences.

Chapter six concentrates on Paul's ethics and how it formed part of his established Christian identity tenets. It examines Paul's ethics as a criterion ordained and shaped by him addressing concerned issues that the Galatians experienced. Identity here refers to the self-understanding that Christians came to develop and how they are to conduct themselves in the light of their belief in Christ. The reflection also endeavours to establish how Paul's ethical teaching resembles the content of Greek and Roman philosophers of his time.

Chapter seven discusses Christian unity of faith and love and freedom as befits the community of Christians that perceived themselves as the "Body of Christ". The sense of oneness which early Christians obtained by means of their close identification with the Risen Christ had many more implications, among other the egalitarian ethos of oneness in Christ. Christological love and freedom points to new life in the Spirit of Christ and it is a life that is lived in union with all believers.

Chapter eight is an attempt to recreate Paul's theological and ethical argument and by so doing measure the theological, social and cultural impact they may exercise in shaping a new emerging South African society that is morally and doctrinally healthy. It wishes to appraise the innovative dynamism and effects the Christian characteristics according to Galatians have in addressing some of the current major social problems experienced by the post-apartheid South African society. Issues such as exclusiveness, gender violence, discrimination, egalitarian ethics and misuse of freedom receive attention.

The final chapter serves as a summary that draws conclusions and makes a statement of conviction that the Christian tenets of Paul's message to the Galatians can be constructively utilized in creating an equitable social and political order in the new South Africa. The thesis does not present the final word on Christian identity characteristics. It is perhaps only a shot in a long continuous journey of Christian identification.

SECTION ONE

THE FORMATION OF GALATIAN CHRISTIAN IDENTITY CHARACTERISTICS

CHAPTER ONE

1. THE CONCEPT IDENTITY-CONSTRUCTION

1.1. INTRODUCTION

The prime purpose of this chapter is to explore the idea of identity and identity-construction or formation, be it of an individual, be it of a corporate body with particular reference to Christianity. It intends to delineate the distinctive characteristics of identity formation and to establish how identity is formed, discovered, preserved and how identity can even go astray and become befuddled. An additional focus of this foundational chapter is to establish mechanisms of managing and maintaining change while at the same time claiming continuity of identity. Establishing this foundational insight will, we hope, assist in the investigation of the follow-up chapter that focuses on how Christianity came to establish her original identity in an environment marked by sameness and difference, in a world that claimed both unity and multiple disparities on various levels. Stephen Neill (1962:36) maintains that the identity of Christianity has to do with what Adolf von Harnack calls *Das Wesen des Christentums*, namely, the essence of Christianity. This same notion is reiterated by Judith Lieu (2004:26) who in relating to the question asserts that to "search for the identity of Christianity is in fact to search for its essence". This is thus the underpinning position of this thesis, namely the understanding that to examine the concept of "Christian identity formation" is in actual fact to explore the "essence of Christianity" as well as establishing the art of maintaining its essence in different periods of time, in varied conditions and different environments.

The task of determining Christian identity is not a lifeless residue of a vanished era that no longer needs to be taken seriously. On the contrary the legitimacy thereof provides validity for Christianity today and for this purpose historical science has to come to the assistance of the search to determine how Christian identity was formed in antiquity. To this end this thesis affirms the view of Stephen Neill (1962:36) who believes that the search for the original Christian identity is to search for the voices of classical antiquity, in fact for the voices of the past in its entirety. He is of the firm opinion that if the Christian identity has to maintain Christian earnestness and liberty, as prescribed by the Gospels, then Christian identity requires firmness of Christian character, which is based on maintaining Gospel values such as faith, hope and love.

1.2. IDENTITY-CONSTRUCTION

The idea of identity-construction is a fairly recent concept in human sciences and can at best be regarded as an intellectual and ideological preoccupation that had entered almost all areas of contemporary discourse. While the idea has become ubiquitous, a broad consensus has been reached that identity formation is better understood and analyzed as a social construct. An elementary definition of either individual identity, or corporate identity, is intrinsically related to those distinctive characteristics that an individual or a group has internalized, that makes the person or a group unique and differentiate them from others. Judith Lieu (2004:12) is of opinion that corporate identity is conceptually dependent on the notions of individual identity. Individual identity, in turn, is constructed during the course of a person's life, from the moment of birth until death, distinguishing one person from another. Personal identity, which can be traced among other things to our particular genes, is inseparable from our bodies, our gender and sexuality, the culture and context in which we live (de Gruchy 2006: 44). As to how far the felt senses of corporate or individual identity are separable, interdependent, or derivative one from the other, that is still considered an open debate among sociologists and others who deal directly with this question. To investigate the formation of a corporate identity one would be expected to look at characteristics such as sameness, boundedness, homogeneity and the recognition of self by self and by others. In the effort to ascertain what defines groups, it will be essential to ascertain whether it falls under the same umbrella of beliefs that relate to nationhood and ethnicity. Awareness of sameness as well as of difference; of shared and agreed values; of continuities and of boundaries, whether physical or behavioural are all present, either implicitly or explicitly, whether people are Romans or Greeks in antiquity, or contemporary nationalities. This is how people view themselves and others, currently or in antiquity.

This research operates from the understanding that the construction of identity is not only about returning to the origins, but it also concerns the mechanism for managing and maintaining change and so to claim continuity of identity. Judith Lieu (2004:13) claims that the "essentialism inherent in the initial definition of identity lends itself to a primordialism according to which deeply rooted sentiments and ties predetermine other sets of relationships as non-negotiable . . .". But to look at the rhetoric of identity is also to explore how identity is discovered, preserved or how identity can be lost. Factors like history and archaeology, she says, have been frequently active or passive players in affirmations of identity, ethnicity or nationhood.

A system of symbols that people hold and that hold people is what constitutes identity and plays an important role in identity formation. The relevant symbols include meaning and values, as well as feelings about the meanings and values that are attached to and embodied in and by persons, things and events. The social system, as a system of symbols, consists of persons, self and others, things (nature, time and space) and events (activities of persons and things) that constitute the consensus reality of a culture (Malina 2001:22). To further this idea, Bruce Malina (2001:11) says: "Symbolism means filling people, things and events with meaning and value (feeling), making them meaningful in such a way that all the members of a given group mutually share, appreciate and live out of that meaning and value in some way". Identity formation is therefore a process of sameness and difference expressed by means of cultural symbols. Cultural symbols denote people, things and events in such a way that all persons in a group share the patterns of meaningfulness that derive from this symbolizing process. This awareness of sameness and difference of shared and agreed values of continuities and of boundaries, whether physical or behavioural were all present either implicitly or explicitly as Romans and Greeks viewed themselves and others. It is believed that Christianity in essence seized the high ground of the Graeco-Roman world and society and in this sense adopted some of the most respected models of the contemporary world, for example embracing elements of Platonism for its doctrines and guidelines to lead a morally pure life.

To have a strong sense of identity is no doubt an affirmative attribute, but according to R. Schwartz (1997:5) the construction of identity is not an entirely positive process by virtue of the fact that the formation of identity also possesses an inherent negative and destructive potential in this sense that it holds the power of labeling and exclusion. Labeling and exclusion are intrinsically discriminatory as they set people apart and focuses on differences and function on the basis of "keeping out" and "keeping in". Connected to this opinion Schwartz pronounces very strongly that: "Acts of identity formation are themselves acts of violence" (1997:5). She bases this assertion on the understanding that an awareness of sameness and of difference, of shared and agreed values, of continuities, of boundaries, whether physical or in behaviour are all present, either implicitly or explicitly in the formation of identity. Schwartz claims, however, that it is precisely this principle of difference and exclusion, the sense of what distinguishes one group from another, as a means of constructing identity that is foundational to establishing identity. This sense of what differentiated 'us' from 'others' goes back very early and the emergence of an 'ethnic identity' or of 'Greek self-definition' is already evident in the 5th century BCE. This must have been critical during the Hellenistic period as horizons extended and people located themselves within the wider world that claimed both unity and multiple differences. This sense of a pervasive self-definition present in the Hellenistic period forms an important factor in this research as it examines the formation of the Christian identity in an environment where there already existed strong established identities. It would be essential to keep in mind these views when ascertaining how much labeling and exclusion; how much focusing on differences; on "keeping out" and "keeping in" and how much violence was done in the formation of Christian identity in antiquity.

In a practical sense Jacques Dupuis (1997:15) explains that Christianity is everywhere conditioned by the historical context in which it exists, together with its cultural, economic, social, political and religious components. To assist his point he states that the roots of biblical religion are deeply implanted in the religious and cultural surroundings of Israel. The sharp self-consciousness in Israel of its religious identity as God's Chosen People often resulted in negative judgments on other religious systems, as they came to perceive other religions as idolatry. He maintains that it was the same powerful sense of identity and authority that prompted negative evaluations of other religions in the New Testament; less validity was attributed to any religious system other than Judaism and Christianity (Dan 7: 13-14; Acts 17:2-8; Rom 1:20).

Connected to the above notion is another important feature that facilitates the formation of identity, namely, the phenomenon of change, as well as the idea of encountering others different from oneself. By encountering different societies with observably strong identity structures and beliefs, one is inevitably confronted with the structures, beliefs and practices of one's own identity. In such cross-identity encounters one faces either change, submersion or resistance or all three. In the nascent environment of the Greeks and Romans, whose identity-construction was very powerfully supported by pertinent factors, they inadvertently or purposefully enticed others who lived in their world and on the margins of their environment into their worldview. Judaism formed part of this same world and the Maccabean literature attests to this encounter with Hellenism. While this encounter with Hellenism marked a new stage in the life of Israel, it ironically was also during that time that it became textually legitimate to speak of the Israelites as Jews. The rich diversity of the Jews, their thoughts, what they believed and organized became most visible, and thereby provoked the continuity of a debate as to what constituted the core of Jewish identity. The diversity of characteristics that constituted Judaism no doubt admitted a probable equivalent diversity in the primary terms of self-definition as they had to measure themselves against the radically alternative self-understanding of the Hellenists of the Maccabean era. In the identity debate, arguments range from whether Jewish identity in the late Second Temple period should be defined as ethnic or as religious or to whether there was a movement between the two forms of identity. Within the late Second Temple period and beyond, Jewish self-definition was evolving within the wider context of the Graeco-Roman world. The actual texts of Hellenistic Judaism reveals a range of nuanced interactions with contemporary strategies and components of self-definition, even while maintaining the distinctive moments and symbols of her own particular story. The diversity within Judaism extended into diversity in her interactions with the complexity of the wider world. No doubt this environment would have constituted the rich ground for the process of Christian identity formation.

1.3. IDENTITY-CONSTRUCTION IS TO OPEN ITSELF TO INTERNAL DIFFERENCE

It is evident that the distinctiveness of Christian identity was formed in a certain cultural milieu where the languages spoken were Hebrew, Greek, Aramaic and Latin and where certain religious practices and rituals formed part of daily living. In conversation with Jacques Derrida, John D. Caputo provides a philosophical reflection on the construction and deconstruction of Christian identity and his stance is that one cannot deny or renounce the idea of cultural identity; hence the idea that the Christian identity is its infancy was culturally bound. However, it had to be at the same time internally differentiated, opened up to divergence and differentiation if it was to become a separate entity. According to Caputo's views identity develops as a consequence of difference, where differentiation has to articulate and distinctiveness has to be named. Often identity is formed when confronted with opposites and the very points of differences become the criteria of identity formation. In his effort to construct and deconstruct the idea of identity Derrida attempts to distinguish an airtight, impermeable, homogeneous, self-identical identity from a porous and heterogeneous identity that differs from within itself (Caputo 1997:114). The question of identity and the development thereof, is to open itself to difference, to the significant opposite other. Developing an identity is similar to Hegel's idea of a W*esen* becoming itself, getting to be *bei sich sein* in and through difference (in Caputo 1997:117). Something that is self-identical is a dead thing, it is immobilized, and it lacks freedom, movement, life and history, such as a stone, a rock, something that is fossilized. Identity by its very nature cannot be a dead entity; though while it remains open to new possibilities and growth, it also remains faithful to the foundational essence that constitutes its original identity. No doubt the formation of Christian identity in antiquity could not escape internal differences, be they cultural or religious, even to the point of conflict.

If, as is presumed for the purposes of this research, Christian identity is based on the Galatian statement of 3:28 " . . . *and there are no more distinctions between Jew and Greek, slave and free, male and female, but all of you are one in Christ Jesus"*, then Christian identity was to wipe out differences, to be beyond nationality and national citizenship, something beyond what is geographically bound. Christian identity would therefore have been obliged to accommodate race, gender, nationality, language, religion 'in a nutshell' (Caputo 1997:117). *"Now there were devout people living in Jerusalem from every nation under heaven, and at this sound they all assembled, each one bewildered to hear these men speaking his own language. They were amazed and astonished. 'Surely' they said 'all these men speaking are Galileans? How does it happen that each of us hears them in his own native language?"* (Acts 2: 5-8).

To have been such a Christian community would it have implied having a common identity? Would this have implied doing away with differences? What constitute this common identity? Significant of the first Christian community according to Acts 2:42-47 is that they *"remained faithful to the teachings of the apostles, to the brotherhood, to the breaking of bread and to the prayers . . . . The faithful all lived together and owned everything in common; they sold their goods and possessions and shared out the proceeds among themselves according to what each one needed. They went as a body to the Temple every day, but met in their houses for the breaking of the bread; they shared their food gladly and generously; they praised God and were looked up to by everyone. Day by day the Lord added to their community those destined to be saved".*

There is, says Caputo (1992:117), an irrepressible desire for people of common purpose to join hands, for women and men who have dedicated or given themselves to an end or purpose to come together to dream of what is to come. A common identity would thus imply having a common purpose in mind.

1.4. IDENTITY-CONSTRUCTION AND CHRISTIANITY

Applying the concept of identity formation or identity-construction to Christianity is a curious phenomenon, and as it is the aspiration of this research to discern the emergence of "Christian identity" in antiquity, it is expected that this research will have to take cognizance of the given social, political, historical circumstances of the time particularly since Christianity interacted consistently with Judaism and her polytheistic neighbours. The formation of Christian identity is nevertheless housed in the proverbial question: how did "Christianity" emerge? How did Christianity come to articulate its own self-understanding with authority, autonomy and self-worth?

While the emergence of a separate Christian identity or self-definition and the sense of being a Christian eventually became apparent, this identity is often connected to the separation that took place between Judaism and Christianity. However, the proverbial question is: when did this separation take place? For Christianity to break away it is presumed that there had to have been some sense of Christian self-awareness or a budding self-definition already in existence. The prevailing question would be: what were the original ingredients that formed the rudiments of Christianity in antiquity?

To discern the identity structures of Christianity would imply ascertaining how to speak of the community centered on faith in Jesus Christ in the first century. The process of identity formation would have to consider whether Christianity initially was a self-contained phenomenon, subject to influences from the ideas of the time, frequently engaged in resistance to them, or whether it was ultimately either victim or beneficiary of external political movements. In ascertaining the identity of Christians it is well to determine whether early Christianity was a Jewish Christianity or a Pauline Christianity, or is there such a phenomenon as Jesus-Christianity? What was the post-Jesus formation of the identity of the Christian religion?

There is a tendency in recent approaches to speak of Pauline, Matthean or Johannine Christianity, leaving unresolved the question of how and when the sense of identity emerged, however theoretical or belonging to something that transcends the local. Does it mean that the approaches of Paul, Matthew or John determine a certain identity of Christianity or is there such a thing as a trans-local identity"? Can we today speak of Jewish Christianity or Pauline Christianity and if that be the case, what are the determining principles on which we base such an allegation?

Embryonically then, how did the formation of Christian identity occur? Was it a subversive course, or was it the result of political or social processes? An additional question to consider is: when did the decisive move occur when Christianity became identifiable in her own right? When did Christianity cease to be the Jesus-Movement within Judaism? When did Christianity and Rabbinic Judaism stop considering themselves and recognizing the other as belonging to the same religion? How much after the parting of the ways can it still be acknowledged that a great deal of the New Testament is an interpretation of Judaism?

Religion, like any social system, is a system of symbols that acts to establish powerful, pervasive and long-lasting moods and motivations in people, formulating conceptions of value objects. How did this occur in the embryonic stages of Christianity's development?

1.5. Conclusion

It is obvious that identity-construction is not a simple process and even to delineate the factors involved in the formation of Christian identity is not that apparent. But if the essence of Christianity is inherent in its identity, then to search for an understanding of how Christianity came to form its own the identity would make this research more than worthwhile. If the Christian identity is to be something porous, permeable, open-ended, affirming of the other, to be amenable to difference, intrinsically free and yet significantly unified, then it must and should be exceptional in its pristine arrangement and nature. The underlying question is: does the Christian identity adhere to the ordinary human procedures of identity formation? The following chapter will look at the Greco-Roman environment in which Christianity established itself. It will look at whether Christianity had to sacrifice or surrender any "essentials" of the Jesus-Movement within Judaism in creating its own identity in an environment where a manifold of identities were already firmly established? The following chapter will investigate the environment into which the followers-of-the-Jesus-Movement moved *on route* to the establishment of Christianity.

CHAPTER TWO

2. IDENTITY FORMATION IN THE INTERFACE BETWEEN HELLENISM, JUDAISM AND CHRISTIANITY

2.1. INTRODUCTION

There is neither Jew nor Greek, there is neither slave nor free, there is neither male nor female, for you are all one in Christ Jesus. And if you are Christ's, then you are Abraham's offspring, heirs according to promise (Gal. 3:28).

The central objective of this chapter is to identify some of the diversity of factors and influences that shaped the nascent New Testament Christian identity in a Jewish-Graeco-Roman world. In this world different societies were confronted with an amalgam of religious practices and beliefs, cross-cultural systems, various philosophical arrangements, together with a multitude of social factors that constituted a wide range of world-views. The all-embracing question is whether nascent Christianity could create a self-governing identity in an environment where a multitude of ideologies, philosophies and religions existed? While it appears that Christianity did manage to establish a distinct identity in its multi-dimensional environment, an additional problematic matter under scrutiny is: what precisely facilitated such a development in a milieu where other religious cults and practices expressed the identities of other multi-faceted civilizations of the time? This chapter therefore sets out to explore how Christian identity formation took place against the backdrop of the Hellenism/ Judaism "dualism", a "so-called dualism" that could not have been avoided in nascent New Testament times.

If identity is constituted by the formation of a group mentality, by the creation of *Gemeinschaft*, by means of kinship, locality, mind patterns, then it is presumed that Christianity in establishing its identity had simultaneously not only to establish itself within, but also to extricate itself out of, a complex network of legal, religious, cultural and moral systems. It is therefore presumed that the rudimentary elements of undeveloped primitive Christianity must have either inserted or extricated itself into and out of the powerful environmental forces of the ancient Hellenistic world. The significance of this inquiry is to determine the elements that favoured the formation of Christianity's distinct self-identity.

From the outset it was clear that the Jesus-Movement that was to become Christianity had to do so within the social, political, religious and ideological dynamics of the world, of which its adherents were inhabitants, namely, the world of the Eastern Mediterranean with its Hellenistic heritage and of the expanding Roman Empire. It was also a world that was in turn configured in its own variety by different worlds. Locating Christian groups within a social context of that time makes it imperative for this research to look at how Christians would have identified their sense of belonging in relationship to other patterns of belonging, for example in an ancient city, as well as in relationship to a variety of voluntary associations (Lieu 2004:4).

At this stage, however, this research intends examining the social settings of the Graeco-Roman-Judaic world, the intellectual forces of the time. It wishes to ascertain the culture and value-based systems as well as the society and beliefs within the context. It looks at the intellectual and anthropological settings of the time, which stressed the relationship between the conditioning environment and human/divine thoughts and actions that must have had an impact on the formation of a Christian identity or at least on the development of some sense of Christianity's self-understanding.

Christianity, in its infant stages, could not have avoided the most powerful, all-embracing forces of Hellenism. Thus the task of establishing its own identity in the light of this all-pervasive environment had either to have been a considerable challenge, or a good match for Hellenism. It is also possible that Christianity inadvertently or deliberately assumed the same *modus operandi* as Hellenism, hence its ability to deal with the force of Hellenistic cultural supremacy. On the other hand Christianity may have answered a need of the time that supported the formation of its own distinct identity.

Christianity and Judaism were always, and in various ways, exposed to foreign multi-faceted influences, and it was in the context of either being attracted or repulsed that their religious identities were established or otherwise strengthened, particularly during the Hellenistic-Roman period when foreign influences were most pervasive. It could have been expected that in the face of foreign stimuli either the influences were integrated into their own faith environment or they were out-right rejected, but whatever the nature of the encounter, it would have made Judaism as well as Christianity more self-conscious, more self-confident, and more self-aware of their own distinctive characteristics. It is also to be expected that in the face of many foreign stimuli the measure of self-identity would either have grown in intensity or would have been weakened or lessened by the deluge of foreign elements, so much so that it would have lost all claim to a distinctive identity. As both Christianity and Judaism are the only two religions of antiquity that survive until today, this fact of survival must be attributed in some way or other to a strong sense of self-identity or to compelling identity characteristics.

No doubt, there would have been some existing factors that were instrumental in shaping the New Testament Christian identity factors such as the historical tradition of Israel, the person of the historical Jesus, the Risen Christ and the influences of Jewish-Hellenism. As Christianity grew out of Jewish soil, additional influences such as Gnosticism, Greek and Oriental mysteries, magic, astrology, pagan polytheism, and popular Hellenistic philosophy would all have been mediated through Hellenistic Judaism. For these reasons it will be well to examine the **cross-cultural, multi-religious, philosophical and social** context of the Judaic-Hellenistic world in which Christianity had its roots. The statement " . . . *among all those who have been baptized into Christ there is neither Jew nor Greek" (Gal: 3:28)* is foundational to the query as to how much early Christianity was Jewish, and how much of it was Greek. By determining the unique interaction between the two cultures it may be possible to determine the distinctive character which Christianity assumed in the spiritual and intellectual confrontation between Judaism and Hellenism.

2.2 THE MULTI-CONTEXT OF THE HELLENISM WHICH LOCATES GALATIONS 3:28.

Just as the Romans were known to have masterminded excellent laws and constructed high-quality roads, so too was the Greek genius during the time of Alexander located in the ability to create and spread Hellenistic language and culture. In the areas of art, culture, government, recreation and religion the process of Hellenization proceeded apace with the Greek language as its main vehicle. "The concept '*Hellenism*' derives from the word *Hellas,* which is the Greek name for ancient Greece. The verb *hellēnizein* means first to speak Greek and then to live like a Greek, to imitate the Greeks in speech, clothing, sport, theatre, art etc," (du Toit 1998:133). According to David Stacey (1956:18), Hellenism was not a religion like Judaism, nor was it a school of philosophy, like Platonism, nor a system of ethics, as Stoicism, yet it affected everything: religion, philosophy, ethics, society, social and government structures, trade, art, language, recreation and culture. In reality it permeated every part of life. Its influence was not only subtle, but also extensive. If this was the cultural scenario into which Jesus came, then there was no likelihood that Christianity in its infant stages of development could have been exempt from the powerful forces of Hellenism. The commencement of Hellenism is generally dated from after the death of Alexander the Great in 323 BC although other historians date it as early as 360 BC. From a political perspective it continued well up to 31 BC although its cultural phase extended well into the time of the Roman Empire. It was Alexander the Great's aim to find a world-empire in which his Macedonians would live side by side with Greeks and non-Greeks, enjoying the same rights, intermarrying, honouring one another's customs and ideas, blending the different cultures into a whole. For this to become a reality he no doubt relied on the ascendancy of the Greek spirit and expected his world-empire to bear a Greek hallmark (du Toit 1998:134).

16

Hellenism, as a *compelling movement* of the time, did not replace the other religions, philosophies and institutions, but undoubtedly coloured, influenced and affected them profoundly. Its *modus operandi* was that it created very little, but modified much that was in existence. In the words of Stacey (1956:18) Hellenism could have been described, as "a way of life, an outlook, a tradition" that was noticeable, but at the same time it was also "elusive and inescapable". Hellenism was without doubt a world force to contend with long before Christianity came onto the scene. It was an all-encompassing power that all religions (new and old), philosophies, societies and political structures would have had to deal with. Given this state of affairs, it would be reasonable to ask whether Hellenism paved the way for Christianity. Did Christianity cleverly employ the legendary *modus operandi* of this great cultural force in establishing her self-identity, or was it possible that Christianity, as a new movement, became a potentially life-threatening force for the future existence of Hellenism? Be that as it may, Hellenism created a new culture whose influence is still prevalent today in the sense that it produced new types of literature, new technical sciences and a channel whereby intellectual attainments and cultural developments became the possession of all cultures and nations. In addition to Christianity, Hellenistic culture became the basis of present civilization.

As stated by de Villiers (in Du Toit 1998:136) the influence of Hellenism can be summed up in the concepts of *cosmopolitan* and *individualist*. One of the most significant characteristics of Hellenistic times is the disappearance of the ancient Greek city-state with its close structure, its own cultic activities and its devotions to gods and heroes. The result thereof was the breaking down of walls and divisions between nationalities, social classes, religion and cultures. Alexander's conquests opened up new worlds and vistas for the conquered people, so much so that people called themselves 'Hellens". Language differences lessened as common Greek, or *koinē allowed* people to understand each other. It permeated all spheres of life e.g., the juridical, the educational, the moral, the commercial, the industrial, and the religious.

Differences in race and social standing were no longer regarded as the primary norm by which someone's worth was assessed. It was a person's character that became the basis of appraisal. Even slaves and the two sexes, male and female, came to experience this change in social life. Slaves were treated as human beings and not as mere merchandise. Despite the fact that this was a slow development, the idea of a woman having the same rights as a man steadily gained ground in practical life, seeing that the man's interest was no longer completely absorbed in the city-state's politics and this allowed him to pay more attention to his domestic life. With the rise of the Graeco-Macedonian and Roman empires, participation in the government of a country was naturally restricted to certain individuals. The ordinary citizen could devote more time to his own affairs, his own home and family, his own occupation and business. With these changes De Villiers (in Du Toit 1998:136) maintains that the basic possibility for the development of personality was now evident.

In conjunction with all the above changes, the development of a free society, furnished with freedom of speech, freedom of association and freedom of professional choice, came into being. This issued in private ownership and a flourishing economic life. The concept 'freedom' became 'depoliticized' and individualized. It was no longer so much a case of external political freedom, but of inward mental freedom. However, this concept of inner freedom, which was attainable by everyone, even the salves, did not abolish slavery. Nevertheless, the real slave was perceived as the one who was inwardly chained by fear and evil. That is why it was possible for the physical slave to be mentally free. The new concept and appreciation of humanity, found particularly among the Stoics, did however eventually lead to slaves being treated better.

In this context one could say that the Christian message was first proclaimed in a world that was in many ways prepared for it by Hellenism. The Hellenistic disposition which guarantied and encouraged freedom of speech, belief and association would have been a fertile environment for Christian ideas to flourish. The adherents of nascent Christianity would have made use of Greek, which was understood everywhere. The appreciation of human beings and their liberty could be linked to the emphasis that this is precisely the Gospel which is intended for all people, of all sorts and conditions, as is evident and contextually expressed in the following New Testament verses:

> Galatians 3:28: *"there are no more distinctions between Jew and Greek, slave and free, male and female, but all of you are one in Christ"*;
> Col 3:11 *" . . . and in that image there is no room for distinction between Greek and Jew, between the circumcised or the uncircumcised, or between barbarian and Scythian, between slave and free man. There is only Christ: he is everything and he is in everything"* . . .
> and that it is Christ that gives true freedom Jn 8:36: *"So if Christ makes you free, you will be free indeed"* and

> 2 Cor. 3:17 *"Now this Lord is the Spirit and where the Spirit is, there is freedom"*.

2.2.1. Hellenism's philosophical and religious environment

As a historical movement Hellenism grew progressively out of a situation where people were looking for some belief system that offered redemption, personal communion and hope for the future. Put plainly, they were searching for a promise of immortality. The composition and nature of the ancient Greek religion could not provide for, or accommodate, this much-needed religious pursuit of the time. In reality the then Greek religion amounted to an uninspiring polytheism, which centered largely on a set of anthropomorphic deities that appeared stronger and more beautiful than mortals, though not more righteous. Educated Greeks did not consider these gods worthy of reflection, so as such Greek traditional religion had to give way to mystery cults which were considered worthy of thoughtful minds. It was easy for foreign mystery religions to take root in Greece, even though their worship was bland, e.g., the mystery cult of Eleusis that was fostered in Athens. By the time the golden age of philosophies arrived, two types of worship existed in Greece namely: the worship of Zeus and the worship of the mystery deities, and according to Stacey (1956:20) both kinds aimed at satisfying the religious instincts of the age. While these mystery cults were mostly uninspiring, they served a purpose for the time, in this sense that they at least offered people freedom, rebirth into eternity, a purified life away from the misery of Hades and some form of moral incentive. It was against this background, says Stacey (1956:20), that the great philosophies of Hellas made their appearance, with as their main objective to reduce the universe to a single force and thus to give it a type of monotheism on the one hand and a materialistic monism on the other. The gods, with their various functions, became redundant and in fact faded into the background and eventually from the scene altogether.

The golden age of philosophy was followed by military and political expansion. While Plato proclaimed the unity of creation as a copy derived from the good, it was the task of Philip of Macedon to make this unity of creation, of civilization, an energetic force. By now Greece had become a united entity, since each city-state, with its local religions, had lost its independence. This unity was the foundational element and life force of Hellenism. When Alexander moved to the East, many barriers of race, language and isolated communities were broken down. One large empire, with a universal organization, a common tongue and a common leader, was established. The Greek empire was held together as a cultural unity by means of the Greek language. The subsequent Roman conquest brought even better organization. A more stable political unity was brought into being. The most important aspect of or key to Hellenism is the desire for "the One", univocity (Martin in Troels 2001:55). Dale Martin (2001:56) is of the opinion that the Greeks themselves, with Platonism as its main perpetrator, saddled subsequent European civilization with the unfortunate desire for oneness, univocity and universalism.

The Greek speaking population of the Hellenistic world inherited from the pre-Alexandrian Greeks a variety of rich traditions in philosophical and religious thought. They were fiercely independent in this sense that philosophical and religious notions competed with one another freely in the market place of ideas (Newsome 1992:23). Despite the fact that there was a pantheon of Greek gods that had been worshiped for centuries, by the time of Alexander very few believed in them seriously. The Hellenistic world was not only a melting pot of diverse philosophical and religious teachings and ideas; it also provided a freedom for men and women to choose whatever doctrines they wished to follow. This insight is illustrated by the somewhat idealized scene in the Acts of the Apostles 17:16-34 which narrates Paul's encounter with the philosophers of the Hellenistic world on the Areopagus in Athens; it show a kind of ideological give and take that was commonplace in the Hellenistic environment.

This freedom of ideas had not existed in the earlier empires of Egypt, Assyria and Babylon. Instead, what existed was the worship of gods which was united to membership in the community of the nation-state, often with the king having the responsibility to promote and maintain the cult. In the case of Rome the emperor was worshipped, but in the Hellenistic society the free flow of philosophical and religious ideas would have had profound consequences for both Judaism and Christianity, especially in the latter's early efforts at expansion. Philosophical systems, important during the Hellenistic period, with deep influences on the development of nascent Christianity were *inter alia* Platonism, Epicureanism and Stoicism. In the effort for Christianity to establish its own identity it had no doubt to be content with the various ideas imbedded in these specific philosophies. There is for example clear evidence in the New Testament that Platonic philosophy found significant expression and influence in the content of the message of Christianity. Plato's ideas had significant influence on John the Gospel writer, while the Stoics could be detected in Matthew and Paul.

2.2.1.1. Hellenism's philosophical schools

As is the case in many societies, the schools of the Hellenistic era were a primary transmitter of culture. Education was sometimes privately provided by individual tutors, but most education was socially centered in the gymnasium where athletic skills and education in the arts were related to the worship of the gods (e.g. the important games such as the Olympic, Pythian, Isthmian were dedicated to various deities) (Newsome 1992:21). In the Hellenistic Kingdoms these gymnasia assumed a special role, as they became centers for the cultivation and perpetuation of all that was Greek, such as food, clothing, drama, literature, music etc. One way to become elevated into the Greek social upper strata was to become a pupil of the gymnasium. Here the young men in particular became "Hellenized" and this process made available new social and financial opportunities that were not accessible to their predecessors. The athletic emphasis of the gymnasia ensured that coveted awards were made available for excellence in performance and that their names were inscribed in prominent places to inspire future generations. It is evident that the author of 2 Timothy was familiar with the Hellenized world when he wrote:

> "I have fought the good fight. I have finished the race, I have kept the faith. From now on there is reserved for me the crown of righteousness, which the Lord, the righteous judge, will give me on that day, and not only to me but also to all who have longed for his appearing (2 Tim. 4:7).

2.2.1.2. The philosophical school of Plato

Central to Plato's (427-347) teaching was the view that ultimate reality exists only in ideas and that particular things we may experience with our senses are impermanent and unreal. The highest ideas are abstractions such as justice, beauty, truth, courage, self-control and goodness, and men and women achieve meaning in life by relying upon their powers of reason to incorporate these ideals into their day-to-day living (Newsome 1992:24). Plato is one of the main sources of the Greek dualistic views of human nature. The well-known dichoctomy in Western thinking between the body and the soul is a product of Platonic tradition (De Villiers in Du Toit 1998:175). He believed that the soul is a non-material entity, which exists apart from the body. He claimed that the soul is indestructible at death; that it existed eternally before birth and will exist after death. His doctrine of the immateriality and immortality of the soul is in line with his theory of the world of forms. In this context he holds that the soul and not the body attain knowledge of forms.

According to this dualistic understanding of human nature, Plato holds that it is logical for a true philosopher to long for death so that the soul would be released from the body as the body impedes the soul's function, especially its pursuit of knowledge. So the philosopher has little regard for the body and longs for the soul's freedom. A person can therefore never attain full potential while s/he is attached to the body. The soul is immortal and is related to the eternal, divine world of ideas (the world of ideas is regarded as the real world and the visible world is only a vague ephemeral reflection thereof). The body belongs to this ephemeral, visible world and is destined to be the servant of the soul. Plato maintained that the human person has to wait until death so that the soul can be freed from the prison of the body. Nevertheless, the soul can begin to free itself from the prison of the body in its lifetime on earth. Plato believed that philosophy is the means whereby humanity may attain this liberation by means of meditation and concentration on the soul. A Platonic way of life recommended self-mortification and self-discipline, to control and negate the senses, to limit the appetites of the body and to concentrate on the world of forms. Platonic philosophy urges the soul not to abandon itself to physical desires and emotions since experiences of joy and sorrow strengthen the bond between body and soul. The more the body is deprived and disciplined the more the soul can liberate itself from the body.

According to Plato the soul is the most important part of the person, the real person. Thus human fulfillment, meaning and destiny are not to be found in this earthly existence, but in the life hereafter. All the same Plato did not regard the body as evil, only that it is the fault of the soul that it is imprisoned by the body, seeing that the soul had erred in a previous existence. The body by itself is good, but is an unsuitable habitat for the soul. Plato believed in the theory of transmigration of souls, metempsychosis, or reincarnation. This philosophy claimed that if the soul had committed offences in the previous life it would be reincarnated in a new body.

Plato also displays some positives about the worth of the body. According to him if the body and soul were to find each other and cooperate with each other, the body would naturally heed the soul and serve it faithfully. If this were done on a regular basis, a good working relationship between body and soul could lead to a balanced life, hence Plato's respect for physical exercise. Yet this is only transient, as the soul will always be restricted. True Platonic spirituality gives preference to the soul; death is a moment of liberation.

Platonism continued as an important philosophical influence for many centuries and had an enormous impact on Christianity, particularly in its teachings on the immortality of the soul. In this philosophy the soul of a person corresponds to the person's body in somewhat the same way as the idea of a tree corresponds to the trunk, the branches and the leaves of the tree which we can see and touch. Since the soul has enjoyed a previous existence, upon a person's death, the soul returns to the realm of ideas from which it came. The Platonic view of the immortality of the soul was to influence later Christian theology in profound ways, many Christians finding it a more satisfactory description of life after death than Paul's doctrine of the resurrection of the body as explicated in 1 Cor. 15:1-58. Plato's immortality of the soul is, however, a natural immortality inherent in the soul because of its quality or nature. The philosophical theory of the immortality of the soul differs from the Christian doctrine of a life after death, the resurrection of the body, and God's gift of eternal life through the merits of Christ (De Villiers in Du Toit 1998:175).

Religion was nevertheless important to Plato; he did not deny the existence of the gods of Greek mythology. On the contrary he stressed the importance of worship, and declared that atheism is a crime punishable by the state. Yet Plato's gods seem to be philosophical abstractions more than living beings, and one senses that Plato's pupils often gave their deities little more than lip service. All ideas for Plato are summed up in one final ideal, which he calls the "idea of the Good", namely the principle of perfection. This idea of the Good can be regarded as Plato's closest approach to the biblical idea of God, but for him the good was a 'form' and not a 'god'. While Plato's thinking was deeply religious, it was the impersonal principle of perfection which he worshiped. However, by referring to the 'First Principle' which is absolute and unchangeable, the true Being, and to the divine principle of order in the cosmos, Plato prepared the way for the religious thinking of the Hellenistic era (De Villiers in du Toit 1998:175) Platonism continued as an important philosophical influence for many centuries (Newsome 1992:24) and evidences thereof may be found in New Testament writings.

2.2.1.3. The philosophical school of Epicurus

During the Hellenistic period it was especially the systems of Epicurus and of the Stoa which held greater attraction because of a shift in emphasis. The purpose of philosophy was no longer concerned with epistemological issues, but with the question: *how can a person live happily?* Ethics became the most important part of philosophy. With the disappearance of the Greek city-state, the state religion lost its significance as a religious factor in the lives of the people. Along with the mystery religions, philosophy offered a way out for those who sought a more personal religious experience. The role of the itinerant philosopher with his street preaching attracted the attention and interest or ordinary people; they became accustomed to this type of teaching. No doubt this practice laid the foundation of the subsequent proclamation of the Gospel by Christian missionaries who linked up with this tradition (De Villiers in Du Toit 1998:117).

The school of the Epicureans was founded by Epicurus (341-270 BC) He was a citizen of Athens who founded a school called "the Garden" because of where it was located. He turned his back on metaphysics, thus displaying differences from Plato and Aristotle, as well as Zeno's school, in this respect that he followed the teachings of Democritus, the Atomist, and regarded the particular arrangement of atoms in the physical universe as fortuitous. He claimed that the soul of the human person was composed of finer atoms, which dissipated at death, thus leaving no basis for any further life.

Ethics had a central place in Epicureanism. For Epicurus the senses may be relied upon, therefore what we see, feel, hear, smell, and taste is true and real. In fact, ultimate reality is to be found in the world of matter, which is composed of minute particles called atoms. Atoms are eternal and, because they differ in size, shape, and colour, they form a material world of varying textures and patterns (Newsome 1992:25).

Contrary to Stoicism, the *summun bonum* of Epicureanism was the pleasure of the senses, not the odd unnatural passion, but the integrated pleasure of the whole sensuous system. The aim of life was therefore the pursuit of pleasure; the avoidance of pain; morality was utilitarian.

The highest good for men and women is to avoid pain and to achieve pleasure. But because human beings are rational beings, mental pleasure is superior to physical pleasure. Because most pleasures that are overindulged create pain, moderation in all things should be considered a goal of the rational person. The highest pleasure is friendship and, in light of this belief, many Epicureans lived in secluded communities to which were admitted only those who embraced their philosophy.

Epicurus affirmed the existence of the gods on the grounds that, since human reason is based on the senses, and the senses tell us what is true, human ideas of the gods must be based in reality. But the gods, like human beings, are composed of atoms and are therefore mortal. What is more, since the gods are not concerned about human life, men and women need have no concern about the gods. Because God, in Epicureanism, was lofty and insensible, most teachers of this school were atheists. It is not surprising, therefore, that Epicureanism was open to corruption and that much self-indulgence occurred in its name. Stacey (1956:21) is of opinion that the self-indulgence that occurred in the name of Epicureanism could have been ascribed to the inadequate grasp of its true teaching. He maintains that if properly understood Epicurean's morals should have assisted a person's freedom and should have led to inward stability and peace. It should have liberated people from the bondage of fatalism and superstition. Epicureanism rejected unjust gods and the propitiation they required. While it offered no answer to death, it did however, soften the blow by stating that when death occurred and reigned there would be no more sorrow, no punishment, no bitterness, not even the regret of the loss of life. With such beliefs it was easier to resign oneself to death. Despite the influential impact of both these philosophical schools, they, failed to provide some credible form of belief system that offered redemption, and hope for the future linked to some kind of existence in eternity.

As stated by Newsome (1992:25) Epicureanism spread throughout the Hellenistic world and was influential well into Roman times, although its adherents were often misunderstood and vilified because of their tendency to seclusion. It is believed that almost none of Epicurus' writings have survived, but the Latin poet Lucretius (96-55 BC) eloquently espoused the Epicurean viewpoint in his long poem *On the Nature of Things (De Rerum Natura)*. The presence of Epicurean and Stoic philosophers is noted by the Book of Acts (17:18) in connection with Paul's visit to Athens as well as in 1 Cor. 15:32 where he writes: "If the dead are not raised,—" let is eat and drink, for tomorrow we die". This is most likely a reference to Epicureanism. Paul contrasts it with the Christian belief in Christ, which has significance for this life and the life to come. It is no surprise then that his audience on the Areopagus would not want to listen further to someone speaking about the resurrection of the dead (Acts 17:18). "Some also of the Epicurean and Stoic philosophers met him. And some said, 'What does this blabber say?" Others said: "He seems to be a preacher of foreign divinities"—because he preached Jesus and the resurrection. In Acts 17:32 it reads "Now when they heard of the resurrection of the dead, some mocked but others said, 'We will hear you again about this'".

2.2.1.4. The philosophical school of Zeno—Stoicism

Just as for Epicurus, for the Stoa the purpose of philosophy resided in the practical life. For the Stoics ethics was also the most important part of philosophy, whereas logic and physics were of minor significance. Stoic philosophy was propounded by Zeno of Citium, on Cyprus (c. 335-265 BC), who came to Athens about the year 300, and by his followers; the Stoics depended on Heraclitus, not Plato. The name of this philosophical school derives from Zeno's favourite place for meeting with his pupils, namely the *Stoa Poikile*, or *"Painted Porch"* in the agora, or marketplace, in Athens. Like the Epicureans, the Stoics were materialists, but they went beyond the Epicureans to identify the material world with God (Newsome 1992:26). In other words, theirs was a type of pantheism which stressed the unity of all forms of being: mind, matter, God, man/woman all constituted a unity. They claimed that the duty of a person is to live rationally, that is, within the laws that govern the material world. These laws were understood by the Stoics to be the Divine Reason or Logos. The highest human good is attained by understanding the nature of Logos and by submitting to it. Human emotions are to the soul as diseases are to the body. One must attempt to be free of fear, desire, pleasure, and the like if one is to attain the inner tranquility which permits one to live in harmony with Logos.

The materialism and the fatalism of the Stoics did not prevent them from expressions of deep beauty and piety. They regarded the soul as the spark of eternal fire. While they adhered to the natural order, the primary, necessary impulses of nature, these adherents in fact ignored inordinate emotional impulses, as they perceived them as unnatural and distracting to good reasoning. They considered reason as the light that enabled a person to distinguish between the good and bad; hence reason was essential for virtuous living. For them salvation consisted in the eradication of needless passions and the dominance of the will.

The Stoics employed the views of Democritus in physics in that they accepted law and order in the material universe. The *anima mundi* was regarded as the ultimate principle of life. The soul had no individuality separate from the *anima mundi* and hence the Stoics produced no doctrine of immortality. In moving from Greece to Syria and Rome, Stoicism picked up strands of other philosophies; according to the opinion of Stacey (1956:21) it ended up showing more non-Greek influences than any other Greek philosophical school.

The Stoics acknowledged the divine as the supreme ruling principle through which the cosmos originated and exists, but, because their theology conflicted with the current ideas about the gods, they sought a synthesis. According to them the goal of philosophy is ethics; and on the question as to how one must live, they answered: one must live in conformity with nature (De Villiers in Du Toit 1998:185). The cosmos for them came into being according to a fixed plan and is a perfect product of divine reason. In it humanity takes its own place and should not disturb the harmony thereof. This can only be achieved by living in concord with nature. It is by virtue of reason that correct insight into the essence of things is supplied and allows humanity to act and live in accordance with nature. While a person is subjected to the unavoidable, one must make oneself independent of everything that binds one to this world. Inner freedom enables the followers of Stoic philosophy to endure everything that happens to them. Stoic counselors encouraged their followers to control their passions, strive for inner harmony, not to fear death and to believe that they had been linked to a higher order. They preached the equality of all people because all share in the Divine Reason. This theory fitted in well in the Roman world-empire with its variety of nations and resulted in greater appreciation of slaves. Both emperor (Marcus Aurelius) and slave (Epictetus, former slave) could both feel at home among the Stoics (de Villiers in Du Toit 1998:186).

It is often asserted that Paul was a strong follower of Stoicism. There is indeed plenty of evidence to bear this out. In Acts 17:28 Luke has Paul say: *"since it is in him that we live, and move, and exist as indeed some of your own writers have said: "we are all his children"*. This quotation is apparently from the Phainomena of Aratus, a poet of Cilician origin (3rd century BC). Cleanthes, the Stoic, (3rd century) used almost identical language[1] In Phil. 4:11-14 Paul writes that he had learnt to be content whatever the circumstances. He says:

> "I have learnt to manage on whatever I have, I know how to be poor and I know how to be rich too. I have been through my initiation and now I am ready for anything anywhere, full stomach or empty stomach, poverty or plenty. There is nothing I cannot master with the help of the one who gives me strength. All the same it was good for you to share in my hardships".

In the words of de Villiers (1998;186) these words hold no evidence of an apathetic Stoic attitude, since Paul immediately added that he was able to do all things through Christ, who strengthened him. The acquiescence taught by the Stoics was quite different from the Christian endurance of which Paul writes in Romans 5:3-6:

> "But that is not all that we boast about; we can boast about out sufferings. These sufferings bring patience, as we know, and patience brings perseverance, and perseverance brings hope and this hope is not deceptive, because the love of God has been poured into our hearts by the Holy Spirit which has been given us".

Stoics disregarded all suffering, attempting to defeat it by a fatalistic and apathetic attitude of life. Christians, according to Paul who uses the Stoic ethos, can however, submit and accept suffering, because

---

[1]   Taken from the footnote in the Jerusalem Bible

Christ has drawn its sting, namely sin. *"Death is swallowed up in victory. Death where is your victory? Death where is your sting? Now the sting of death is sin and sin gets its power from the law"* 1 Cor. 15:55. *"Christ abolished death and he has proclaimed life and immortality through the good news . . ."* 2 Tim 1:10. Christians, says Paul, believe that Christ freed them from the dread of death. *"These are the trials through which we triumph, by the power of him who loved us. For I am certain of this; neither death nor life, no angel, no prince, nothing that exists, nothing still to come, not any power, or height or depth, not any created thing, can ever come between us and the love of God made visible in Christ Jesus our Lord"* (Rom 8:37-39).

The Stoic theory and practices obtained a large following. They certainly exercised a significant influence on the teachings of Paul. Paul adapted Stoicism to his Christian faith and this had a definite influence of his presentation of Christianity.

2.3. HELLENISM AND RELIGION

Religion in the Hellenistic world was not given to a fixed system of beliefs. As confidence in the old gods of Mount Olympus diminished and disintegrated new forms of philosophy, those with a mystical bent particularly were attracted to new religions which flourished in the Hellenistic period and beyond. There existed a teeming mixture of faiths and counter-faiths that often appeared mysterious and contradictory, but for the Hellenists themselves it was all a part of the robust, sometimes violent, energy that characterized their lives. Although religious systems competed with each other and with the various philosophies for adherents, they could at the same time also be flexible and adaptive when the need arose. Consequently, says Newsome (1992:27), it was often not considered unusual that a given individual might identify with more than one religious cult and/or philosophical system, or that the worship of a given deity in one place would have a quite different character from the worship of that same deity (who might, moreover, be known by a different name) in another place. Except, however, for the state religions which, to one degree or another, regarded the ruler as god and therefore had certain civil and political implications, there was usually no central hierarchy that defined "orthodoxy" or attempted to enforce it. As a result the lines between one Hellenistic system of faith and another are frequently blurred (Newsome 1992:27). Noteworthy of this was that Hellenism lacked religious dogmatism, resulting in the absence of a reliable religion. While Hellenism tolerated every kind of god in the Greek empire, none of them could exist and reign in single splendour as the rights to rivalry were both respected and tolerated. It was an age of wonderful religious freedom and this aspect was practiced with liberality. As there existed a perfect passion for cults that offered secrets of immortality, people could practice cult after cult, but no specific cult was in control or paramount.

Most significant of Hellenism was that, in the midst of the welter of religions and religious tolerance, there was at the same time a dominant and widespread search after monotheism, One God. In fact it was a search after one united religious truth. A main aspiration of philosophy at the time was to draw all the strands of religion together into one systematic whole. While Alexander was successful politically, in his efforts to transcend national states, to transcend national cults, to transcend one empire and clamour for one "inhabited world", one culture, worshipping one god, it was the search for religious unity that proved to be the greatest challenge for him and Hellenism. This search for the fusion of one god with another and to combine the divinity behind them became a typical characteristic pursuit of Hellenism. Many religions were solicited to make their contribution towards the process of syncretism. People of the time searched through many gods to find the perfect and living truth, the true way of life.

While Hellenism excelled in the process of syncretism, of endless combinations, drawing all foreign cultures together, the idea of religious syncretism proved far more complex for the ideologies of the day. Hellenistic syncretism included Gnostic systems, Babylonian mythology, Persian dualism, Egyptian mysticism and occultism, Orphic cosmology, Jewish theology, Greek philosophy especially Platonism and Pythanagoreanism. In spite of it all, no ideal combination was ever discovered. No faith won universal support until Christianity became the religion of the Empire of Constantine. No arrangement was found that could elicit widespread conviction or that dispensed with inferior elements.

This failure of a religious syncretism, so characteristic of the Hellenistic Age, gave rise to a deeper and more urgent longing for freedom, for redemption and for inward light. This sense of failure threw the later Greeks back upon their own soul, upon the pursuit of personal holiness, upon emotions, mysteries, and revelation, into a dream world where there is no sin and corruption. Civilization was seeking a truth that would show all others to be partial. It is against this background that Christianity was to establish itself, with Paul in the forefront. He incidentally in 1 Cor. 10:11 proclaimed that *"the ends of the ages has come"*. Paul was a fervent adherent of Judaism. For him the Greek and the Jewish worlds were not two separate entities. These two worlds were inextricably mingled and thus the followers of Jesus, and in particular of Paul, were at the same time both Jew and Hellenist. This combination of being both Hellenist and Jew was an ideal arrangement in answer to Alexander's problem in providing religious syncretism. Christianity entered the Hellenistic world characterized by so-called mystery religions that seemed to have met the needs of both men and women of the time. What significant contribution did Christianity bring, and to what specific need did it seem to respond in the midst of this religious mix?

2.3.1. The Mystery Religions.

The so-called mystery religions of the Hellenistic world enjoyed a wide following. No other form of religious expression of the time did. The detail of the manner in which each mystery was observed was a closely held secret and the knowledge was limited and reserved to the initiates of the particular cult. The word mystery derives from the Greek verb that means *"to close,"* in this instance *"the lips"*. Because of this secrecy, the information that became apparent about the mysteries became known through the detractors and, for this reason, has to be carefully weighed. In spite of this, certain features are recognizable as common characteristics of the mysteries as a whole. These recognizable features include:

- a rite of initiation or purification by which the individual is rendered worthy of participation in the activity of the mystery;

- a sense of personal relationship with a deity or group of deities whom the initiate now claims as his or her own; and

- the hope of life beyond death (Newsome 1992:27).

Some of the Mysteries were centered upon devotion to deities who had been venerated as part of the Greek pantheon for centuries before the Hellenistic period, while others focused upon gods and goddesses whose homes had originally been in the East or in Egypt. While there were many Mysteries in existence at the time, it is well to focus on two of the most significant Mysteries, namely the Eleusinian and Dionysian Mysteries for the purposes of illustration.

2.3.2. The Eleusinian Mystery.

This Mystery was practiced in Athens at a shrine in the town community of Eleusis and to a lesser extent, at cultic centers in many places throughout the Hellenistic world. It is clear that, in the beginning at least, this was a fertility cult based upon devotion to the goddess of the grain harvest, Demeter, and her daughter Kore, who is also called Persephone. What made the Demeter cult more than just another fertility religion was the process of acceptance, by a rite of initiation, into membership in the cult. Several stages appear to have been involved in the new member's initiation, but a climax came in a grand procession in which the members of the cult walked from Athens to the shrine at Eleusis, a sacred parade which was an impressive sight to see and an even more impressive experience in which to participate. Membership in the Mystery implied more than a simple association of like-minded persons; it included the promise of release from earthbound concerns and of life beyond death. It may be that the Eleusian beliefs included some expectation of a personal rebirth (as in the annual "rebirth" of the earth), but they certainly held out the promise that, for the believer, existence both in the present and beyond the grave was of a different order than for nonbelievers. Famous people that had been initiated into the Eleusian mysteries included the Roman orator Cicero and several Roman emperors including Augustus. They maintained that membership of this cult educated them out of a life of barbarous rusticity into civilization. The initiation ceremonies apparently provided them with principles of living and gained for them a way of living in happiness (Newsome 1992:28-29).

2.3.3. The Dionysian Mystery

The Dionysian Mystery was another popular Mystery Religion which was widely observed in the Hellenistic world, so much so that many local varieties flourished and by so doing a great variety of stories were produced that hardly cohered with one another. The symbols associated with this god of intoxication and fertility were the grape and the ivy plant, while rebirth and intoxication, even madness, were experiences often associated with them. Apparently Dionysus had a miraculous birth in that the great god Zeus rescued him as a fetus from his dead mother and sheltered it in the flesh of his own thigh until the child's birth. Because of his special relationship with Zeus, Dionysus could also claim to be "god's son".

Dionysus, who learnt the art of making wine, made his knowledge known throughout the whole world and survived a number of incredible adventures. Back in Greece he was greeted with hostility and was even put in prison. Various versions claim that he suffered a violent death at the hands of the god Perseus, who threw him into the sea. Other versions claimed that he is raised to life by his father Zeus and becomes born again.

It was not until Hellenistic and Roman times that this cult gained wide popularity. Several Dionysian festivals were celebrated throughout the year. There were often debaucheries of the most extravagant kind. The Roman senate felt compelled at one stage to curb the excesses of their rites by means of legislation. On the positive side as Dionysian rituals involved role playing by various participants. They laid the important foundation of Greek drama (Newsome 1992:29).

While the celebrations of Dionysus were associated with drunken brawls and orgies, the veneration of this god also functioned as a kind of Mystery through which the participants hoped to gain immortality. 2 Macc. 6:7 reflected the prominence of this cult among Greek speaking people when attempts were made to Hellenize Jerusalem. These in turn led to the Hasmonean revolt. It is an example how the Hellenistic religious expressions were forced upon the Jewish people:

On the monthly celebration of the king's birthday, the Jews were taken under bitter constraint to partake of the sacrifices; and when a festival of Dionysus was celebrated they were compelled to wear wreaths of ivy and to walk in the procession in honour of Dionysus (2 Macc. 6:7-9).

> "People were driven by harsh compulsion to eat the sacrificial entrails at the monthly celebration of the king's birthday; and when a feast of Dionysus occurred they were forced to wear ivy wreaths and walk in the Dionysiac procession".

2.3.4. The worship of the Ruler

One of the religious expressions worth noting during the Hellenistic period was that of "worship of the ruler", a practice that both Jews and Christians resisted persistently. The cult of worshiping special individuals always had a prominent preserve in Greek culture such as an "individual of superior wisdom and skill who benevolently but firmly rules the state" (Newsome 1992:31). The idea of attributing divinity to the ruler gained wide acceptance in the wider Hellenistic world more so than in Greece itself. However, the acclaim attributed to Alexander during his lifetime and thereafter provided new strength to the idea that the ruler was some kind of god. Sanctuaries and temples of worship of the dead Alexander sprang up, various places within the Hellenistic world and in particular in Alexandria, his final place of burial. This cult received additional acclaim from non-Greek people such as the Egyptians who regarded the pharaohs as divine since deep antiquity. Since Alexander conquered Egypt, his reception as the new pharaoh accorded him immediate divine status. In addition his designation as "Son of Ammon" was an early step towards his own deification as well as towards divine status.

2.4. HELLENISM AND JUDAISM

Since Hellenism were such an all-encompassing, powerful, movement, it would be academically naïve to think that Judaism would have had the capacity to escape the brunt of its influence altogether Israel, before and after Jesus, was subjected to even greater powers such as the Persians, Greeks and Romans. From the 4th century BC when Alexander the Great, King of Macedonia, conquered the Persian Empire, Israel was under the control of the Ptolemies in Egypt between 301-200. From 200 to 63 BC, the Seleucids governed Syria: the arrival of the Romans implied the collapse of Syria. Israel was under Roman rule from 31 BC and by AD 6. Judea was a province of the Herodians.

Of all the nations that conquered Israel, Persia, Greece, Rome, the Greeks, as claimed by Barnett (1999:48), presented by far the greatest challenge to her cultural and religious survival. The subtle influences of Hellenism (300 BC to AD 6) threatened Israel's covenantal loyalty to Yahweh. Israel was surrounded, indeed permeated, and penetrated by Hellenism. While Roman power was imposed from above, Hellenism seeped in from all sides, potentially effecting people from within.

Under Greek influence the Jews modified many of their ancient institutions as testified in 1 Macc. 1:11-15.

> Antiochus Epiphanes, son of King Antiochus, once a hostage in Rome, became king in the one hundred and thirty-seventh year of the Kingdom of the Greeks. It was then that there emerged from Israel a set of renegades who led many people astray. "Come", the said "let us reach an understanding with the pagans surrounding us, for since we separated ourselves from them many misfortunes have overtaken us". This proposal proved acceptable, and a number of the people eagerly approached the king, who authorized them to practice the pagan observances. So they built a gymnasium in Jerusalem, such as the pagans have, disguised their circumcision, and abandoned the holy covenant, submitting to the heathen rule as willing slaves of impiety".

They tried at all cost to resist the Hellenistic supremacy, but it was a futile battle. Clothing, music, architecture, recreation, games, legislation, all external things conformed to the Hellenistic ethos, though it is believed by some that when it came to faith and worship, the Jewish people stood firm in their resistance. However, judging from the nature of Hellenistic infiltration in the external, there appear to be enough ground for the hypothesis that there was a similar influence on thought and faith. The Greek language was spoken by many Jewish people of the time. It was used in the synagogues, in rabbinic colleges. The Talmud alone contains more than 1,100 Hellenistic words. Hellenistic synagogues and rabbinic schools in existence at the time taught Greek wisdom side by side with the Talmud. In fact the Scriptures circulated in Greek. But the Qumran texts were written in Hebrew and Aramaic.

It is common knowledge that the Jewish philosopher Philo acted in accordance with the syncretism of the age. He laboured to reconcile Judaism with philosophy. As a Jew he was of opinion that all wisdom was contained in Israel's divine revelation, but as an Alexandrian he learnt Greek philosophy and accepted as many of the tenets of the philosophy as was possible for a Jew of his day. In fact Stacey (1956: 23) claimed that Philo acted in accord with the syncretism of the age. In so doing, Philo tried to demonstrate that the truths of philosophy were already hidden in the Scriptures. To accept the one was to accept the other. Judaism and Hellenism could be joined without the loss of anything.

Greek learning was also evident in the rabbinic learning of Gamaliel who had exceptional close relationships with the Greek authorities. It is known that upper class Jews gave way to the practices peculiar to Epicureanism since there is reference to this in the Mishnah, i.e. the licentiousness of Jews as Epicureans. While the will to resist Hellenism was there Hellenization took place unwittingly. Yet, some tried to keep the fundamentals of Judaism unaffected.

2.5. HELLENISM AND JESUS

As previously mentioned Hellenism was pervasive in Israel before and after Jesus and as such Jesus was not exempt from its encompassing influences. Israel was subjected to even greater powers such as Persians and Romans. Our research looks at Jesus against the backdrop of the historical and cultural influences of that time. The conglomeration of Hellenistic powers that ushered in foreign influences during the time of Jesus stretches as far back as the 4th century BC when Alexander the

Great conquered the Persian Empire. Israel came under the control of the Ptolemies, 301-200, and under that of the Seleucids from 200 to 63. Roman rule was a reality in 31 BC, with Judea as a Roman Province in 6 AD.

Of all the nations that conquered Israel, namely, Persian, Greece, Rome, the Greeks presented the greatest challenge to her cultural and religious survival. The subtle influence of the Greek culture (named Hellenism) from (300 BC-800 AD) threatened Israel's loyalty to Yahweh as she was not only surrounded by, but also permeated and penetrated by, Hellenism. Jesus came onto the scene when Hellenism had seeped in from all sides and when Roman power had been imposed by military force.

Although Jesus was a Jew steeped in the Jewish Scriptures and religious practices, the culture and customs of the covenantal people, much of the environment of Galilee owed its character to Greek influence. Indeed the greater part of the economic, administrative and cultural landscape of the Galilee of Jesus' era was Greek rather than Jewish (Barnett 1999:48). Greek was the *lingua franca* of the eastern Mediterranean. As a language Greek would have been familiar to Jesus, even though there is no evidence that he was proficient in speaking the language. In the new Hellenistic cities various academic schools famous for Greek philosophy, history, mathematics, literature and science arose, and one of these centers of learning was Gadara, east of the Sea of Galilee. Jews of the upper echelons not only learnt *koinē*, the common religious language of the Hellenistic period, but also came to love things Greek, including religion and philosophy. Those who lacked the skills of Hellenism were conscious of their disadvantage. Various Jewish resistance movements against Hellenism sprang up during this time out of covenantal apocalypticism (Barnett 1999:50).

By the time of Jesus, many considered Hellenism, and certainly Greeks and educated people of the time, to have transcended smaller ethnic boundaries. While they may have had their own language, ancestral customs and religious rites, Jews were regarded as one *ethnos* among many, such as Lydians, Carians, Egyptians, Persians and Scythians (Martin in Troels 2001:30).

It was as Christ, and not as Jesus, that Jesus made his impact on the Greeks and Romans. Christians were called after him and as such the name was highly significant in the formation of identity. For the Greeks Jesus was the first name and Christ the title. For the Greeks this title was incomprehensible as for them it meant "the smeared one". To accommodate the cultural needs of the Gentiles, says Barnett (1999:21), the title became the surname, hence for them Jesus Christ. This very title aggravated the Jewish authorities who regarded it as a criminal offence. The identity formation of Christianity was largely due to the *kerygma* about Jesus, the Promised One of Israel.

2.5.1. The Jewish Jesus before Christianity

The complexity of the world of Jesus offers a fundamental orientation to the self-understanding of Christianity in antiquity. Hence to determine some form of understanding of Christianity in antiquity it is imperative to understand Jesus in his Jewish context. To capture an understanding of the historical Jesus is not easy. But some knowledge of first century Judaism may provide a fuller and more textured portrait of Jesus. Mary C. Boys (2000:87) is of the critical opinion that Jesus is not sufficiently situated in the complexity of the first century Jewish world and claims that knowledge of Judaism is imperative to ancient Christian self-understanding. Thus to establish and appreciate Christian identity characteristics in antiquity requires information about Judaism. This places the rudiments of ancient Christianity inherently within Judaism. It also requires us to engage in the complicated work of restoration, "removing the layers of supersessionist claims that have obscured the Jewish Jesus" (Boys 2002:137).

The principal factors of Jewish life, namely, the Sabbath, circumcision and purity laws would have been intrinsically part of the "Jewishness" of Jesus. Pivotal to Judaism at the time of Jesus would have been the belief that God had made a covenant with Israel. This was a dominant metaphor for Israel's relationship with God. Belief in monotheism was another firm cornerstone of the covenant with God as well as the Torah as expressed in the Shema (Deut. 6:10).

During the time of Jesus the treatment of Jews in the Roman Empire varied from toleration to protection, freedom of religion was permissible and they were subjected to heavy taxation. Judaic practices such as circumcision, observances to the Sabbath and dietary laws set the Jews apart from others nations in the Roman Empire. The Jesus-Movement with Jesus at the helm was started with the intention to reform Jewish life. Such an intention was not an unusual phenomenon during this time as groups such as the Pharisees both bore a similarity with Hellenistic philosophical schools and envisioned a way of reforming Jewish life. The adherence to Torah rules and engaging in these practices not only set the Jews apart from other groups, but also set the boundaries that enabled Jews to deepen their sense of identity lest they be absorbed into Hellenistic-Roman society.

Characteristic of Jesus' movement would have been a vision of a renewed Israel. This would have been similar to the renewal movements of his contemporaries, especially the Pharisees, but his teaching and life form would have been distinctive to himself. At the center of his preaching was a God whose reign was imminent. Jesus was an eschatological prophet who summoned Israel to live more justly in view of the judgment at hand.

In the words of Mary Boys (2000:140), the eschatological language of that period, the advent of the divine rule, did not necessarily mean a catastrophic end to all realities, but could instead refer to a revolutionary transformation of the world itself whereby the righteous and beneficent will of God comes to reign. The revolutionary transformation means reversals, the powerful dethroned and the lowly roused, the hungry receiving their fill and rich sent away empty (Luke 1:52-53).

Bruce Chilton (1997:12-13) puts forward five coordinates whereby God's reign was made manifest in Jesus' teaching.

1. The first is that the finality of time, God's rule, which exists in the heavenly realm (Psalm 96:10), is so near that it impinges on our experience. For this reason God's rule is to be prayed for as it is the divine imperative that in the long run will make sense of our lives.

2. God's rule is transcendent, transforming as silently and surely as yeast in dough.

3. Judgment is inherent in divine rule and like all other prophets Jesus calls on people to live ethical lives.

4. In addition to right living, Jesus also calls people to purity of heart.

5. To be included in the reign of God involves radiance or holiness because as people are transformed in purity the holiness of God is manifested. For Jesus the reign of God was not a concept but "divine activity itself".

6. A divine intervention in history. (Viviano 1988)

The Gospels create the impression that Jesus longed passionately for Israel's renewal and for this reason had little involvement with the Gentiles. In Matthew 10:6 Jesus thought in terms of the restoration of Israel, though he did not specify the means by which this restoration would happen. For this reason the mission of Peter, John and James to the Gentiles after committing themselves to preparing Israel for the coming of God's rule is regarded as consistent with Jesus' preaching. As pointed out by Boys (2000:142) the overwhelming impression is that Jesus started a mission which later, after his death (and resurrection) came to see the Gentile mission as a logical extension of itself. In this regard she claims that it is better not to attribute any explicit viewpoint to Jesus at all if one is to understand the debates among the early Christians. Jesus' renewal for Israel was based on an intimate relationship with God who is gracious and merciful.

However, the revolutionary power of Jesus' preaching contained the innovatory power of inclusion of the marginal (a characteristic that will be taken up by Paul's Christianity according to his letter to the Galatians). Jesus put forward God's awareness of the marginalized. Jesus' teaching on love of enemies and on non-violence, showed his anger at the condition of the oppressed, and this testifies to his emphasis on the inclusion of the marginal. In fact, as pointed out by Boys (2000:137), Jesus placed relatively little stress on the Jewish boundary markers in comparison to some of his contemporaries, regarding purity and Sabbath. Rather Jesus placed more stress on the nearness of God's reign, thereby revitalizing all institutions and that includes the Temple as well as the rule of the Romans.

2.6. Hellenism and Paul

Many scholars regard Paul as the Hellenizer of Christianity. Scholars regard Paulinism as the first step in the Hellenization of Christianity. For Christianity to obtain its own hegemonic position and specific identity it had to supersede both Hellenism and Judaism, though it would be expected for many reasons that Paul would have been directly influenced by the culture, philosophy and practices of Hellenism. Yet Eusebius, in his *Preparation for the Gospel*, insisted that Christianity is "neither Hellenism nor Judaism" but a new and true kind of divine philosophy, bringing evidence of its novelty from its very name. He perceived Christianity as superior to Hellenism, because he regarded Greek religious practices as polytheism. Because Christianity rejected idolatory he placed Christianity as a third way between Hellenism and Judaism. This was his way of identifying Christianity. His claim that Christianity is neither Hellenism nor Judaism is supported by his argument that Christianity contains the best part of both. Eusebius regarded it as true 'philosophy' on the one hand and the 'true faith' of the Hebrew patriarchs on the other hand. He maintained that if influence had to be considered it was Christianity that had influenced both Hellenism and Judaism (Martin in Troels 2001:32). If Paul were regarded as a product of Hellenism and Judaism, then Stoic philosophy would have been pervasive in the milieu of Paul in Tarsus. Paul's rabbinic training would have increased his knowledge of Hellenism. His letters bear witness to the revolutionary effects of the religious worldview of a Messianic movement *in statu nascendi*. Paul was both a mystical thinker and a messianic thinker.

Tarsus, the hometown of Paul, was a Hellenistic city with a reputation for scholarship. It boasted schools of rhetoric, teaching Stoic philosophy and the Greek language. Paul was a citizen of Tarsus and he was also a Roman citizen. This was somewhat unusual since Jews, according to Barnett (1999:259) did not become citizens in Greek cities unless they were quite wealthy and able to pay 500 drachmae, which was an equivalent of two years wages at that time. So for Paul to have been a Roman citizen meant that he belonged to the social elite of Cilicia.

Tarsus had a strong rhetorical tradition. It is presumed that Paul would have received a good education in Greek tradition, as residents of this city would have been required to possess some expertise in Greek speech and reading. Saul's family in Tarsus were *diaspora* Jews, though of strict temper in this sense that they were Hebrews, Israelites, descendents of Abraham, members of the tribe of Benjamin, circumcised on the eight day (Phil. 3:5). According to Acts 26:4, Paul became a Pharisee and a disciple of rabbi Gamaliel (Acts 22:3).

Paul displayed the mind of a Roman and appeared to have favoured Roman colonies as centers of his ministry. Towns, such as Tarsus, Antioch, Pisidia, Iconium, Lystria, Troas, Philippi, these were all capitals of Roman provinces like Antioch-on-the-Orontes, Thessalonica, Corinth and Ephesus.

If Paul was a Roman citizen, then Roman culture has to be considered in Christian identity formation. Many issues in Pauline Christianity can be pursued more in the light of Roman than Greek cultural background such as teachings about slavery and its metaphors; patron client structure; household structures and symbols; roles of women and their access to public life; the imperial cult along with its ideology and public presence and, indeed, the symbols of empire itself. According to Dale B. Martin, to ask questions about Hellenism or Judaism and to ignore Roman cultural factors or to collapse them into Hellenism, will not do (Martin in Troels 2001:30).

Monotheism, an identity characteristic of Christianity, was an attraction to Greeks, and hostility between Jews and Greeks like Antioch, between 30-40 AD, worked to the advantage of Christianity establishing itself (Barnett 1999:265). This would have turned on the issue of circumcision. Some Christians preached a Gospel which was free from the Mosaic ceremonial law; circumcision was part of that law.

For Paul the blessings of righteousness and the Spirit came by faith in Christ through hearing the Word of God. For him the truth of the Gospel, faith in Christ, was important. Paul had a confrontation with Christian Jews versus Gentile Jews, uncircumcised and circumcised, eating separately. Jewish Christians demanded that Gentiles become Jews first before they become members of the Messianic community of Israel. Newcomers from Jerusalem demanded the circumcision of Gentiles as a qualification of their inclusion of the people of the Messiah (Gal. 2:11-14) (Barnett 1999:285).

In trying to establish Christian identity, confrontation over Judaism had to take place with Judaic Christians. The circumcision party was composed of Pharisees who had become members of the wider community of the Messiah in Jerusalem. Paul also had been such a Pharisee. Paul insisted that no condition such as circumcision could be imposed on a Gentile to become a Christian.

Paul insisted that the truth of the Gospel and not the "works of the law" must be made obligatory for Gentiles. He was adamant that the free Gospel must be presented to the Gentiles. Faith in Christ is what justifies a person; the level ground is Christ, the love of Christ, who gave himself for our sins (Gal. 1:4). Being a person in Christ, Paul is now raised, justified with Christ to a new life of relationship with God.

> In other worlds, through the Law I am dead to the Law, so that now I can live for God. I have been crucified with Christ and I live now not with my own life but with the life of Christ who lives in me. The life I now live in this body I live in faith: faith in the Son of God who loved me and who sacrificed himself for my sake (Gal. 2: 19-20)

It is clear, however, that Paul was not a one-sided product of Hellenistic Judaism, but was stamped by a Palestinian Jewish apocalypticism that does not stand in opposition to the rabbinical tradition (Hengel and Barrett 1999:24). Paul, however, functioned out of Hellenistic Judaism, but posed no threat to Jewish monotheism. Paul, as a Jewish thinker, was a penetrating theological thinker, rooted also in Jewish mysticism and apocalypticism, though a revolutionary Jewish mystic (Hengel and

Barrett 1999:25). Paul's understanding of the economy of salvation, his growing eschatological universalism, in which he views the evangelization of the Gentiles as a kind of acceleration of the eschaton, are likewise rooted entirely within the scope of Jewish tradition.

Paul's ideas, dominated by the "antithesis of flesh and spirit", could be indications of Greek influence. The Baur and post-Baur school are of opinion that Paul's Christianity was Hellenized Christianity. There are of cause arguments that Paul was more a product of Judaism and his inner conviction testifies to this fact. While some scholars claim Paul for Hellenism, others claim him entirely for Judaism. Others, such as Albert Schweitzer, maintain that the Hellenization of Christianity only started after Paul, in the second century. To substantiate such a view Schweitzer claimed that Paul's thoughts came from Judaism. But Schweitzer posits different kinds of Judaism such as Old Testament Judaism, Hellenistic Judaism, Rabbinic Judaism and apocalyptic (Martin 2001:37).

2.7 JUDAISM AND EARLY CHRISTIANITY

Early Christianity, like Judaism, was always and variously exposed to foreign religious influences, but it was in such a context of attraction and repulsion that their religious identity was first established and strengthened. This is particularly true of the Hellenistic period in which foreign influences upon Judaism are said to have reached their climax. Foreign stimuli or influences were either integrated or rejected, but such encounters effectively made Judaism more self-confident and influential. In the words of Hengel and Barrett (1999:2), Christian self-identity grew stronger in the face of foreign stimuli. In other words, the more Christianity was exposed to foreign influences, the stronger her sense of self-identity became.

The burning question here is how much of early Christianity is Jewish, and how much of it is Greek? What is the peculiar interaction between these two cultures, which, as Meeks (2001:16) says, were habitually taken as opposites? Is it correct to assert that Christianity became the intellectual and spiritual battlefield on which Judaism and Hellenism fought their battles with unprecedented intensity?

Early Christian Jews came to believe in Jesus based on their Jewish roots and on their Christian experiences. Paul was one of them. Paul was not a one-sided product of Hellenistic Judaism, but stamped by a Palestinian Jewish apocalypticism that does not stand in opposition to the rabbinical tradition. Paul's original Christophany experience added distinct characteristics to Christianity. His revelatory experience of Christ as an eschatological Redeemer, the Messianic ministry, crucifixion and resurrection and the expectation of Jesus' coming as Judge and Redeemer, enabled Paul to bring the two worlds of Judaism and Hellenism together through Christianity.

It should, however, be noted that primitive Christianity did not simply take over the Jewish and Hellenistic terms, as would have been expected. Primitive Christianity reworked them and filled them with new content. Like every creative movement, they constructed to a certain extent their own language by coining words and thus developed their own Christian terminology (Goppelt 1970:65).

This Gospel was open to question Mosaic Law, so as to develop a Gospel free from the ritual Law for both the Jews and the Gentiles. This Gospel had to unite the message of Jesus and the Old Testament into a consistent unity (Goppelt 1970:66). In Antioch the Christians had detached themselves from the law for a reason just as obscure as that which had caused the Jewish believer in Jerusalem to continue to observe it. Both communities could only protect themselves from floundering into syncretism on the one hand and Judaism on the other by means of the theological development of the Gospel.

Paul was uniquely conscious of being called to this task. For this reason he emphatically referred Hellenized Christianity in Corinth, which was sinking into syncretism, to the Old Testament history of redemption (1 Cor. 10:1) and, the tradition of Jesus who had appeared in history (1 Cor. 15:1ff). Paul also rejected decisively any obligation to the ritual Law on the part of those who believed (Gal. 2:21).

Paul operated as a theologian, because he was an apostle to the Gentile people. He had given the Gospel of Jew and Gentile its fundamental character. Entirely on the basis of the Gospel he created the fundamental identity and structure of the Gentile Church. When Paul entered the Roman Church which had arisen completely independent of him, his kerygma, says Goppelt (1970:67), was recognized by its Hellenistic Christianity as authoritative.

2.8. CONCLUSION

The Jewish and Hellenistic environment formed the setting in which Christianity was to establish its own identity. The Hellenistic environment itself was subjected to various influences and Hellenistic Jewish Christianity did not represent a closed unity. However, the transition from Jewish Christianity to Gentile Christianity was fluid. On the one hand they showed this by the adoption of Gentile Christian forms by Jewish Christians, and on the other hand by the Judaizing of Christians from the Gentile sphere (Bauer 1996:243).

CHAPTER THREE

3. THE JEWISH-MESSIANIC-UNIVERSALIST MOVEMENT: NASCENT CHRISTIANITY.

3.1. INTRODUCTION

Relating the beginnings of Christianity to the context of Jewish history of this period constitutes the essential background in which Christianity established itself. As it was an offspring of Judaism, we expect it to carry features thereof forward into establishing Christianity's identity. In addition the process of Christian identity formation would also have relied profoundly on the central figure of Jesus Christ, the corpus Paulinum, the Acts of the Apostles, the corpus Johanneum, the Gnostic texts and the Fathers of the second century up to Clement of Alexandria and Tertullian. Directly and even indirectly these texts have the task to illumine the characteristics and motives of early Christianity. While Christian self-identity is a matter for open discussion, it is understandable that the early Christians were not simply a reformed group of Jews or Messianic Jews. This, says Hengel (1995:79), would seem to underestimate the degree of newness and discontinuity which they reflected. In Hengel's view Christianity may have produced some innovative ideas, something new over the Judaic and Pagan world; the movement was "something distinct and separate from Judaism (Hengel 1995: 80). Nevertheless, in 1 Cor. 10:31-32, Paul did not think of Christianity as a new, distinct religion, as a new group between Greeks and Jews. Instead he refers to Christians as the Church, as "the Israel of God" (Gal. 6:16).

In early Christian consciousness there existed a consciousness of faith as a universal movement and in this milieu Jewish particularism associated with election did not fit. Hengel (1995:80) argues that while the Jews used the Torah as a dividing wall, a fence or hedge that protected the identity of Israel, the Pauline Christians saw themselves as overcoming Jewish particularisms and saw themselves as faithful to God's revelation in the Scriptures. The charismatic, eschatological self-understanding of Jesus' followers enabled them to perceive themselves as having a mission to the Gentile world, indeed the whole world, and therefore there had to be no compromise with legalistic provisions such as circumcision. Jewish circumcision is a distinctive cultural ethnic identity that is valid for Jews, but not for others.

The emergence of Christian self-identity or of self-awareness was also born out of 'a crisis of identity' precipitated by the encounter between Christian and 'Gnostic' movements. The Gnostic faith was deeply anti-Semitic and anti-Hellenistic. The rejection of the radical solution of the Gnostics was important in the self-definition of Christians. The first phase of identity formation was to bequeath to Christianity a doctrinal and ecclesiastical structure sufficiently defined and sufficiently homogeneous to demarcate Christianity from sects.

In establishing Christian identity the line had to be drawn between Christians and Gnostics. The world of Christianity stood much closer to the tradition of Graeco-Roman thought than to the Gnostics. It was imperative for them to resist the temptation of allowing themselves to be sucked into the whirlpool of the esoteric sects that were prepared to be assimilated into the pagan world. The threat of being assimilated into Gnostic sects was a greater threat to the identity of Christianity than establishing orthodoxy (Markus 1980:7).

Christians in antiquity constructed a new world and did so through the evolution of a mode of living and a communal discipline that carefully distinguished Christians from their Greek and Jewish neighbours. They could do this partly through a discourse that was itself constantly brought under control and disciplined and again: "Christ was the Word, and Christianity was its discourse" (Avril Cameron). In this context, texts or literary material played a pivotal role in shaping Christian identity and in turn the texts were also shaped by the self-understanding of communities. This research will endeavour to ascertain the ways in which these texts function, but also how it can be manipulated in the creation and maintenance of identity. To identify identity, or a sense of identity, or to construct a sense of identity from literary texts, remains a difficulty since it only deals with the emergence of facts out of literary sources. Studies of identities in antiquities have focused on texts, not only because it is these that survive, but also because of the recognition of the constructive role of texts in that world, particularly of the Roman Empire. Texts, says Lieu (2004:28), would have shaped the self-understanding of audiences. By looking at Paul's letter to the *Galatians* as a major text, our research may come to recognize how Christians constructed a sense of distinctive Christian identity. It may be able to discern how a distinctive identity was constructed, an identity that came to be labeled as Christianity.

3.2. THE JEWISH-MESSIANIC-UNIVERSALIST-MOVEMENT: CHRISTIANITY AS SHARED IDENTITY WITH JUDAISM

Christianity is, no doubt, of shared identity with Judaism; the absorption of Judaic past into Christian present was one of the strongest statements of an urgent Christian hegemony. They possessed shared patterns of self-understanding. The Christian reading of Jewish texts read those texts as Christian texts and by so doing Jewish self-understanding informed Christian self-understanding. In the case of the Jewish self-understanding that was construed by literary strategies, these would have included rabbinic literature, the Dead Sea Scrolls including the Temple Scroll. Because Jews and Christians shared a common sub-culture and the literary focus was the Jewish Scriptures, Scripture would have played a major role in the formation of Christian identity. Christianity's construction of identity occurred under the impact of a biblically shaped literary culture, though it was not limited to biblical exegesis. While this reliance on Jewish literature was crucial for the establishment of Christianity in the beginning, in the construction of her own identity she had to go beyond the adoption, the interpretation and the expansion of Scriptures received. In fact the formation of identity required that she developed her own new literary corpus, with its own claim to authority, which will generate further adoption and interpretation. The actualization of self-understanding and self-identity relied on the formation of texts and later on the production of the New Testament canon.

Texts, asserts Judith Lieu (2004:7), played a central role not just in the documentation of what it meant to be Christian, but also in the actual shaping of Christianity. In fact she maintains that it was through Christianity's remarkable literary creativity and productivity that a multi-faceted self-conscious identity was produced. While the Jewish Scriptures played a pivotal role in the construction of Christian identity, the formation of Christian identity had a broader context: e.g., the literary constructions such as that of the Graeco-Roman world, as well as the wider account of the relationship between identity and texts (Lieu 2004:28). The Scripture provided the vocabulary of their Jewish and then Christian identity, and thus for those of Gentile background this invited a radical resolution or re-acculturation (Lieu 2004:40). In many senses it can be stated that the formation of Christian identity is in fact a re-alignment and maintenance of Jewish identity under new circumstances (Lieu 2004:75).

The construction of a Christian identity would therefore be associated with early Christianity participating in the rewriting, remembering and forgetting of scriptural history that was a feature of the diverse Judaism during the period of Christian antiquity. The preservation by Christians of the Scriptures in their Greek translation (the Septuagint) and also a range of other Jewish literature, from the centuries immediately prior and contemporary with their own emergence, was itself an assertive act of remembering. Lieu (2004:64) claims that remembering and forgetting is both essential in the construction of the narrative of identity as both include and exclude acts of power. The recovery of history, which is part of the construction of identity, involves a remembering that brings with it a new consciousness that in fact shapes a new identity and by interpreting the past is in fact one way of constructing the future.

Just as the Sinai experience (Ex. 19:5-6) could be considered as the identity-defining event of the Israelites, confirmed by Hosea (1.6, 9: 2, 25) stating that Israel is established as a people who once were no people but now a people (λάos) of God. These very sentiments are re-interpreted and expanded by Peter when he addressed the Christians as a "chosen race, a royal priesthood, a holy nation, a people set apart". For the author of 1 Peter there is a definite continuity between the time of the prophets and that of the audience of the letter. In this sense Scripture provides the vocabulary of Jewish identity, but for those of Gentile background this invited a radical resolution or re-acculturation (Lieu 2004:40).

For Christianity to obtain its own hegemonic position, its own identity, this thesis is of the opinion that it had to supersede both Hellenism and Judaism. Although the standpoint of our present research acknowledges the proposal of the History of Religion school of Göttingen, which claims that Christianity had its beginning with the purely Jewish circle of the earliest Jesus-Movement and ending with the wide world of syncretistic Hellenism, our research does not settle with all-inclusive certainty that this provided for the entire establishment of Christian identity. Dilbert Burkett (2002:57) writes that the Jesus-Movement was initially regarded as a sect of Judaism. Jesus was, of course, a Jew and as was expected he, no doubt, practiced the Jewish religion. His earliest followers were Jews and they continued to practice Judaism; the difference was, however, that they eventually came to believe in Jesus as the Messiah. The Jesus-Movement in due course became a new religion distinct from Judaism when the Gentiles joined and became more numerous than the Jews. It was only after the Gentiles entered the movement that the members received the name "Christians" (Acts 11:26), but Paul speaks of "those who are in Christ"; he did not use the term "Christians. Before that, in Palestine, it was called "the sect of the Nazoreans" (Acts 24: 5; cf 24:14; 28:22).

The Jesus-Movement, as a sect of Judaism and the foundation of Christianity, shared many similarities with other Jewish groups. With the Pharisees they shared belief in the resurrection of the body; they believed with the earlier Pharisees that the Law had a central core. Jewish Christians also shared similarities with the Qumran community in this respect that both groups believed they lived in the last days and regarded themselves as the people of the new covenant of the light as opposed to those of the dark. It was not surprising therefore that the

Jewish Christians felt the need from time to time to define themselves over against other groups or to defend their practices against the criticism of other groups. Significant of this struggle towards a sense of self-definition or self-justification were the so-called "controversy stories" (e.g. Mark 2:1-3:6-7:1-23:13-34). Many of these stories defend a particular practice and have the same literary form, namely:

* Jesus and or his disciples performed some action
* The opposing group criticized them
* Jesus uttered a short paradigm, apophthegm[2] that justified the practice
* Representatives of some group ask Jesus a question about some issue of Jewish belief or practice
* Jesus gave an answer that silenced his opponents (Burkett 2002: 58).

Characteristic of the Jesus-Movement was that it was perceived as a group of "wondering charismatics" supported by settled communities and had a message that reflected an ethos of homelessness, alienation from family and social units, and criticism of wealth and property. Between Jesus and his missionaries there existed a dependent-independent relationship in which the Holy Spirit provides a crucial link. Later on it became obvious that the Jesus-Movement differed from Gentile Christianity simply because the world of Palestine and the world of Paul differed vastly. Politically the world of Paul was one of cities and integrated urban centers and in Paul's world the sayings of Jesus mattered little and the Kingdom of God did not form a central metaphor. The pluralism and diversity within the Jesus-Movement were also unsuitable to the Pauline situation and it was precisely the notable differences between Jewish and Gentile Christianity that got Paul into arguments with Peter and the Galatians among others.

There can be no doubt that the Jewish movement functioned as a cultural and religious critique movement and when it became Christianity this function of the Jewish movement went into decline. Can it be that Christianity in antiquity deviated from the basic principles

---

2   A terse saying that embodies an important truth

of the Jesus-Movement and that later institutional Christianity became a distortion of the "traditional Jesus-Movement"? The perception that the principles of the Jesus-Movement and that of Christian origins should have had an impact on the formation of Christianity in antiquity goes along with the question as to how much of the principles of the Jesus-Movement had to be rescinded to make way for Christianity. Based on the assumption as pointed out by Luke Timothy Johnson (1996:55) that the origins define the essence implies that "the understanding of Jesus was necessarily better than any following; the original form of the Jesus-Movement was naturally better than any of its developments".

3.3. THE INTERLACEMENT BETWEEN JUDAISM AND THE JEWISH-MESSIANIC-UNIVERSALIST MOVEMENT.

Ever since the radical attempt of Hellenistic reform after 175 BC which threatened the Torah and the Temple (the heart of Jewish religion), and called into question the identity of Israel as a people belonging to and chosen by God, the Jews reacted distrustfully to any real or imaginary attack on their God-given entrusted benefits that set them apart from other nations and people. The Messianic movement with its claims by Jesus' disciples that he was the Crucified Messiah, the liberator from sin and death, resurrected from the dead, called into question again the most important Jewish faith tenets, though for different reasons. While the Hellenists did not threaten monotheism they did call into question directly the immanent coming of the Kingdom, the eschatological fulfillment of the Old Testament prophecy, the significance of the Temple and Torah. In this instance faith and obedience were no longer directed to the law, but to a messianic person, a mediator proclaimed by Isaiah 64:1. The new Messianic movement claimed that this prophecy was fulfilled (Hengel and Barnett 1999:9). This new Messianic movement of the Nazarenes, which claimed for itself the eschatological gift of the prophetic spirit, was also able to lay claim to some of the central doctrines of Israel's faith and did so with some measure of success. Both the novelty and the danger of the enthusiastic messianic *haireseis tōn Nazoraion* (Acts 24:5) lie in this central point of the person of Jesus, the Messiah, the *Mešīhā Yešua,* Christ Jesus, and the universal redemption that was put into effect. Later on Paul was regarded as the ringleader, the instigator of rebellion among the Jews (Tertullian) *"Messiah contra*

Torah". It was no longer Moses and the Law that mediated between God and humanity, but the Messiah, Jesus, the bringer of the new covenant (cf Jer 31-34). According to Romans 10:4, "Christ is the end of the law". The Messiah made salvation universal, for all, not exclusively to Jews only (Rom 3:20). Tension between the Messiah and the Torah e.g., the stoning of Stephan (Acts 6:13), caused the Jewish Hellenists to be expelled from the metropolis of Judea, so they became missionaries of the new Messianic Gospel in the synagogues of Syria.

This Jewish-Messianic-universalist movement, motivated by the new eschatological motivated mission, and which preached the effective reality of the Kingdom of God, shifted emphasis from Israel's exclusive existence and the earthly ethnicity of the Jews as a distinct political unit to a new eschatological and universal consciousness (Gal. 3: 26,28; Phil. 3:20; Rev. 21,22). Classical Judaism received its identity from emphasizing the unity of the exclusive Torah-bound religion and political ethnicity. This identity proved to be stronger than all other religious groups of antiquity; this reality is evident in the fact that of all ancient Palestinian religions only Judaism and Christianity survived (Hengel and Barnett 1999:12).

The identity of Judaism was deeply rooted in its belief that a personal God intervened in the life story of Israel. The Old Testament makes explicit use of 'covenant' terminology with the term *berith* referring to the free, gratuitous, personal, salvific intervention of God in the history of Israel. The covenant, according to Jacques Dupuis (1997:31), created the identity of Israel as the People of God. Therein one finds the foundation of Israel's religious experience, the beginning of a dialogue with God in the history of salvation. "I shall be your God and you shall be my people" (Lev. 26:12), such is the theological meaning of the covenant. The religious awareness, that the covenant has been attained between Yahweh and Israel, is really the consciousness that God and his people belong together in a community of life. This awareness of the personal irruption of God into the history of his people served in Israel as a point of departure for a reflection on the identity of Yahweh for them.

Another criterion for identity of Israel was their *monotheistic faith*. Old Testament monotheism was based on Israel's experience of

Yahweh's saving deeds. Rahner (1961: 93-94) explicates this point by stating that it became progressively clear to the Israelites that God was not only a powerful God to them, but to all the peoples, that God is "the transcendent cause of all reality . . .". The theological formulation of Israel's monotheism is found in the *Shema*: "hear O Israel: the Lord our God is one God . . ." (Deut. 6:4; Mark 12:29). This obliged Israel to preach Yahweh's exclusive dominion and the non-existence of other gods. This awareness on which Israel's identity is based and its vocation toward the nations raises the question of the *universalism versus the particularism* of Judaism. It was with the figure of Jesus that the centrifugal forces surging within the Scriptures break out into the non-Jewish world. Christianity, which emerged out of this Jewish-Messianic-universalist movement, become known as the new messianic, mission-oriented movement. The novelty of the movement was that it was able to call into question and challenge the existence of Israel as a distinctive, elected people, i.e. as a political-religious unity separated from the nations of the world. This novelty was later borne out by Paul who believed that the election of all believers is a reality in Jesus Christ (Rom. 11:26). This messianic, mission-oriented movement grew progressively in its awareness of the universality of its mission. The disciple first preached the good news of the Kingdom to the Jews; thereafter they spread it to the Jewish-Hellenistic world and then to the Greeks. However, the attitude of the early Christians towards the Gentiles was often complex and ambivalent (Acts 10:34-35) and when Peter preached to the household of the Cornelius at Caesarea, the Holy Spirit fell on all and this was a sign to Peter that they also were called. A vision brought Peter to the realization that the Gentiles too can be acceptable to God. In Acts 17:22-31 there is a witness to an open attitude of the apostles towards the "religiosity" of the Gentiles. In Paul's speech in Athens Paul refers to the one God who made the world and everything in it . . . and he refers to God's proximity to all people and that the religions of the nations are not bereft of value, but find in Jesus Christ the fulfillment of their aspirations. This type of attitude, claims Dupuis (1995:50), amounts to recognizing in the Greek tradition (Platonic and Stoic) a genuine "feeling after God". The speech of Paul inaugurated a missionary strategy based on a positive approach to the religiosity of the Greeks. This attitude also indicates the two great axes of continuity and discontinuity. Discontinuity places the stress on the radical newness of Christ and his resurrection; continuity underlines the homogeneity of salvation unfolding according to God's plan.

3.3.1. The Jewish-Messianic-movement's universalism and inclusiveness versus Judaic exclusiveness

The significant differences between the Jewish Messianic movement and Judaism surfaced instantaneously. As one of the attributes of Judaism lay in its identity as a nation, it became apparent very soon that Christianity could not be identified with a particular race or nation, since it professed universalism and inclusiveness. Characteristic of Jesus was that he possessed a moral sense that is universal, it was broad; his unconfined humanity and divine exaltation gave his person its ultimate significance. Very soon it was realized that the national Messianic idea of Judaism had a narrow and cramping influence on Christianity. The distinctive identity characteristics of Christianity become evident as it embraced universalistic traits and understandings. While Christianity concerned the individual, it was also truly universal and could therefore not esteem the particularities of any one specific nation, race or religion. Once the movement was distinguished from Judaism, it took on universalism and inclusiveness and Paul could thus express the same notion in the sentiment that in Christ there is "neither Greek nor Jew, slave nor free . . ." (Gal. 3:28).

3.3.2. The Jewish-Messianic-movement's freedom from the law versus Judaic adherence to the law.

A very strong and significant characteristic of the Jewish Messianic movement and later Christian identity that emerged was a Gospel free from the ritual Law and later also freedom from ritual circumcision as a compulsory identity practice for the followers of Jesus. Jesus' disciples established a religious movement, a messianic conventicle within the Jewish nation that was first faithful to the law and to the Temple. They considered themselves as the New Israel upon whom God's salvation had already dawned. Leadership constituted an enormously important role in the self-understanding of the early Christians. While the leadership was varied it was a true expression of their self-understanding as members of the Jewish movement. After the first Apostolic Council

(Gal. 2:1) a new form of leadership emerged: namely that of James in Jerusalem, Peter in his Mission to Israel, and Paul in his Mission to the Gentiles. However, the form of leadership that Peter exercised collapsed and disintegrated through the death of James in 44 AD together with Peter's flight and separation from Jerusalem.

According to Leonhard Goppelt (1970:300), Jesus who in fact came to fulfill the law (Matt 5:17-20) also admonished that people should keep the law. This juxtaposition is evident in the early struggle for an independent identity as the Christians went vacillated in their development towards the cultic and ritual. The initial perception of the developing Christian identity was not contradicted by their keeping of the Law and Temple observances. To the contrary it supported its self-understanding and even to a certain degree expanded it ordinances. First, as is pointed out by Goppelt (1970:30), was the freer attitude of mind towards these cultic and ritual observances evident in the struggles concerning the Sabbath controversies, clean and unclean food, circumcision and uncircumcision.

In the initial years of Jesus-Movement the disciples gave themselves entirely to what was new. In so doing they also permitted the old to remain. Through their witness they summoned Israel to repentance and ignored at first Jesus' demand for repentance from legalism. They were primarily concerned in their conduct to give a good account of their faith and their love and by so doing they also kept the law as this formed part of their life (Goppelt 1970:31). The first community made Jesus' critical statements about the law a part of its identity. Jesus' earthly ministry and with him breaking the Sabbath law did not mean that Jesus annulled it (Matt 3:16). To the contrary, his action demonstrated that total obedience transcended the law; in this sense the law's validity and invalidity belonged together. Jesus' affirmation of the law obliged the Christians as clarified by Paul in Rom 13 to live according to the law, but according to the pronouncements of Jesus Christ. This obviously implied a lot of tension and conflict with relation to the worldly order and especially in relation to the Mosaic Law (Goppelt 1970:31).

In the effort to establish Christian identity the Christian community had to confront the earliest Church environment whose social order was the

Mosaic Law, it was also the redemptive order of the Sinaitic Covenant. This was evident when Stephen brought forward the side of the message critical of the law and for Peter to abandon the commandment concerning clean and unclean food laws in order to remain obedient to Jesus' instruction of salvation for all by means of faith (Goppelt 1970: 32). The High Priest's executioner in the Temple killed the Lord's brother, because he remained to the end a witness of Jesus in spite of his obligation to the Law and the people under the Law. The Jewish Christians used the practice of the Law as the dividing line, just as the early Christians used only the confession of Jesus as the Bringer of Salvation who simultaneously confirmed and annulled the Law.

3.3.3. The Jewish-Messianic-universalist-movement's Missionary witness crossed Israel's boundaries.

Another identifiable characteristic of the Jewish-Messianic-universalist movement and later Christianity in antiquity is that the apostles whom Jesus had commissioned to carry out the mission, soon thereafter commissioned itinerant missionaries. They were commissioned by the Spirit to do so. The fact that every baptized member had become a missionary witness accounted not only for the spread of the faith, but also for identity formation (Acts 11:1 and 31).

The separation between Judaism and the particular communities that became "Christianity" was not a rapid process nor painless as is evident in the fact that Judaic boundaries such as circumcision, dietary laws, the role of the Temple, were among the issues that were passionately disputed by the believers of Jesus, both Jews and Gentiles. The conflict about what it meant to be "one in Christ Jesus" exacerbated tensions not only within the community of Jesus' followers as displayed between Peter and Paul (Gal. 2:11-14) and with other Jews (e.g. the polemical denunciation of the Pharisees (Matt. 23:1-36). Considering all the tensions the separation was quite prolonged and the boundaries between the two traditions remained quite fluid. In fact the parting is best described by Boys (2000:146) as the "Jesus Renewal Movement" that evolved into "Christianity" through a gradual, lively and complex process. While doing so, it drew from its primordial source namely the wellspring of Jewish life. Mary Boys (2000:147) claims that: "'Early

Christians' is an umbrella term for diverse believers in Jesus who held different views about their relationship to Judaism and who imaged themselves in varying modes". With the development of time this relationship took on different and new hues and so did the identity characteristics of unfolding Christianity, though for a long time the "Jesus Renewal Movement"/Christianity remained the so-called fraternal twin of Judaism.

The separation of the Jesus Renewal Movement/Christianity from the Judaism occurred in varying ways and degrees and not according to the popular misconception that this separation occurred in one fell swoop. There were no abrupt clear cut demarcations between Judaism and Christianity that brought about a sudden divorce at a given moment in history. On the contrary the separation was filled with such complex and multifarious overlays of issues that the parting of ways should not be oversimplified. The process of separation was not between just one group and another; it appears that it was a sporadic separation among different groups or communities and often for different reasons and this occurred also at different times.

Mary Boys (2000:150) puts forward a diverse number of issues that had been identified for the severance of splinter Jesus-Movement groups from Judaism. One of these was the fact that the early believers-in-Jesus possessed diverse points of view such as their views related to the synagogue. Their parting reasons, argues Boys, were neither orderly nor sequential. Mark could give the impression that the year 70 C.E. as the decisive date, while Matthew and John provide a more continuing argument about the synagogue issues.

Another point of interest is that the believers constantly had to explain their relation with Judaism while the Jews were not preoccupied with explaining their relations with the early Christians. The Christians perceived themselves as the rightful heirs of Judaism and yet had to defend themselves for not accepting everything in relation to Jewish custom, laws and rituals. After all the first believers in Jesus were Jewish Christians who confessed that he was the Messiah.

It can, however, be stated with reasonable conviction that Christianity's development in its initial stages was neither a unitary nor a cohesive process. The two religious entities were not two conceptually different religions with clear boundaries, separate identities and cohesive communities. The believers in Jesus communities lived in various relational degrees with the Jewish communities. Some separated themselves sooner than others. Others constantly drew upon Jewish communities for religious meaning and identity.

If Christians were to adapt to Jewish methodology of spreading belief in God, it would have set parameters to the Gospel message of the early Christians. For this reason the mission of the early Christians went beyond the boundaries of Israel. The Apostolic *Kerygma* (1 Cor. 15:3; Acts 2:5) which shaped the apostles' earliest preaching, namely the death of Jesus, the Resurrection and Easter witness, the *parousia*, the gathering of the redeemed community and the single eschatological event shaped the earliest Christian identity. The first preaching was also accompanied by miracles. For Paul the acts of miracles were signs that referred to the redemptive event and its proclamation (Acts 3:2). Only the witness of the Spirit in whom the Witnessed One worked substantiated the witness of the disciples. Through the witness of the Spirit the message became *kerygma*, that is a compelling and self-understanding authenticating address from God.

The distinctiveness of Christianity, also its unique identity, protected it against its multi-religious environment. This meant that its distinct identity which was first shared with ancient Israel, at the same time demonstrated that Christianity not only climaxed, but also fulfilled that which was true of Judaism (Meeks 2001:21). While the Jewish-Messianic-universalist movement, which grew out of Jewish soil, could be regarded as the earliest form of Christianity it was not called Christianity. This earliest form of Christianity, and later on, Jewish and Gentile Christianity, together with other influences evident in the New Testament, were mediated through Hellenistic Judaism. Jewish Christianity came in a variety of forms and not all displayed the same attitude towards the Jewish heritage. The new Messianic movement that consisted of Jewish-Christian membership from Palestine demonstrated knowledge of Judaism of both Palestine and the diaspora.

Evidence of this is apparent in the work of Paul, John, Mark, Matthew and Luke. It is believed that the author of the letter of the Hebrews was a rhetorically versed Hellenistic Jew who masterfully employed the Alexandrian art of allegorical and typological exegesis. Similarly too with the author of the first letter of Clement in Rome, who showed evidence that he must have been familiar with the liturgy and scriptural tradition of the synagogue. Hengel and Barrett (1999:6) are of opinion that what is often described in the New Testament as Hellenistic could very well have stemmed from Jewish sources that remained embedded in the religious *koinē* of the time. In fact Jerusalem had its own brand of Hellenism, which was different from Alexandria's, in that it was more strongly shaped by the ethos of the Holy Land, the Temple and its cult. Palestinian Judaism in turn also differed from Judaism of the Hellenistic Diaspora.

A significant identity characteristic of early Christianity was its strong eschatological emphasis, but it was nevertheless characteristically Jewish in detail. While the building was new, the stones by which it was built were intrinsically Jewish. The conflict between the growing normative Judaism and the new Messianic movement concerned central religious concerns, Judaism questioned Jewish theological belief, hope and practice. It had to do with the relation between messianic redemption and the traditional validity of the temple and the Torah.

In antiquity the identity characteristics of Christianity were shaped more progressively when Christianity was transplanted from Jewish territory to Greek and Latin territory. The transplantation of the Gospel from East to West was largely due to the work of Paul and by so doing he made Christianity "intelligible not only to the Greeks but to all people generally . . ." (Von Harnack 1996:177).

3.4. THE SEPARATION OF THE JESUS-MOVEMENT/CHRISTIANITY FROM JUDAISM: A DEFINITE STEP TOWARDS IDENTITY FORMATION?

The parting of ways between the Jews and Christians constituted an important step in the formation of Christian identity, yet as previously mentioned this process was relatively prolonged and quite complex. The coming into being of Christianity should not be regarded as a process whereby Christianity replaced Judaism and by so doing provide a reason for Christian triumphalism.

While there is a lack of resources that permit us to establish when precisely Christianity separated from Judaism, there are certain instances and inferences that enable one to indicate that partings took place.

The expulsion of the "Messianic Jews" by the conventional synagogue communities caused the Jewish-Messianic-universalistic movement to form independent conventicles. The believers in Jesus were not always of one accord in their own attitudes towards the synagogue. It was most likely that Jewish Christians went to synagogues on great feast days and also attended the new eschatological conventicles. Very soon it became clear that the new eschatological sect had become more than just a new synagogical assembly with some strange, but also many familiar, customs. There were already notable changes that the new Messianic community brought about. For example they read the old Scriptures with entirely new prophetic eagerness; they prayed according to the trusted form, but also in the name of Christ; they sang the Psalter, but also with Christological hymns; they lived according to the same ethical commands of Scriptures, but with new emphasis upon the commandment of love and they also abhorred idolatry and pagan vices (Hengel and Barnett 1999:31). Eventually they distinguished themselves by the good biblical term "*Ekklēsia*". *Ekklesia*, meaning the *qahal adonai*, understood as the "New Israel of God", the eschatological assembly of God that awaited the coming of the Lord.[3]

The growing distance that developed between the synagogue and the Messianic movement furthered the apparent identity-divide between Judaism and Christianity. This took place by means of various practices, *inter alia* liturgical rituals. A significant change was that the Messianic

---

[3]   Speaking about the Jews and the Greeks the New Testament makes a difference between the ethnic name, the Jews that is ethnic, political Ioudaioi and Israel, which is the holy name of salvation history. Ekklesia, drawn from the Septuagint, translated mainly qahal but sometimes edah, translated synagoge—with their eschatological consciousness, the Christians, as early as the Hellenists, deliberately chose the word ekklesia, in an eschatological sense as referring to the last true people of God.

liturgy was celebrated on the Messiah's Resurrection and a simpler codex was used for liturgical readings. The sense of a generational shift and the progressive estrangement that made the shift and the rift gradually unbridgeable was concluded by the destruction of Jerusalem together with the gradual new consolidation of Judaism in Palestine and Syria. The expulsion of Jewish Christians from the synagogue as well as the Jewish Christianity's concurrent loss of predominance put some finishing touches on the separation (Hengel and Barrett 1999:40). The consolidation of Judaism caused the gradual expulsion of nonconforming Jewish groups, groups such Sadducees, Boethusians, Essenes, Zealots all disappeared from history and the Jewish Christians were pushed into separation.

When Christianity became a predominantly non-Jewish sect (or community) the most important task was to define itself in a world that was profiled by late Hellenistic culture together with frontiers of the Roman Empire. The most urgent and complex task of early Christianity was to define itself as a distinct entity. and this says Hilary Armstrong in Markus (1980:74) was forced upon them. The believers in Jesus as explained by Mary Boys (2000:151) had to explain their relation with Judaism, whereas (other) Jews were not preoccupied with explaining their relationship with Christianity. The manner in which Christians understood themselves in relation to Jewish traditions was an internal matter, for example, the way they interpret Scriptures and building on Jewish prayers. Christians had to defend their relation with Judaism because they were criticized as claiming to be the rightful heirs of Judaism, while rejecting its community, laws and customs.

The self-definition of Christianity in relation to Judaism had important effects when the Christians of antiquity came to work out its attitude to Hellenism, both popular and philosophical and of the *oecumene, namely* the Roman Empire. One of the identity characteristics was firmly imbedded in the naming of the Jewish Messianic movement. The term Christianity, *Christianoi*, is a tag given to this Judaic Messianic movement by the pagan authorities of Roman Antioch in the late 30's AD. The term was in no way self-descriptive, but derived from the Greek suffix *ianoi* equivalent to the Latin ending *iani meaning* followers or adherents. The association of these Christian followers with Christ was a most prominent characteristic towards the identity of Christianity. They were followers of their leader, Christ (Barnett 1999:29). [4]

On the other hand, the Jewish description *nósrîm/ nasrâyyâ/Nazoraioi*, is derived from the origin of Jesus of Nazareth and usually appears like the Greek *Nazarēnos* as an epithet for Jesus in Hebrew. Noteworthy during the trial of Paul the rhetorical prosecutor from Jerusalem chosen by the High Priest Ananias, speaks of the Jewish sect as the *Nazarenes* (Acts 24:5) *hē ton Nazōraion hairesis (24:15)*. Whereas King Agrippa the Second during his interaction with Paul used the word *Christianos* (Acts 26:28), saying to Paul "a little more, and your arguments will make a Christian of me" (Hengel and Barnett 1999:7). It was hardly expected that the Messianic movement of the *Nazarenes* or *Christianoi* would result in a new religion alongside and in opposition to the Jews. It is not in the New Testament but in the apologists of the second century that the notion of the Christians as a third race or people alongside the Jews and Gentiles is encountered in the *Kerygma of Peter and Aristides*. What kept the Jewish Messianic movement from separating earlier was the thought of the coming *parousia* of Christ. It was the burning expectation of Christ's return that kept the inevitable separation at bay.

---

[4]   In the New Testament the term *Christianoi (Christiani)* occurs only three times and of these twice in the context of encounters with the Roman State. For the Greek ears the term should rather have been *Christaioi* or *Christenoi*. It was not until AD 114, that the Gentile martyr, Ignatius used the word with frequency and distinguished, also for the first time, between Christianity *(Christianismos)* and Judaism *(Ioudaïsmos)*. It is interesting that only towards the first decades of the second century that separation between Judaism and Christianity was finally completed and the former Jewish eschatological movement had been transformed into a new, more universal religion. The separation between the synagogue and the new enthusiastic messianic movement was a long and complicated process, but around this time 114 AD Pliny, in writing to Trajan about his views on Christianity, described it as a *superstitio prava et immidica (a degenerate and extravagant superstition)*. Thereafter Suetonius calls the Christian movement a *superstitio nova et malefica (a new and magical superstition)* but Tacitus still reports that this *exitiabilis superstitio (detestable superstition)* began in Judea (indicating its Jewish origins).

3.5. THE PARTING OF CHRISTIANITY FROM JUDAISM

Co-existence and confrontation, proximity and distance would have described the developing relationship of Christianity in relation to Judaism. The development of Christian identity was neither unitary, nor cohesive; no clear boundaries were evident in the first two centuries as various Christian communities lived in varied relationships with Jewish communities. Some separated themselves earlier from Judaism and others drew constantly upon their Jewish roots. What all these groups had in common is that they all wrestled with the fundamental problem of Christianity's relationship with God's People Israel (Boys 2000:152).

James Dunn (1991:24) proposes four pillars of Judaic faith whereby the Jesus-Movement had constantly to refine themselves in relation to mainstream Judaism and thus to a lesser or greater degree "Christianity" and "Judaism" eventually parted ways. The four pillars identified by Dunn are: *Monotheism* (God is One); *election* (a covenant people and a promised land); *a covenant focused on the Torah* (covenantal nomism) and *land focused in the Temple*. In addition to this Dunn discerns three so-called partings or separations between the Jesus-Movement and Judaism: the first happened over the Temple, the second in regard to the Gentile mission (involving covenantal nomism and election) and the third because of the Christian movement's affirmation of Jesus as the Divine Word/Wisdom-becoming flesh (Dunn 1991:35). While these are the views of James Dunn there is no conclusive evidence that these issues brought about the definitive and universal separation of Christianity from Judaism. However, it is worth examining the proposition.

3.5.1. The Temple expulsion

Though Jesus was very critical in his actions and words towards the temple cult with regard to the purity rituals and norms, he was not alone in this. Even though the Gospels recount his fierce priestly reaction to the cleansing of the Temple, these events do not suggest that Jesus' teaching required a break with the Temple. The Jesus-followers remained loyal to the Temple. The collision came between the Hebrews and the Hellenists who were divided over the role of the Temple and the preaching and martyrdom of Stephen initiated a radical critique of the Temple and its role in the life of the young Christian movement. Stephen asserted: "Yet the Most High does not dwell in houses made with human hands" (Acts 7:48). This, according to Dunn, implies that Stephen regarded the Temple as an idol *(cheiropoieton)*. It is most likely at this time that the Hellenists like Stephen focused on their own house liturgy and regarded it as more meaningful than the Temple and its sacrifices, because Jesus' death brought an end all other sacrifices.

Paul also contributed to the interpretation of the Temple by giving it an additional slant in the sense that he transposed the Temple from a geographical place to persons and their relationship with God through the Spirit. In 1 Cor. 3:16-17 he says: "Do you not know that you are God's Temple and that God's Spirit dwells in you? If anyone destroys God's Temple, God will destroy that person. For God's Temple is holy, and you are that Temple". For Paul the divine presence lodges in the person of Christ rather than in the sacred building represented by the Temple (1 Cor. 12:12-30). He speaks of Christ's death as a sacrifice that precludes the Temple sacrifice (Rom 8:3; 2 Cor. 5:21). While Paul spiritualized or transposed the Temple sacrifice, the writer of the letter to the Hebrews subverted it completely by claiming that Jesus' sacrificial death superseded the traditional Jewish rituals of repeated sacrifice performed by the Aaronic priests. This indicates that a new era has dawned for the followers of Christ who maintained that a Judaism that focused on the Temple and its cult is no longer of relevance as it had been supplanted by new meanings provided by the life and death of Jesus Christ. This as discerned by Dunn provided a "decisive breach" from the essentials of Judaism.

3.5.2. Covenantal nomism and election

The second determined argument, put forward by Dunn, that provided a basis for the believers in Jesus to part from Judaism was the issues surrounding the covenant and in particular the matter of circumcision which was regarded as the outward sign of the individual's covenantal commitment to God. There were also other very important everyday markers in the form of dietary laws and regulations, ritual cleanliness or purity laws that were fundamental to the daily practices of Jewish life. These particular rituals and practices became the very problematic obstacles to include those who were not Jewish, but believers in Jesus. Were they to be included in the Jewish community? As will be observed in detail at a later stage in this research Paul addressed this issue in his letter to the Galatians in a very commanding manner, referring to his conflict with Peter concerning this very topic (Gal. 2:11-14).

The conflict that existed over the covenant was felt in different camps: for James and for Peter (to a certain extent) the logic of the covenant meant that God's covenant with the Jewish people can be extended to those not Jewish, on condition that they keep the law that governed that life of the Israelites. Paul's logic seemed to differ in this sense that he believed similar to James and Peter that one enters into the membership of God's people through faith, however, and this is where they began to differ, Paul did not regard circumcision as a necessary means to enter this covenantal relationship. Paul argued that belonging to the people of the covenant rests on faith, not on the laws about food and the community of the table (Boys 2000:156). In the words and opinion of Dunn (1994:133), Paul's view that faith in Christ "is the climax of faith; faith should not be made to depend in any degree on the believer living as a Jew".

These views of Paul indicated a definite break with other leaders and their traditional views. The covenantal relationship and the practice of circumcision and other related issues that commanded obedience to the law constituted one of the foundational pillars of the Jewish community life and religion. While Paul was not opposed to the law or against any form of "good works" he was dead against interpreting the law in a manner that limits God's grace and prevents the Gentiles from participating fully in the covenantal life with God. Paul does not deny that God had called the Jewish people in a very special way, but now God had extended this calling to others, who are not Jews, as well. What emerged at this early stage already is that "inclusivity" is regarded as foundational to Paul's original principles for Christianity. (This principle will receive detailed attention at a later stage in the research.)

Dunn is nevertheless of opinion that this matter did not constitute sufficient cause for a full split between the followers-of-the-Jesus-

Movement and Judaism, and what ultimately made the split inevitable was the theological reflection on the resurrection and incarnation.

3.5.3. The declaration of Jesus as the Divine Word/ Wisdom-becoming flesh

While Jesus claimed insights into God's will, professing to speak on behalf of God, he remained firmly within the boundaries of Judaism which did not become Christianity. Moreover, the initial Christology that arose out of the resurrection remained within Jewish categories, however, the emphasis on Jesus' oneness with God, Jesus as the Son of God, his manifestation as wisdom incarnate was perceived as threatening to the revelatory status of the Torah and the embodiment of divine Wisdom (Boys 2000:157). These Christological claims, evident in the Gospel of John, resulted in a debate around the understanding of God and indeed about monotheism. These Christological claims caused the rabbi's to defend the unity of God and ultimately to claim simultaneously to be a "follower" of Jesus (a Christian) and a Jew became increasingly more difficult to hold in balance. The understanding about God steered directly towards a separation, but the parting was not clear cut, it did not occur in one swoop moment. In fact there exist no evidence of a clean delineation of separation between Christian and Jews.

Nevertheless, while there are attempts among scholars to delineate an exact time when a definite separation took place between Jews and Christians, the overwhelming impression is that early followers of Christ experienced no apparent difficulty in combining allegiance to Jesus with a respect for Judaism. This was often evident in the fact that ordinary Christians in antiquity took active part in the life of the synagogue, upheld Jewish customs and celebrated Jewish festivals. The divisive issues appeared to be concerns more of those who held positions of power and those who claimed religious authority.

The separation between Jews and Christians cannot be oversimplified as this forms part of an erroneous understanding of the formation of Christianity in antiquity. While such issues as the divinity of Christ did become a theologically divisive issue between Jews and Christians, the actual separation occurred much later. Often there were problems experienced between Jews and Christians that were also problems among Christians themselves such as worship in the Temple and food laws.

3.6. CONCLUSION

Christianity in antiquity was a complex phenomenon and was found both in the Palestinian and Hellenistic environment and it was no doubt subjected to various influences. Early Christianity in all its diversified appearances, including its so-called orthodox developments, was a thoroughly syncretistic 'religion' due to the fact that it assimilated and absorbed a staggering quantity of outside influences. In the opinion of Helmut Koester (1971:115) to label the most earliest form of Christianity as Jewish Christianity is misleading since everyone in the first generation of Christianity was a Jewish-Christian and thus both Jewish traditions and Jewish thought, including the Old Testament, continued to exert considerable influence upon almost all the development of early Christianity and for a long time since. While the very early Christian congregations understood themselves as part of the religious community of Judaism there was nevertheless no uniformity in beliefs and institutions (Koester 1971:120). How then did Christianity in antiquity develop a distinctive identity if it was known as a religious movement, the Jesus-Movement, which is syncretistic in appearance and conspicuously marked by diversification from the beginning? What the individuality of Christianity was to become, could, according to this research, not be taken as an established priori since Christianity in antiquity was understood as a heretical diversification and aberrations from the original true anachronistic formulation of the Jewish faith.

The environment wherein Christianity owes its origins were marked by divisive conflicts of early Christianity which initially centered on the circumstances of Stephen's martyrdom (Acts 6:1-8; 5); the Apostles' Council in Jerusalem and the incident in Antioch. After Stephen's death only the "Hellenists", namely the Greek speaking Jews from the diaspora were persecuted, and were forced to leave Jerusalem, whereas the circle around Peter and James remained untroubled because both of them remained in the realm of the Law, its observance and temple cult, while the Hellenists did not. Stephen was martyred because as a Christian he rejected the law and ritual of his Jewish past.

The Apostolic Council highlighted some other topics responsible for the break between Hellenistic Jewish Christians and Jewish Christians. The mission of the Christian Hellenists had grown in number and the newly created churches in membership, and they were not adhering to the law that required circumcision. This lack of adherence to the law created impediments because the observance of the law was deemed essential by the Christians in Jerusalem as well as by other law-abiding Christian groups. It became increasingly apparent that observance to the law, particularly marked by circumcision, could no longer be regarded as a characteristic mark of Christians since it was open to all nations and not all new members adhered to circumcision. No solution was reached and the immediate agreement was that Paul became the Apostle to the Gentiles and promised to collect money for the Jerusalem Church (Gal. 2:7-19). A third group would not sign the agreement as they were convinced that the ritual law of the Old Testament is binding to all, both Jew and Gentile.

Another incident that also illustrated a cause of division in the early Christian environment was the incident where Peter visited Antioch and when he ate with the Gentiles (Gal. 2:12). By dispensing with the dietary laws Peter displayed a truly liberal attitude, but then Peter withdrew from the table with the Gentiles. Paul regarded this action as hypocritical. Peter and Barnabas were not altogether willing to forego the demands of the dietary laws (Gal. 2:12-13). Koester (1971: 120) is of opinion that in Gal. 2:15 ff Paul illuminates the problem (based upon his concept of the law), namely: the transition from the law to observance to life "in Christ". His concern was not so much Peter's withdrawal from the table, but the disruption of the unity of the one community that is made up of both Jews and Gentiles.

Hellenistic Christianity did not represent a closed unity. However, the transition from Jewish Christianity to Gentile Christianity was fluid as, on the one hand they showed by the adoption of Gentile Christian forms by Jewish Christians, and on the other hand by Judaizing of Christians from the Gentile sphere (Bauer 1971:243)

More conflict between Jewish Christianity and Greek Christians is evident in the statements of the Pauline letters such as Galatians, Philippians and

Romans. Apart from Pauline Christianity, there existed Jewish Gnosticism as well. The heretical Gnostic Jewish-Christian group rejected marriage plus the eating of meat. The fundamental acknowledgement of the Old Testament Law was assured. According to Bauer (1971:254) the heretics of the *Didascalia* were "Judaizing Christians" who had adopted some aspects of Jewish observance, but not the totality of Jewish regulation. They did in fact not actually live in association with Judaism and are not to be designated as Jewish Christians.

As it was a characteristic of Jewish-Christian self-understanding to affirm the continuity between Christianity and Judaism, Jewish Christianity had a legalistic outlook. The struggle between Jewish Christianity and Gentile Christianity was that Jewish Christians claimed and approached the Gentile mission with legalistic Jewish trends. Legalistic Jewish Christianity wavered between a basically tolerant attitude that granted Gentile Christians freedom from the law and other attitudes that expect Gentile Christians to maintain Jewish observance. The self-identity of Jewish Christianity was marked by Jewish observance, namely the observance of circumcision and Sabbath, months of purification, though for Gentile Christianity baptism serves as a rite of initiation, not circumcision.

In Walter Bauer's (1971:285) opinion the view that "the Judaists soon became a heresy rejected with conviction by the Gentile Christians and that the Jewish Christians were repulsed by Gentile Christianity needs to be corrected. Not only is there 'significant diversity' within the Gentile Christian situation, but the same holds for Jewish Christianity that was a "polymorphic entity".

The quest for identity criteria coincides with the quest for the essential identity characteristics of early Christianity. To identify the essential characteristics, the individuality and singularity of Christianity is inevitably bound up with the problem of the historical Jesus. Christianity did not begin with a particular belief, dogma or creed, or canon; rather Christianity started with a particular person, his works and words, his life and death: Jesus of Nazareth. Creed and faith, symbol and dogma are more the expressions of a response to this Jesus of history, despite that it was often understood as the heretical diversifications of early

Christianity and as aberrations from one original true and orthodox formulation of faith.

However, without continuity there can be no 'identity' or 'identity formation' which is a form of self-understanding or the narrative of self-understanding that comes out of the retrieving of the remembering of the Scripture stories of the past. Identity formation comes from remembering and celebrations such as jubilees, festivals, the Passover. Jubilees prove that people in the process of searching for a new identity desire to be placed, together with laws and feasts, within a well—defined historical and social setting. These practices present something of a variation of the theme of invention on tradition. Creative remembering, ritual practices such as circumcision, food laws, identity forming are reinvented and reformed. In the view of Judith Lieu (2004:75) the formation of Christian identity is in fact a re-alignment and maintenance of Jewish identity under new circumstances. Does it mean that a joint culture like Judaism and Christianity pointed to a shared identity?

This is precisely the focus of the next chapter that strives to look closely at Paul's letter to the Galatians. Herein it is hoped that it will become clear that the previous identity factors peculiar to Judaism had to be renewed in creating and making space for new identity factors that will constitute Christianity.

CHAPTER FOUR

4. CHRISTIAN IDENTITY FORMATION AS OFFERED BY PAUL'S LETTER TO THE GALATIANS

4.1. INTRODUCTION

It can be argued that Paul never used the term Christianity in any form and least of all to indicate a new religion implied by the term Christianity. What this chapter tries to establish is not Paul's Christianity, but Christianity according to Paul's writings to the Galatians. While it may be the case that Paul never used the term "Christianity" to indicate a new religion, he did, however, play a key role in transforming Christianity from a Jewish sect into a universal religion with its own identity features. In addition it can be argued that Paul did not become a Christian since there were no Christians at the time of his 'conversion'; in the strict sense of the term his conversion implied becoming a follower of Jesus Christ and thus a member of the Jesus-Movement. It is understood that Paul knew only two categories of human beings, namely Jews and Gentiles. So it can be reasoned that to import the category "Christian" at that time would have been a violation of his experiential and thought world as that would have amounted to introducing a foreign concept. It is understood after Paul's conversion he was not only a believer in Jesus Christ, but he also became an Apostle to the Gentiles and he did so as a member of the Jesus-Movement, which was considered as a so-called sect within Judaism. As claimed by Gager (2000:25), Paul never spoke of Christianity and he insisted that God had not rejected Israel. Paul's conversion was a conversion within a religious tradition, seeing that his conversion did not cause him to take leave from Judaism. When Paul persecuted the followers of Jesus, he was intent on destroying the movement since it was apparent that the Gentiles caused deep divisions and disputes within the Jesus-Movement, so much so that Paul was a central figure in these controversies. The question which was intensely debated within the movement (because they were largely Jews) was whether Gentile followers-of-the-Jesus-Movement needed to become Jews first i.e. whether male members needed to undergo circumcision? Did the Gentile members need to observe the Torah; the Law of Moses and so become full members of the Jesus-Movement? In view of his personal situation Paul was adamant that it was not a requirement for the Gentiles to adopt Jewish practices such as circumcision or to follow the Jewish Law. It is precisely *inter alia* this issue that Paul addresses directly in the Letter to the Galatians).

Reflecting on Paul's conversion, Gager (2000:27) maintains that the model of conversion that Paul followed was that of "trans-valuation / reversal of values". According to this model the convert moves from one pole of opposing systems to another and this in general takes place within either a religious, political or social context. In this particular model of conversion the negative pole becomes positive and the positive becomes negative. He claims that the typical language that testifies to this type of conversion is reflected in Philipians 3:7-8: *"But whatever gain I had, I counted as loss for the sake of Christ. Indeed I count everything as loss because of the surpassing worth of knowing Christ Jesus my Lord . . ."* According to this model of conversion the convert does not move to something new and unknown, but to a deep, emotional and religious engagement. Gager (2000:27) is of opinion that the entire system remains intact, but is turned upside down. So in Paul's instance what changed for him was not his view of the Law, or of the Law in relation to himself and to Israel, but the law in relation to the Gentiles or how it concerned the Gentiles. Paul regarded himself as an Apostle of the Gentiles and this mission or awareness of himself is a direct consequence of his personal conversion experience (Gal. 1:16 also Rom. 1:5; 15:15-16). In fact Paul's conversion, his apostleship, centered on his Gospel to the Gentiles.

For Paul, Jesus was the real founder of Christianity, despite the fact that he, Paul, drew many of his ideas from earlier tradition. He was the first major figure to deny that Jewish Law provided the path of salvation.

He states in Gal. 2:21 that if justification were through the law then Christ died for no reason. He interpreted Jesus death in sacrificial terms as atonement for sins (Burkett 2002:291). Generally Paul's Christianity had an eschatological orientation as he looked forward to the imminent dawning of a new age inaugurated by the return of Christ. Creation would be redeemed from bondage, and death would be eliminated. Christ would reign and believers would share in his glory.

While Paul had formulated several doctrines that became central to the proto-orthodox tradition of Christianity, he is regarded as one of the first who clearly enunciated that salvation came through faith in Jesus Christ rather than following the Jewish Law to its finest detail. All the same Paul was not, as is often claimed, the father of Christian anti-Judaism, even though the letter which he wrote to the Galatian community was "both a product and producer" of controversy" (Puskas 1993:35). His vehement arguments were directed not against Judaism, but as stated by Gager (2000:79), against competing apostles in the Jesus-Movement who demanded that the Gentiles be circumcised and so conform to Jewish Law in order to be saved. Anti-Pauline apostles within the Jewish movement had persuaded members of the Galatian community to accept circumcision and to follow at least some of the elements of the Mosiac law: "*Unless you are circumcised according to the custom of Moses, you cannot be saved*" (Acts 15:1). The cause for writing the letter to the Galatians was occasioned by the debate over whether Jewish circumcision should be a prerequisite for Christian salvation. No doubt this controversial issue precipitated the eventual separation of Christianity from Judaism. Paul, as Apostle to the Gentiles, regarded circumcision as an obstacle to the conversion of Gentiles and dietary regulations as an obstacle to full fellowship between Jewish Christians and Gentile Christians. The insistence on adhering to these Jewish practices so as to become a Christian was, according to Paul's reasoning, not conducive to inclusivity, which was to become a secure feature of Pauline Christianity as is indicated by the letter to the Galatians. By declaring the Law superfluous and even unnecessary, and by placing the salvation of Jew and Gentile on the same basis, Paul in fact made it easier for Gentiles to accept the message and by so doing removed the barriers that kept Jew and Gentile apart (Burkett 2002:295). It was however, Paul's perspective that was adopted by the Gentile proto-Christian tradition and which subsequently became a significant part of orthodox Christian teaching; it was also this step that decisively affected the future of the Jewish-Christian movement. As Christianity unfolded, it could not for long in nascent times be considered a sect of Judaism since it developed systematically into a distinct religion with its own identity characteristics.

4.2. BACKGROUND TO THE LETTER OF PAUL TO THE GALATIANS

In the "Letter to Galatia" Paul addresses the "churches of Galatia" i.e. a group of communities in the region or the larger Province of Galatia (Brown 1996:471). In the work of Hubert Richards (1979: 86-87) he states that the Galatians were a Celtic tribe that had its origins in ancient Gaul or France, which was known as 'Galatia' by the Greeks. Apparently Three hundred years before Christ they migrated east across northern Italy, "Yugoslavia" and Bulgaria and settled in what is today called Ankara in Northern Turkey. They formed the "Province of Galatia" under the Roman Empire and in a stricter sense the immigrants also called themselves Galatians or Celts. However, in the Province of Galatia, southern Turkey, where Paul started a community in the year 45, it is possible when he referred to the Galatians that he meant it in the wider sense which included the Celtic Galatians.

By 57 AD the estimated year when the letter was written, the Gentile communities consisted of new converts still burgeoning in their Christian identity and practices and this marked the environment that necessitated the letter to the Galatians. Being young in their faith in Jesus Christ and struggling with the rudiments of embryonic Christian principles they appeared to be particularly susceptible to many influences. The Judaic Christians arrived on the scene with an array of moral and ceremonial observances that appeared critical and necessary for identity formation as a People of God. The Jewish Christians were highly skeptical of Paul's teaching and insisted, as already mentioned, on circumcision as a sign of the covenant relationship with God. On receiving the news Paul, unable to visit the community immediately, wrote a letter, and although it adheres to the basic components of an early Christian letter, it also differs from his other letters in that it lacks a thanksgiving section. It is dominated with argumentation that defends the authority of Paul and reasserts his own teaching (Puskas 1993:37). Paul felt that his original teaching, which claimed salvation by grace, was at risk of being cast aside. He perceived himself as a target of attack in Galatia and hence he made a personal response and wrote in anger, discarded diplomacy, used vigorous language and imagery. In so doing Paul not only defended his stance but he also explained the principles of how he perceived Christianity was to be lived and understood.

The letter to the Galatians is no doubt one of the earliest documents in the New Testament and in it fundamental features of Christian identity and theology were presented. Apart from the basic Christian tenets that become apparent in the letter, it also provides the readers with more personal and autobiographical information of Paul than any other letters of him (cf Gal 1 and 2). He impresses the readers with his self-understanding as an apostle (1.1). At this juncture one learns of his earlier life as a stringent adherent to Judaism as well as a zealous persecutor of the Church of God (1:13-14). He informs the reader of his entry into the Christian faith and the preceding conversion experiences (1:15-16). He relates his previous encounters with the Christian leadership in Jerusalem (2:1-10) as well as his highly contentious confrontation with Peter in Antioch (2:11-14). He also advises us about the previous visits to Galatia (4:12-20), his strenuous life (6:17). In so doing he presents us with a picture of himself as both missionary and theologian.

4.2.1. The recipients and purpose of the letter

Although it is clear that Paul's addressees of the letter are the "Galatians" (I: 2; 3: 1), their specific identity remains uncertain. What is clear is that they were Gentiles and not Jews (4:8). According to Dunn (1993:6) they belonged to the region of Galatia in the heartland of Asia Minor, the central plateau of (modern) Turkey. Many scholars are of opinion that they were descendants of the original Gallic/Celtic settlers or they could also be from the Roman Province of Galatia that extended further South. Apart from their background, Paul knew them as previously they welcomed him with great warmth and they were sympathetic towards his poor physical condition (4:13-15). The

Galatians responded to Paul's powerful preaching and claimed to have had significant faith experiences of the Spirit during his visit (3:2-5).

The purpose of the letter seems therefore to be an immediate response to what Paul perceived as an urgent crisis among the Galatian churches (1:6-9). It was, as Puskas (1993:35) says, "both a product and producer of controversy". The letter was a substitute for a personal presence (4:20). It was a personal letter or message delivered by Paul as he regarded it as urgent and since his own circumstances made it impossible for him to visit in person.

As the first followers of Jesus were Jews, the Jesus-Movement was regarded as nothing more than a branch of Judaism. Because they are to inherit the promises of the Old Testament they remained within the Jewish tradition and while recruitment was confined to Jews the Jewish Christians perceived themselves as an enclave within Judaism (Richards 1979:89). Once others not of Jewish persuasion joined the Jesus-Movement, conditions for admittance were questioned. Paul was of firm opinion that while the Jesus-Movement was regarded as a reform movement within Judaism, for him it was more than that, it had some radical departure features. The Jesus-followers had to take advantage of this newness so as to assert their independence from Judaism. Paul regarded this as being faithful to the Gospel's deepest insight and universal potential. As already evident in his first missionary journey Paul welcomed people into the Jesus-Movement without any reference to the traditional Jewish customs and practices which had been adopted by Jewish Christians as a matter of course. Paul claimed that the logic of the Gospel demanded this (Richards 1979:89).

Jewish Christians regarded Paul's views as a betrayal of their past and even the past of Jesus. The Jewish Christians were firmly intent to protect the Gospel, to keep the links with Judaism and to save it from mavericks like Paul. It is evident from the letter to the Galatians that the issue came to a head between the Christians of strong Jewish persuasion and Paul whom they regard as presenting a mutilated presentation of Jesus' message. While Paul is outraged, the letter also testifies to his principles of Christianity that would provide the identity features of Christianity as he preached it to the Galatians.

In a state of total rage Paul calls the Jewish Christians "sham Christians and interlopers (2:4). He even goes as far as attacking the entirely of Judaism (1:8; 3:13; 5:10). He maintains that the Jewish practices are a form of infantilism and enslavement (3:23, 4:9; 5; 1) and there should not be a (magical) reliance on them. The immediate cause for writing the letter was occasioned by the debate over whether Jewish circumcision should be a requirement for Christian salvation. The Jews insisted on the traditional Jewish identity terms for Gentile acceptance into the Jewish movement and they thus demanded circumcision of a proselyte precisely because it was so fundamental to Jewish identity. In addition to their insistence on circumcision they also insisted on the observance of calendrical feasts (4:10). Paul was gravely offended by these insistences. This controversial issue hastened the eventual separation of Christianity from Judaism. As the Gentile converts were as yet not well established in their new-found faith in Christ, and presumably not completely versed with Judaic practices either, they were found to be susceptible to Jewish-Christian influences. The Jewish Christians and all their ceremonial observances made the Galatians to believe that the solution to their apparent difficulties is to turn to Jewish practices. The Jewish Christians were highly suspicious of Paul's teaching, as for them he was not Judaic enough in the interaction with the Gentiles, and they insisted on the obligation to practice circumcision as a sign of the covenant relationship with God and as it had become a corporate identity feature of being Judaic, now appears to be a requirement laid down by Jewish Christians in becoming a follower of Christ. The principles that Paul had put forward in response to a crisis would form the rudiments of the identity features of Christianity according to Paul's writings to the Galatians.

The original teaching of Paul that emphasized salvation by grace appeared to be at risk and thus on hearing of the events in Galatia and being unable to visit the community directly, Paul considered a personal letter of immediate necessity. He regarded the Jewish Christians, who insisted on the Galatians adhering to Jewish practices, as opponents of the truth of the Gospel and thus regarded them as "troublemakers" or "agitators" (Gal. 1:7; 5.10, 12). As it came into view that these very Jewish-Christian "troublemakers" enjoyed a fair amount of success in persuading Paul's Gentile converts on the need to be circumcised, Paul felt impelled to set the records straight and to remind the Gentiles of the essentials of being a follower of Jesus and what this required from them and that the requisites did not necessarily include Jewish customs and rituals.

The Jewish Christians considered themselves to be preachers of the Gospel of Christ (1:6-9) and they agreed with Paul on the importance of faith in Christ and of the cross of Christ (6:12). However, these Christian Jews understood that their part of the missionary task was to ensure that the Gentile converts to 'the way' (to the Jesus-Movement) had to be converted properly, i.e. that they had to understand the full implications of the Jewish faith, and by so doing they claimed the authorization of the Jerusalem Church's leadership for their mission. According to their view the Galatian converts could not claim participation in the full heritage of Israel's blessing simply as God-fearers; they must become full proselytes. Paul was of full conviction that these views are to be addressed but before he did so he had to set the record straight by informing them of his identity. Hence, Paul being a Jew himself and now a follower of Christ, a Christian Jew, of similar religious background as the so-called "troublemakers", felt it necessary at the beginning of the letter to declare his Jewish identity and personal history with utter conviction, to inform them of his conversion and of him being now a believer in Jesus as Messiah and a follower of his 'way' (Acts 24:14, 22). He subsequently deemed it necessary to give attention to some of the unresolved issues that the Christian Jews struggled with, namely:

- "How can Gentiles and Jews relate to each other within the purposes of God?"
- How should Gentiles relate to the God of Israel?
- How can Gentiles participate in the blessings God promised through Abraham?
- Who belongs to Israel now that the Messiah Jesus has come and on what terms?
- Is circumcision to continue as a key identity factor that marks out the chosen of God's people? (Dunn 1993:9).

Very important to note at this stage is that in the process of addressing the problem issues that the Galatians encountered, Paul simultaneously made apparent the identity features of Christianity. Very significant is that Paul's Gospel is one "without legalism", without adhering to the Law, and he intended to make the Galatians a people of the Spirit liberated from the evil world (4:3-6). They are to be recipients of God's Spirit and salvation merely by trusting in Christ as God's agent of salvation.

The first characteristic stressed by Paul was his conviction that the Galatians were to be liberated from the ritual details of the Law and this would bring along the freedom of the Spirit. However, the deficiencies in the Christian experience of the Galatians soon became evident to many since in this new-found freedom the Galatians experienced some transgressions (6:1) that are related to problems with, as stated in Galatians with the "flesh" (5:13, 15, 26; 6:9) which was most likely in relation to some misconduct or immorality. These problems constituted an abuse or exploitation of their Christian freedom. In addressing the legal ethical problems, Paul communicated the Christian principles to the Galatians and thus to all other Christians.

In opposition to Paul the Jewish-Christian missionaries were of strong opinion that because the Galatians did not adhere to Jewish ritual Law and customs they fell victim to unreserved freedom and as a result turned into lawless sinners. This position of the Jewish-Christian missionaries became very influential since these zealous Jewish Christians believed that immorality was a natural consequence of not observing the law. According to their perception Paul's Gospel was lawless and this had made Christ a "servant of sin" (2: 17, 21). Hence their insistence that the Galatians must accept the Jewish law and observe the rite of circumcision in order to be partakers of the Sinai covenant and all the securities that would come with it. Speaking into this situation Paul stressed how circumcision and the dietary laws and adherence to Jewish customs constituted a recipe for exclusiveness and Christianity is above all about inclusiveness and unity among all believers.

In providing his apologetic responses on the issues at stake in the letter to the Galatians Paul in actual fact presented his theological principled arguments and by so doing he presented the fundamentals of Christianity (according to Paul's Gospel to the Galatians).

Christian mystical ethics, another constituent of the basic tenets of Christian identity, are based on the Galatians' experience of the Spirit through faith in Christ. This Paul regarded as sufficient unto the course as according to Paul's reasoning if they adhered to his interpretation of the Gospel the Galatians would be recipients of God's salvation and its benefits without conforming to Jewish laws. The Galatians are reminded, before Paul gives his proofs, that he was appointed by Christ himself to preach this Gospel without legalism and to bring salvation to the Gentiles. (The specific characteristics that constitute the distinctiveness identity features of Christianity according to the letter to the Galatians will be dealt with in finer details in the subsequent chapters of this thesis).

What follows is a brief structural outline of the letter to the Galatians.

4.3. THE STRUCTURE OF THE LETTER

Although this Letter of Paul to the Galatians adheres to the basic components of an early Christian letter, it also differs from his other letters as it lacks a thanksgiving section. It is dominated with argumentation that defends his authority and him trying to reassert his own teaching (Puskas 1993:37). As pointed out by Puskas, Paul employed the language of Greco-Roman courtroom judicial language. His persuasion was concerned with the justice of a wrong-doing committed in the past. Both Jews and Gentiles of the Hellenistic period were familiar with this genre as it was part of the Greek way of conducting court issues. In the letter Paul defended his position using well-formulated arguments.

It is claimed that Paul most probably wrote his letter from Ephesus to the Christians of North Galatia around AD 53-54. As already mentioned it was written in response to a crisis in the Galatian churches founded by the apostle. In the effort to deal with their problems they assumed a complete system of legal requirements as advocated by Paul's opponents: the Judaizing Christians. In his attempt to defend his ministry and the spiritual experiences of the Galatians, Paul writes his letter by organizing the arguments in a manner similar to the judicial or courtroom rhetoric of Cicero and Quintilian.

The Galatians were confronted with a choice: after reading the letter they were to make a choice between the curse and the blessing. The letter itself serves as the carrier of both the curse and the blessing. However, reading the letter will automatically produce the "judgment." The readers who are in reality both the judge and the jury will either be acquitted or freed or will be sent to the cosmic prison (cf. 4:1-10). By conveying this imagery, Paul repeats the initial confrontation with the Gospel. Having read the letter, they see themselves transferred back into the moment when they first encountered the Gospel. As a result Paul's defense of the Spirit coincides with the proclamation of Jesus Christ.

At this stage it is useful to take a brief look as to how the content of the letter is structurally organized, and to illustrate that it followed a judicial setting familiar to both Jews and Greeks of the time, this research will use the outline as proposed by Puskas.

4.3.1 The organizational structure of the content of Galatians

Puskas illustrates the judicial setting of the letter by means of the following outline:

1.	*The defender of the case is*:	Paul
2.	*The accusers are*:	the Judaizers
3.	*The jury*:	the Galatians
4.	*The forum is before*:	Christians: Gentile and Jew
5.	*Paul's defense is*:	that the experience of the Spirit through faith is sufficient for the Galatians.

The organization structure of the content of the letter corresponds closely with the components of judicial language of the time. The style is lucid and passionate

1. The Epistolary Prescript (1: 1-5)

The letter of Paul to the Galatians contains epistolary features in both 1:1-5

> *Paul an apostle—not from human beings or through a human being, but Jesus Christ and God the Father who raised Christ and God the Father from the dead—and all the brethren who are with me.*
>
> *To the churches in Galatia: Grace to you and peace from God the Father and our Lord Jesus Christ, who gave himself for our sins to deliver us from the present evil age, according to the will of our God, and Father to whom be the glory forever and ever. Amen*

And 6:11-18

> *"See with the large letters I am writing to you in my own hand. It is those who want to make a good showing in the flesh that would compel you to be circumcised, and only in order that they may not be persecuted for the cross of Christ. For even those who receive circumcision do not themselves keep the law, but they desire to have you circumcised that they may glory in your flesh. But far be it from me to glory except in the cross of our Lord Jesus Christ, by which the world has been crucified to me, and I to the world. For neither circumcision counts for anything, nor uncircumcision, but a new creation. Peace and mercy be upon all who walk by the rule, upon the Israel of God. Henceforth let no one trouble me; for I bear on my body the marks of Jesus. The grace of our Lord Jesus Christ be with your spirit, brethren. Amen*

At the same time it also includes the symbolic devices of restating Paul's argument as stated in (6: 12-14)

> *It is those who want to make a good showing in the flesh that would compel you to be circumcised, and only in order that they may not be persecuted for the cross of Christ. For even those who receive circumcision do not themselves keep the law, but they desire to have you circumcised that they may glory in your flesh. But far be it from me to glory except in the cross of our Lord Jesus Christ, by which the world has been crucified to me, and I to the world.*

By so doing it achieves pity or emotional appeal as illustrated in (6: 17). Henceforth let no one trouble me; for I bear on my body the marks of Jesus.

2. The Exordium or introduction to the case (1:6-10).

Paul's opening statements about the problem at Galatia (1:6-10) constitute the exordium or introduction to the case.

> 6. *I am astonished that you are so quickly deserting him who called you in the grace of Christ and turning to a different Gospel⁷ not that there is another Gospel, but there are some who trouble you and want to pervert the Gospel of Christ. 8 But even if we, or an angel from heaven, should preach to you a Gospel contrary to that which we preached to you, let him be accursed. 9 As we have said before, so now I say again, if anyone is preaching to you a Gospel contrary to that which you received I let him be accursed.*

> 10 *Am I now seeking the favour of people, or of God? Or am I trying to please people? If I were still pleasing people, I should not be a servant of Christ.*

As it was customary to mention one's adversaries and the seriousness of the case (including threats), Paul follows protocol. As a smooth transition often occurs from the introduction to the narration (description), it is clear that this provides some rationale for a division between v 10 and v 11.

> 11 *For I would have you know, brethren, that the gospel which was preached by me is not man's gospel.*

3. The Narration (1:11-2:14).

In the narration, Paul states his argument and explains that his Gospel was not flippant, but came to him through a revelation of Jesus Christ (vv 11-12).

> 12 *For I did not receive it from humans, nor was I taught it, but it came through a revelation of Jesus Christ.*

Since Paul's life in Judaism and his activity as persecutor of the Church (vv 13-14) are not under question, the information here serves as a transition to the actual facts of the case (1: 15-2: 10).

13 For you have heard of my former life in Judaism, how I persecuted the church of God violently and tried to destroy it; 14 and I advanced in Judaism beyond many of my own age among my people, so extremely zealous was I for the traditions of my fathers.

The account of Paul's birth, conversion, calling and his apostolic ministry (1: 15-24: 2:1-10) serves a number of functions, as such it:-

a. provides a preceding history that led to the present situation

15 But when he who had set me apart before I was born, and had called me through his grace, 16 was pleased to reveal his Son to me, in order that I might preach him among the Gentiles, I did not confer with flesh and blood, 17 nor did I go up to Jerusalem to those who were apostles before me, but I went away into Arabia; and again I returned to Damascus.

18 Then after three years I went up to Jerusalem to visit Cephas, and remained with him fifteen days. 19 But I saw none of the other apostles except James the Lord's brother. 20 (In what I am writing to you, before God, I do not lie!) 21 Then I went into the regions of Syria and Cilicia. 22 And I was still not known by sight to the churches of Christ in Judea; 23 they only heard it said, "He who once persecuted us is now preaching the faith he once tried to destroy." 24 And they glorified God because of me.

b. substantiates the thesis statement in 1: 11-12. Gal 2: 11-14

2. Then after fourteen years I went up again to Jerusalem with Bar'na-bas, taking Titus along with me. 2 I went up by revelation; and I laid before them (but privately before those who were of repute) the Gospel which I preach among the Gentiles, lest somehow I should be running or had run in vain. 3 But even Titus, who was with me, was not compelled to be circumcised, though he was a Greek. 4 But because of false brethren secretly brought in, who slipped in to spy out our freedom which we have in Christ Jesus, that they might bring us into bondage—5 to them we did not yield submission even for a moment, that the truth of the Gospel might be preserved for you. 6 And from those who were reputed to be something (what they. were makes no difference to me; God shows no partiality)-those, I say, who were of repute added nothing to me; 7 but on the contrary, when they saw that I had been entrusted with the Gospel to the uncircumcised, just as Peter had been entrusted with the Gospel to the circumcised 8 (for he who worked through Peter for the mission to the circumcised worked through me also for the Gentiles), 9 and when they perceived the grace that was given to me, James and Cephas and John, who were reputed to be pillars, gave to me and Bar'na·bas the right hand of fellowship, that we should go to the Gentiles and they to the circumcised; 10 only they would have us remember the poor, which very thing I was eager to do.

(c) concludes the *narration* and prepares for the *proposition.*

11 But when Cephas came to Antioch I opposed him to his face, because he stood condemned. 12 For before certain men came from James, he ate with the Gentiles; but when they came he drew back and separated himself, fearing the circumcision party. And with him the rest of the Jews acted insincerely, so that even Barnabas was carried away by their insincerity. 14 But when I saw that they were not straightforward about the truth of the Gospel, I said to Cephas before them all, "If you, though a Jew, live like a Gentile and not like a Jew, how can you compel the Gentiles to live like Jews?".

4. *The Proposition (2:15-21).*

As stated by Puskas, Paul's statements in Gal. 2:15-21 function adequately as the proposition, which generally occurs between the narration (1:11-2:14) and the probation (3:1-4:31). Along with the summarized expositions that are to be elaborated later (2: 19-21), the proposition contains points of argument (2: 15-16) and disagreements (17-18) shared between the defendant and accusers.

15 We ourselves, who are Jews by birth and not Gentile sinners, 16 yet who know that a man is not justified by works of the law. but through faith in Jesus Christ, even we have believed in Christ Jesus, in order to

be justified by faith in Christ, and not by works of the law, because by
works of the law shall no one be justified. 17 But if, in our endeavour to
be justified in Christ, we ourselves were found to be sinners, is Christ then
an agent of sin? Certainly not! 18 But if I build up again those things
which I tore down, then I prove myself a transgressor. 19 For I through the
law died to the law that I might live to God. 20 I have been crucified with
Christ; it is no longer I who live, but Christ who lives in me; and the life
I now live in the flesh I live by faith in the Son of God, who loved me and
gave himself for me. 21 I do not nullify the grace of God; for if justification
were through the law, then Christ died to no purpose.

5. The Probation (3:1-4:31).

The central section, which contains most of Paul's doctrinal or theological teaching (3:1-4:31), corresponds to the *probation* or proofs of the case. In forensic speeches, the *probation* is the most decisive section because in it the main arguments of the case are presented. Six arguments are detected:

* an appeal to "the reception of the Spirit, "an experience undisputed by both Paul and the Galatians (3: 1-29); 4:2).

   O foolish Galatians! Who has bewitched you, before whose eyes Jesus
   Christ was publicly portrayed as crucified? 2 Let me ask you only this"
   Did you receive the Spirit by works of the law, or by hearing the faith?
   3 Are you so foolish? Having begun with the Spirit, are you now ending
   with the flesh? 4 Did you experience so many things in vain?—If it really
   is in vain. 5 Does he who supplies the Spirit to you and work miracles
   among you do so by works of the law, or by hearing with faith.

   6 Thus Abraham "believed God, and it was reckoned to him as
   righteousness." 7 So you can see it is men of faith that are the sons of
   Abraham. 8 And the Scripture, foreseeing that God would justify the
   Gentiles by faith preached the Gospel beforehand to Abraham saying, "In
   you shall all the nations be blessed." 9 So then, those who are men of faith
   are blessed with Abraham who had faith.

10 For all who rely on good works of the law are under a curse; for it is written, "Cursed be everyone who does not abide by all things written in the book of the law, and do them." 11 Now it is evident that no man is justified before God by the law; for "He who through faith is righteous shall live"; 12 but the law does not rest on faith, for "He who does them shall live by them" 13 Christ redeemed us from the curse of the law, having become a curse for us—for it is written, "Cursed be everyone who hangs on a tree", 14 that in Christ Jesus the blessing of Abraham might come upon the Gentiles, that we might receive the promise of the Spirit through faith.

15 To give a human example, brethren: no one annuls even a man's willing or add to it, once it has been ratified. 16 Now the promises were made to Abraham and to his offspring. It does not say, "And to offsprings," referring to many; but, referring the one, "And to your offspring," which is Christ. 17 This is what I mean: the law, which came four hundred and thirty years afterward; does not annul a covenant previously: ratified by God; so as to make the promise void. 18 For if the inheritance is by the law it is no longer by promise; but God gave it to Abraham by a promise.

19 Why then the law? It was added because of transgressions, till the offspring should come to whom the promise had been made; and it was ordained by angel through an intermediary. 20 Now an intermediary implies more than one; but God is one.

21 Is the law then against the promises of God? Certainly not; for if a law had been given which could make alive, then righteousness would indeed be by the law. 22 But the scripture consigned all things to sin, that what was promised to faith in Jesus Christ, might be given to those who believe."··'

23 Now before-faith came, we were confined under the law, kept under restraint until faith should be revealed. 24 So that the law was our custodian until Christ came that we might be justified by faith. 25 But now that faith has come, we are no longer under a custodian; 26 for in Christ Jesus you are all sons of God" through faith. 27 For as many of you as were baptized into Christ have put on Christ. 28 There is neither Jew nor Greek, there is neither slave nor free, there is neither male nor female; for are all one in Christ Jesus. 29 And if you are Christ's, then you are Abraham's offspring heirs according to promise.

4. I mean that the heir, as long as he is a child, is no better than a slave, though he is the owner of all the estate; 2 but he is under guardians and trustees until the date set by the father.

This is an argumentation from Scripture by citing passages from Genesis, Leviticus, Deuteronomy, and Habakkuk. This is evident in Gal. 3:6-14:

3 So with us, when we were children, we were slaves to the elemental spirits of the universe. 4 But when the time had fully come, God send forth his Son, born of a woman, under the law, 5 to redeem those who were under the law, so that we might receive adoption as sons.

6 Thus Abraham "believed God, and it was reckoned to him as righteousness." 7 So you see that it is men of faith who are the sons of AbrahaIl1-. 8 And the Scripture, foreseeing that God would justify the Gentiles by faith, preached the Gospel beforehand to Abraham, saying, "In you shall all the nations be blessed." 9 So then, those who are men of faith are blessed with Abraham who had faith.

10 For all who rely on works of the law are under a curse; for it is written, "Curse be everyone who—does not abide by all things written in the book of the law, and do them." 11 Now it is evident that no man is justified before God by the law; for "He who through faith is righteous shall live"! 12 but the law does not rest on faith,-for "He who does them shall live by them." 13 Christ redeemed us from the curse of the law, having become a curse for us for it is written, "Cursed be everyone who hang on a tree"-14 that in Christ Jesus 'the blessing of Abraham might come upon the Gentiles, that we might receive the promise of the Spirit through faith.

• What follows is an example from human practice (3:15-18; with 3:19-25, a short digression on the function of the law:

15 To give a human example, brethren: no one annuls even a man's will, or adds to it, once it has been ratified. 16 Now the promises were made to Abraham and to his offspring. It does not say, "And to offsprings," referring to many; but, referring the one, "And to your offspring," which is Christ. 17 This is what I mean: the law, which came four hundred and

91

thirty years afterward; does not annul a covenant previously: ratified by God; so as to make the promise void. 18 For if the inheritance is by the law it is no longer by promise; but God gave it to Abraham by a promise.

19 Why then the law? It was added because of transgressions, till the offspring should come to whom the promise had been made; and it was ordained by angels through an intermediary. 20 Now an intermediary implies more than one; but God is one.

21 Is the law then against the promises of God? Certainly not; for if a law had been given which could make alive, then righteousness would indeed be by the law. 22 But the scripture consigned all things to sin, that what was promised to faith in Jesus Christ might be given to those who believe.'"

23 Now before-faith came, we were confined under the 1aw, kept under restraint until faith should be revealed. 24 So that the law was our custodian until Christ came that we might be justified by faith. 25 But now that faith has come, we are no longer under a custodian;

- Paul recites reminders of their favoured status as Christians (3:26-4:11);

26 for in Christ Jesus you are all sons of God through faith. 27 For as many of you were baptized into Christ. 28 There is neither Jew nor Greek, there is neither slave nor free, there is neither male or female for you are one in Christ Jesus. 29 And if you are Christ's then you are Abraham's offspring, heirs according to promise.

4 I mean that the heir as long as long as he is a child, is no better than a slave, though he is the owner of all the estate; 2 but he is under guardians and trustees until the date set by the father. 3 So with us; when we were children, we were slaves to the elemental spirits of the universe. 4 But when the time had fully come, God sent forth his Son, born of woman; born under the law, 5 to redeem those who were under the law, so that we might receive adoption as sons. 6And because you are sons, God has sent the Spirit of his Son into our hearts, crying, "Abba! Father!" 7 So through God you are no longer a slave but a son, and if a son then an heir.

8 Formerly, when you did not know God, you were in bondage to beings that by nature are no gods; 9 but now that you have come to know God, or rather to be known by God, how can you turn back again to the weak and beggarly elemental spirits, whose slaves you want to be once more? 10 You observe days, and months, and seasons, and years! 11 I am afraid I have laboured over you in vain.

- He also makes a personal appeal to friendship (4:12-20); and

12 Brethren, I beseech you, become as I am, for I also have become as you are. You did me no wrong; 13 you know it was because of a bodily ailment that I preached the Gospel to you at first; 14 and though my condition was a trial to you, you did not scorn or despise me, but received me as an angel of God, as Christ Jesus. 15 What has become of the satisfaction you felt? For I bear you witness that, if possible, you would have plucked out your eyes and given them to me. 16 Have I then become your enemy by telling you the truth? 17 They make much of you, but for no good purpose; they want to shut you out, that you may make much of them. 18 For a good purpose it is always good to be made much of, and not only when I am present with you. 19 My little children, with whom I am again in travail until Christ be formed in you! 20 I could wish to be present with you now and to change my tone, for I am perplexed about you.

- an allegorical argument from Scripture (4:21-31).

21 Tell me, you who desire to be under law, do you not hear the law? 22 For it is written that Abraham had two sons, one by a slave and one by a free woman, 23 But the son of the slave was born according to the flesh, the son of the free woman through promise. 24 Now this is an allegory: these women are two covenants. One is from Mount Sinai, bearing children for slavery; she is Hagar. 25 Now Hagar is Mount Sinai in Arabia; she corresponds to the present Jerusalem, for she is in slavery with her childfree. 26 But the Jerusalem above is free, and she is our mother. 27 For it is written,

"Rejoice, 0 barren one who does not bear; break forth and shout, you who are not in travail; for the children of the desolate one are many. more than the children of her that is married."

28 Now we, brethren, like Isaac, are children of promise. 29 But as at that time he, who was born according to the flesh, persecuted him who was born according to the Spirit, so it is now. 30 But what does the Scripture say? "Cast out the slave and her son; for the son of the slave shall not inherit with the son of the free woman. So, brethren, we are not children of the slave but of the free woman.

6. The Exhortation (5:1-6:10).

The ethical exhortation or *paraclesis* (5: 1-6: 10) is a distinctive element of Paul's argumentation although it has a similar function as deliberative persuasion in rhetorical handbooks. *Paraclesis or the ethical exhortation* was used a great deal in philosophical dialogues and it forms part of Paul's argument in the letter to the Galatians. It can be argued that Gal. 5:1,13,25 repeat the conclusion of Paul's *probation* in 4:31 (which he alludes to arguments 3:9,14,24,29; 4:7) and contains warnings against adherence to the Jewish Torah (5:1-12) and corruption by the flesh (5:13-24). All of the above are effective arguments for the sufficiency of the Galatians' spiritual experience without legalism.

5 For freedom Christ has set us free; stand fast therefore, and do not submit again to a yoke of slavery.

2 Now I, Paul, say to you that if you receive circumcision, Christ will be of no advantage to you. 3 I testify again to every man who receives circumcision that he is bound to keep the whole law. 4 You are severed from Christ, you who would be justified by the law; you have fallen away from grace. 5 For through the Spirit, by faith, we wait for the hope of righteousness. 6 For in Christ Jesus neither circumcision nor un-circumcision is of any avail, but faith working through love. 7 You were running well; who hindered you from obeying the truth? 8 This persuasion is not from him who calls you. 9 A little leaven leavens the whole lump. 10 I have confidence in the Lord that you will take no other view than mine; and he who is troubling you will bear his judgment, whoever he is. 11 But if I, brethren, still preach circumcision, why am I still persecuted? In that case the stumbling block of the cross has been removed. 12 1 wish those who unsettle you would mutilate themselves!

13 For you were called to freedom, brethren; only do not use your freedom as an opportunity for the flesh, but through love be servants of one another. 14 For the whole law is fulfilled in one word, "You shall love your neighbour as yourself." 15 But if you bite and devour one another take heed that you are not consumed by one another.

16 But I say, walk by the Spirit, and do not gratify the desires of the flesh. 17 For the desires of the flesh are against the Spirit, and the desires of the Spirit are against the flesh; for these are opposed to each other, to prevent you from doing what you would. 18 But if you are led by the Spirit you are not under the law. 19 Now the works of the flesh are plain: fornication, impurity, licentiousness, 20 idolatry, sorcery, enmity, strife, jealousy, anger, selfishness, dissension, party spirit, 21 envy, drunkenness, carousing, and the like. I warned you before, that those who do such things shall not inherit the Kingdom of God. 22 But the fruit of the Spirit is love, joy, peace, patience, kindness, goodness, faithfulness, 23 gentleness, self-control; against such there is no law. 24 And those who belong to Christ Jesus have crucified the flesh with its passions and desires.

25 If we live by the Spirit, let us also walk by the Spirit. 26 Let us have no self-conceit, no provoking of one another, no envy of one another.

6 Brethren, if a man is overtaken in any trespass, you who are spiritual should restore him in a spirit of gentleness. Look to yourself, lest you too be tempted. 2 Bear one another's burdens, and so fulfill the law of Christ. 3 For if anyone thinks he is something, when he is nothing, he deceives himself. 4 But let each one test his own work, and then his reason to boast will be in himself alone and not in his neighbour. 5 For each man will have to bear his own load. 6 Let him who is taught the word share all good things with him who teaches.

7 Do not be deceived; God is not mocked, for whatever a man sows, that he will also reap. 8 For he who sows to his own flesh will from the flesh reap corruption; but he who sows to the Spirit will from the Spirit reap eternal life. 9 And let us not grow weary in well-doing, for in due season we shall reap, if we do not lose heart. 10 So then, as we have opportunity, let us do good to all men, and especially to those who are of the household of faith.

7. The Conclusion (6:11-18).

A final defensive weapon envelopes the letter and dramatically intensifies Paul's argument. In the exordium (1:8-9) Paul invokes a curse for those who follow legalism and in the conclusion (6:16) invokes a blessing on those who follow the "rule" of freedom (cf. 3:9; 4:7; 5:1, 13). This conditional curse and blessing gives Galatians a magical potency over the reader. Parallels to the binding force of the curse or blessing can be found in both the Jewish writings of Qumran (1 QS 2.517) and the Greek Hippocratic oath.

Applied to the situation of the Galatians the curse/blessing probably had the following effect. The Galatians are confronted with a choice. After reading the letter they will make a choice between the curse and the blessing. The letter itself serves as the carrier of the curse or the blessing. Reading the letter will automatically produce the "judgment." The readers who are both the judge and the jury will either be acquitted or freed or will be sent to the cosmic prison (cf. 4:1-10). By conveying this imagery, Paul repeats the initial confrontation with the Gospel. Having read the letter, they see themselves transferred back into the moment when they first encountered the Gospel. As a result Paul's defense of the Spirit coincides with the proclamation of Jesus Christ.

> *11 See with what large letters I am writing to you with my own hand. 12 It is those who want to make a good showing in. the flesh that would compel you to be circumcised, and only in order that they may not be persecuted for the cross of Christ. 13 For even those who receive circumcision do not themselves keep the law, but they desire to have you circumcised that they may glory in your flesh. 14 But far be it from me to glory except in the cross of our Lord Jesus Christ, by which the world has been crucified to me, and 1 to the world. 15 For neither circumcision counts for anything, nor circumcision, but a new creation. 16 Peace and mercy be upon all who walk by this rule, upon the Israel of God. 17 Henceforth let no man trouble me; for I bear on my body the marks of Jesus.*

> *18 The grace of our Lord Jesus Christ be with your spirit, brethren. Amen*

8. Summary

From Paul's defense of his interpretation of the Gospel certain issues emerged that could be termed identity features of Christianity in antiquity according to letter to the Galatians. The defense places the spotlight on certain matters and as a result clarified certain questions.

While the first Christians who were Jews saw themselves as an enclave within Judaism, Paul was, however, convinced that what Jesus had brought about was not merely a reform movement within Judaism, but something new which may imply a departure from Judaism so as to cultivate its universal attribute. This may be the reason why Paul welcomed people who were not of Jewish persuasion into the Jesus-Movement without insisting that they comply to Jewish practices first. Paul was perceived by Jewish Christians as mutilating the Gospel message and thus regarded the Gentile's Christianity as incomplete. According to the Jewish understanding not to be circumcised placed them out of bounds with a right relationship with God. They therefore accused Paul of not having known the Jewish Jesus and for not having grasped the meaning of the Gospel. This caused Paul to retaliate by calling the Jewish Christians "sham Christians and interlopers" (Gal. 2:6). The question is whose form of interpretation of the Gospel message will shape Christianity in antiquity. What paramount characteristics will arrange Christianity and are these characteristics faithful to the principles of the Jesus-Movement.

The opposing views of Paul and the Judaizers centered primarily on the centrality and the observance of the Law. The Galatians, as recipients of Paul's *Gospel without legalism*, (without adhering to the Law), became what Paul called a *people of the Spirit* who was liberated from the evil world (4:3-6). They became recipients of God's Spirit and salvation merely by trusting in Christ as God's agent of salvation. In Paul's view to remain bound to a system of law-keeping would be to refuse to accept a loving God who was revealed in the death and resurrection of Christ. The position of Paul's opponents, the Jewish missionaries (Judaizers), was equally influential. From the perspective of the Judaizers, those who live apart from the Jewish law and customs are lawless sinners. For these zealous Jewish followers of Christ, immorality is a natural consequence of not observing the law. As they saw it, Paul's Gospel is lawless and has made Christ a "servant of sin" (2: 17, 21). They were of firm opinion that the Galatians must therefore accept the Jewish law and observe it especially the rite of circumcision in order to be partakers of the Sinai covenant and all the securities that would come with it. It is clear from Paul's letter that the Galatians experienced some transgression in their midst (6:1) related to problems with the "flesh" (5:13, 15, 26; 6:9) probably concerning some misconduct or immorality. These problems hence indicated an abuse or exploitation of their Christian freedom. To live under the law allows no freedom, and Paul claims that the Law stood in as our guardian until Jesus came and thereafter we are justified by faith. Paul says in Galatians 3:23;-5:13 that we are called to liberty. The true Christian, according to Paul, sees him or herself as freed from any merely external determination. The Christian is animated by another principle namely the "Spirit of Christ" or the Holy Spirit. The true Christian is self-determined and therefore free, because the Christian has put on another self which recognizes the absolute demands of the only absolute, namely love.

Paul's apologetic response can be outlined in the following arguments which claim that the Galatians' experience of the Spirit through faith in Christ is sufficient. By responding to Paul's Gospel they have become recipients of God's salvation and its benefits without conforming to Jewish laws. The Galatians are reminded, before Paul gives his proofs, that he was appointed by Christ himself to preach this Gospel without legalism and to bring salvation to the Gentiles.

It has often been suggested that the Christianity of Paul was a complex and distorted version of the simple message which was preached by Jesus and his disciples. Paul in his letter to the Galatians is prepared to defend and challenge this understanding. He claimed that what he taught was not be radically different from what Peter, James and John taught, though the Christianity that he planted throughout his journeys would have had a very specific Pauline flavour. For the purposes of this research five identity elements of Christianity according to Paul's letter to the Galatians had been identified and will be explored in detail in the second half of this study.

The first significant identity characteristic of Christianity according to the letter to the Galatians is that of "Inclusiveness". The second identifiable characteristic is that of "legal ethics" explored in chapter six and the third characteristic that of "mystical ethics" as a foundation of Christian identity will be attended to in Chapter Seven. The fourth characteristic is that of "unity as presented by the notion "Body of Christ" and the final characteristic is the "value of love". By exploring these identifiable characteristics of Christianity presented according to the letter to the Galatians it is hoped that by relating it to some established notions of the Jesus-Movement one would be able to come to some measure of understanding of what Christianity appeared like in antiquity and how we may have deviated from it or comply with it in present day forms.

SECTION TWO

THE FORMATION OF A DIASTRATIC SOCIETY BASED ON GALATIANS CHRISTIAN IDENTITY CHARACTERISTICS

CHAPTER FIVE

5. "INCLUSIVENESS" AS A BASIC CHRISTIAN IDENTITY CHARACTERISTIC OF GALATIAN CHRISTIANITY

5.1. INTRODUCTION

In ancient Christianity a plurality of adherents to the Jesus-Movement came to use the teachings of Jesus Christ in multiple forms. It is therefore vital to discern what beyond this plurality was common and what characterized the collective factors which constituted an emergent Christian identity. In the developing scenario of Gospel diversity a cohesive Christian identity could hardly be articulated since a potential identity came to subsist in relation to other structural religious, social and cultural identities. This is precisely what needs to be discerned in this research as according to Paul's letter to the Galatians the Jewish Christians insisted that Gentile believers first had to adhere to Judaic beliefs, laws and practices before they could rightfully make a claim on a potential Christian identity. This research is thus of opinion that within the framework of developing Christian identities the Judaic claim to exclusivity was directly challenged as it became increasingly apparent that the **"inclusive nature"** of Christianity was beginning to establish itself as an identity characteristic in nascent Christianity.

While emerging Christianity awaited a definite identity arrangement the initial configuration of a sense of identity emerged together with a sense of something that transcends the local and the ordinary. As previously established, the Gospels possessed an inner resistance to being confined to the conventional, and this was made very evident in

Paul's affirmation stating that in Christ *"there is no Jew nor Greek, there is no slave nor free, there is no male and female, for you are all one in Jesus Christ* (Gal. 3:28). This statement in one sense sealed *'inclusiveness'* as a definite Christian identity characteristic.

The literary context for Gal. 3:28 is not confined to the letter to the Galatians as the reference "baptized into Christ" is also paralleled in 1 Cor. 12:12-13 stating that all believers are "baptized into one body". This identification of "one body" with Christ affirms that the baptized are incorporated in the inclusion process. In 1 Cor. 12: 12-13 Paul also lists similar pairs as is found in Gal. 3:28 (except for male and female"), here he also makes no distinction between "Jews or Greeks" and "slaves or free" in relation to how the Spirit endows people with gifts (1 Cor. 12:11). In Colossians 3:9-11 there appears a similar pairings of distinction, but in addition with *circumcised and uncircumcised, barbarian and Scythian.* By putting on this "new person', becoming one in the body of Christ, the behaviour undergoes an ontological change, which forms part of his/her essential ethical character. It is thus possible that the Pauline quotation was uttered with Joel 2:28-29 as a backdrop which advocated for the removal of distinctions between Jews and Gentiles. Joel spoke: " . . . *And it shall come to pass afterwards that I will pour out my spirit on all flesh; your sons and your daughters shall prophesy, your old men shall see visions. Even upon the menservants and maidservants in those days, I will pour out my spirit".* The negation of the distinctions between Jews and Gentiles, male and female, slave and free as cited in Gal. 3:28 may serve for Paul as the concrete application of the initial vision for the formation of early Christianity and for the Church as expressed in Acts 2:16-18. Peter's citation from the prophet Joel at the beginning of the creation of the Church was obviously not lost on Paul. Seeing that the Spirit was poured on all people, Jews and Gentiles alike, male slaves and females alike, he declared all possible divisions null and void from the onset of the Christian Church.

Comparable Hellenistic and Jewish sayings that intended to distinguish within humanity were not uncommon in the Hellenistic and Jewish world of antiquity and certainly not unfamiliar to Paul. The sayings reflected ways of differentiated humanity among both Greeks and Jews, male and female and formed part of common prayer and daily sentiments. The specific formula used by Paul may dated even earlier, as it seems to have been modeled on a Hellenistic formula going back as far as Thales and Plato (6th century BC). It is reported by Hermippus that the philosopher gives thanks first to have said that there were three things for which he was grateful to fortune: *that he was born a human being and not of the brutes; born a man and not a woman, a Greek and not a barbarian (3rd Century AD. Diogenes Laertius Viate philosophorum 1:33 quoted in* Bruce1982:187).

A similar common expression of gratitude also formed part of the Jewish cycle of morning prayers quoted by R. a Judah b El ai (ca 150 CE). There are three blessings one must pray for on a daily basis:

> "Blessed (art thou) who did not make me a Gentile;
> Blessed (art thou) who not make me a boor (i.e. an ignorant peasant or a slave, uncultured);
> Blessed (art thou) who did not make me a woman."

Is it possible that this may well have been familiar to Paul previous to the above date?

There were, however, also evidences of positive statements of distinctions of humanity within Rabbinic Judaism:

> "If a poor man says anything, one pays little regard: but if a rich man speaks, immediately he is heard and listened to. Before God, however, all are equal: women, slaves, poor and rich."

It is most likely therefore that Paul's three couplets (Jew or Greek, slave or free, male or female) was also recognition of this common way of perceiving the division of humanity. It is therefore not unlikely that Paul himself would have been brought up thanking God that he was a Jew, and not a Gentile, a freeman and not a slave, a man and not a woman. Obviously this formula had some considerable importance in Judaism but in using it Paul affirms that in Christ they are of no relevance.

Curiously, however, an initial reading of Gal. 3:28 appears to undermine much of the uncertainties of an emergent Christian identity while at the same time it asserts a distinct identity already in the making. Paul immediately draws on the distinctive symbolic world of Jewish identity (3:29) "You are the seed of Abraham". This investigation has thus identified **"inclusiveness"** as a primary identity characteristic of nascent Christianity. The inclusiveness, typified by Galatians (3:28), is a powerful annunciation based in Christ and in the offspring of Abraham:

> "For as many of you as were baptized into Christ have put
> on Christ. There is neither Jew nor Greek, there is neither
> slave nor free, there is neither male nor female, for you are all
> one in Christ. And if you are Christ's then you are Abraham's
> offspring, heirs according to promise" (Gal. 3:28).

The above statement Gal. 3:28 including 1 Cor. 7:19; 1 Cor. 12:13, pairs concepts that separate people and keep them divided or at enmity with each other. In this instance Paul refers to:

- racial differences namely "Greek and Jews";
- religious differences, the "circumcised and the uncircumcised";
- cultural differences, "barbarian and Scythian" (Col 3:9-11);
- social differences, "slave and free"; and finally;
- sexual differences, "male and female".

While these differences are by far not the only ones that would divide humanity, they do, however, offer a representative sample and include other factors that separate humanity or place them in different camps. Paul does not erase differences between people; to the contrary he includes the differences by stressing unity over and above disunity. The same sentiment is expressed by Matthew 25:31-46 and 1 John 4:20 who states that by being in Christ humanity forms one organism and for this reason human beings should be in human relationship with each other. In fact the calling to become "all things to all people" (1 Cor. 9:22), could this amount to equality in Christ?

According to the view of the early Christian Jews the so-called full privileges of early Christianity were to be enjoyed only by those who were circumcised (Gal. 1:5-11). Christianity was therefore to be confined to the covenanted people i.e. the circumcised people of Israel, who perceived themselves as the only legitimate children of God. Since Gal. 3:28 combated exclusivity, the Jewish Christians would no doubt have perceived the statement as heretical. In this regard Paul outlines that physical lineage is not a criterion when God calls, because in the new covenant when God calls through Christ (John 6:44) the call of the Gentiles appears to be just as valid as that of an Israelite. According to Gal. (1:11-19-2:1-14) Paul counters what he calls the "evil influences of the Judaizers in Galatia" (Gal. 3:4:31) showing that this doctrine of exclusivity is destroying the very essence of Christianity, and by so doing is lowering the spirituality of Christ to an outwards ceremonial system. Christianity in the making, as proposed by Paul's writing to the Galatians, made no provision for population or racial exclusiveness epitomized by the statement that *"in Christ there is no Jew or Greek"*, Paul's principle of Christian—or even human—inclusiveness is based on the new principle of baptism. He argues that by means of baptism Jesus Christ had introduced a radically new departure from the Old Testament where only the male person through circumcision was regarded as the direct carrier of the covenant. In the new dispensation offered by Jesus Christ both men and women share equally in Christ and so become equal members or participants of the Kingdom of Jesus Christ. Characteristic therefore of Christianity in antiquity, and reinforced in Paul's letter to the Galatians, *the inequality of differences* between Greek and Jews, circumcised and the uncircumcised", slave and free"; and "male and female" is of no avail in Christianity; to the contrary it was a matter of **inclusions**. Inclusiveness based on God's impartiality, which incorporates all of humanity as full participants in the body of Christ.

5.2. THE CONCEPT "INCLUSIONS" AND GALATIANS

In the light of Galatians, "inclusiveness" as an identity characteristic of nascent Christianity lends itself to a natural specification of being a follower of Christ. By placing Galatians 3:27-28 in its Hellenistic cultural context and by following it through with a reflection on parallel verses of ancient Christianity, namely Col 3:11, 1 Cor. 12:13 and 1 Cor. 11:11-12 the concept "inclusions" identifies baptism as a principal and foundational characteristic of Christian identity" (Gal. 3:26). While many interpreters would view Gal. 3 as Paul intended to depreciate the

Mosaic Law, this research assumes the position that Paul's argument is against those who misused Mosaic Law to exclude the Gentiles and to impose prohibitions upon them.

Paul's new-found faith in Christ has greatly influenced the way in which he envisioned society. He came to realize that for those bound to Christ, not only are previous religious distinctions removed, but all social distinctions as well (3:28). Hence his strong conviction that one does not have to go via Judaism, or the Jewish Law, into Christianity because there is a more direct way for Gentiles to enter the Kingdom of God apart from the law and that is by means of faith. "Righteousness comes to all who believe through the faith of Jesus Christ" (Rom 3:23), this include all God's people as the promise of Abraham is fulfilled by the faithfulness of Christ in bringing the Gentiles into the Kingdom of God (Buckel 2002:125). God's righteousness included all nations, but the so-called troublemakers of Galatia sought to exclude the Gentiles. Paul's strenuous objection to their insistence on performing the works of the law as a means of obtaining righteousness was not only because it created a division in humankind but it also prevented the universal unity that was promised to Abraham.

Inclusions do not necessarily imply the removal of differences; instead Paul also argues for differences to be accommodated within Christianity. The negation of differences should not be equated with the removal of differences between Jews and Gentiles, male and female, free and slave, circumcised and uncircumcised. His argument is that becoming a follower of Christ does not result in undifferentiated humanity as differences will always remain, but within Christ they are of no avail (Gal. 5:6; 6:15; 1 Cor.7:19). Circumcision or no circumcision; male or female; Jew or Gentile; free or slave are irrelevant conditions for becoming a Christian, and such distinctions and categories are irrelevant to entering the body of Christ. The prime factor for Paul is not to remove differences, but to emphasize that these differences are not of importance to be included into the life of Christ. What underlies the assertion here (Rom.10:12) is the recognition that "God shows no partiality" (Rom.2:11; 10:11-13). This appeal to inclusiveness is also evident in Luke's description of Peter's encounter with Cornelius when he was persuaded to preach the Gospel to the Gentiles (Acts 10:24, 38;

11:9-12). Although this characteristic of inclusiveness is portrayed by God's impartiality it has at the same time implications for how the participants in Christ relate to each other within emerging Christianity. The attitude of inclusions played a strong and important role in emerging Pauline Christianity as this radical negation of partiality he describes as a "new creation" or a "new person". This "new creation" does not refer to an alteration in the physical nature of believers, or to the inward individual change at the level of what it means to be human, but rather to be the "renewed people" of God.

Another point of value is that inclusiveness may not be the same as equality and does not carry similar associations in the Gal. 3:28 contexts. The so-called assertion that Gal. 3:28 proclaims the equality of men and women, free and slave, circumcised and uncircumcised was most likely an uncommon concept and whether early Christianity recognized and practiced equal worth or even equal authority of masters and slave, male and female is hard to discern. It is possible that the first century's claim to equal status in salvation may not necessarily have translated to equal claim to social, political or religious status. What is clear is that Gal. 3:28 is intricately woven into the fabric of Paul's epistles; its meaning and significance cannot be detached from the larger tapestry of the New Testament. Characteristic of early Christianity as expressed by Paul in Galatians is that being "baptized into Christ" highlights an incorporation process and makes no distinction regarding the differences between "Jews and Greeks", "slave and free", "male and female".

At this stage it will be useful to explore Galatians 3:26-28 in its original context together with its interpretative associations and sub-texts. Though the text has a tradition, it is believed that Galatians 3: 26-28 was reworked and written by Paul, harking back to its traditional baptismal saying. Paul worked it specifically for the situation of the Galatians in which they found themselves. Similar accounts such as 1 Cor. 12:13 and Col 3:9-11 may not have been written by Paul, but may have been dependent on the Galatians statement written by Paul.

The redactional account of the statement: For as many of you as were baptized into Christ have put on Christ. There is neither Jew nor Greek, there is neither slave nor free, there is neither male nor female, for you are all one in Christ. And if you are Christ's then you are Abraham's offspring, heirs according to promise" (Gal. 3:28).

- *Baptized into Christ*
- *Put on Christ*
- *Men and women*
- *Male and female*

The Sitz im Leben (or the performative setting) is baptism, but limited to the sub-classifications of primitive Christainity.

MacDonald (1987) states that there are at least three proposals into which this text can be placed namely:

- Paul's own circle
- Paul's communities
- Parties opposed to Paul

5.2.1. Neither Jew nor Greek

Buckel (1993:3) alleges that Paul envisioned a Christianity in which there is no distinction between Jew and Gentile, slave and free, male and female and for this reason he informed the Galatians that they have been freed from enslavement of sin and death so that they can love more fully. Gal. 3:28 embodies a shift from an old world to a new creation characterized by Christ. Indeed the language implies a radical reshaping of a new world shaped by a Christian perspective based on the life and death of Jesus Christ.

The cleavage between Jew and Gentile was for Judaism the most radical within the human race. While it was possible for a Gentile to become a Jewish proselyte, to bring them close to the Torah, the gulf still remained (Bruce 1982:188). It is obvious from the writings of Paul and the records of Acts, that to realize the principle of equality between Jew and Gentile was a struggle in early Christianity. The insistence of influential members that Gentiles Christians conform to the same practices of Jewish proselytes before they would be admitted to Christianity was perceived as indiscriminate evangelization of Gentiles and unwise in Paul's view of the Gospel. Paul's position of clear since the law's inability to impart life there was no distinction between Jew and Gentile before God in respect of their moral bankruptcy or of their need to receive God's pardoning grace (Bruce 1982:188). According to him the Law-free Gospel put both on the same level before God so that "in Christ" there was "neither Jew nor Gentile" (cf. also Rom.1-16; 3:22; 10:12; 15:8f; 1 Cor. 1:24; Eph. 2:13-22; 3:6; Col. 3:11).

Paul may be quoting another piece of common confessional faith, namely, 1 Cor. 12:13

> For by one Spirit we were all baptized into one body—Jews or Greeks, slave or free—and all were made to drink of one Spirit".

It is clear that Paul gave this text a particular twist here as "neither Jew nor Greek" formed part of the controversy in which he was embroiled in Galatia. To be identified with Christ who relativized the traditional distinctions of race, social status and gender, including, and not the least, that between Jew and Greek, which was such a feature of the epoch of Israel under the law meant that the idea of separateness and distinctiveness are to be obliterated. Paul emphasized that Christ, his ministry and particularly in his death had abolished the curse which divided covenant member from outsider (Gal. 3:13). Faith in Christ, as commitment to Christ and belonging to Christ, ensured full participation in the heirs and heritage of Abraham (Gal.3:39) (Dunn 1993; 93). The inclusiveness of Christianity involves becoming like Christ, finding one's identity in Christ, no longer in Judaism, the old identity, but personal meaning and identity is found in Christ as part of the new creation which implies putting on Christ.

The big questions that needed to be confronted by the Jewish Christians were:

- How can Gentiles and Jews relate to each other within the purposes of God?
- How should Gentiles relate to the God of Israel?

- How can Gentiles participate in the blessings God promised through Abraham?
- Who belongs to Israel now that the Messiah Jesus has come and on what terms?
- Is circumcision to remain to be the key identity factor which marks out the assemblage of God's people and do converts to Christianity have to adhere to this practice?

The "troublemakers" (as Paul called the Jewish Christians) insisted that converts to Christ should first take on, and practice the "identity features" of Judaic ideology, before they can take on Jesus in baptism. The Christian Jews understood it to be their missionary task to ensure that Gentile converts were properly converted, i.e., that they had properly understood the full implications for the Jewish faith, and that they acknowledged the authorization of the Jerusalem Church's leadership for their mission. According to their view the Galatian converts could not claim participation in the full heritage of Israel's blessing simply as God-fearers; they must become full proselytes, which implies first adhering to the religious identity features of Judaism. A strategic factor of their preaching was that they insisted on circumcision and adherence to Jewish calendrical feasts (4:10). The Galatians must therefore accept the Jewish law and become inclusive partakers of the Sinai covenant and all the securities that derive from being an active participant in the Abrahamic covenant's rite of circumcision. This distinction between Jew and Gentile should be understood in a religious sense primarily, centering in the Abrahamic covenant's rite of circumcision. Without circumcision the Gentiles were regarded as spiritually depraved and lost in the world (Eph. 2:11-13).

Paul was aware of Joel 2:28-29 as a backdrop for the removal of distinctions between Jews and Gentiles. As this quotation from Joel formed part of Peter's original vision of the Church, Paul saw the situation in Galatia as a concrete necessity for the implementation of this initial vision of Church. This significance of no distinctions can thus not be equated with the removal of differences; but it is rather a matter of inclusion versus exclusion.

5.2.1.1. Circumcision as a form of inclusion or exclusion

While circumcision was a fundamental tenet of Jewish identity, in
Paul's mind it was certainly not a requirement for anyone to become
a believer in Christ. It is obvious from his vehement writings to the
Galatians that he was gravely affronted by the insistence of the Jewish
Christians who impressed on the Gentile Christians to adhere to the
identity practices of Judaism. For him the Old Testament rules and
regulations that isolated Israel from other ethnic groups are no longer
of the essence. Hence his heated opposition to Jewish Christians
insistence on the Gentile Christians to succumb to traditional Jewish
terms so as to be accepted into the Christian faith. He is opposed
to their commanding insistence that the Gentile proselytes should
undergo physical circumcision as the obligatory means of becoming a
follower of Christ.

It is fair to say as pointed out by Van Der Watt (2006:109) that within
the Gospel narrative there are many identifiable action lines that reflect
shared custom, irrespective of whether the person is a follower of
Jesus or of Moses. Certain behavioural practices are assumed to have
been operative on the basis of a commonly accepted value system.
The disciples and Jesus partook in these events without showing any
signs of distancing themselves from Jewish socio-cultural, religious
and judicial activities. It is possible that the Jewish Christians would
have adhered to common Judaic religious practices and circumcision
would have fallen under the list which included visiting the Temple or
synagogues and celebrating certain religious feasts. As circumcision
was an identifiable practice that determined a conspicuous degree of
inclusion or exclusion and precisely because it functioned inherently
as a Jewish identity feature, according to Paul's way of thinking it
cannot just be translated as a Christian identity feature. He preaches
that in Christ the Gentiles have also become heirs in equal measure to
the promises of Abraham despite the fact that national and religious
distinctions remain an obvious reality. By the death of Christ the
Gentiles have received pardoning grace and have in so doing become
heirs of the Abrahamic promises. This is so even though the national
distinctions remain intact (Gal. 6:16; 1 Cor. 10:32).

Paul struggled with the Judaizing Christians from Jerusalem who challenged Gentile members of the Galatian community to become circumcised. Some preachers of Gnostic persuasion also advocated circumcision as a mystical rite that would bring the Galatians to a higher state of perfection with or without the Law (Gal. 6:13).

Since circumcision and uncircumcision are irrelevant conditions for entry into the Body of Christ, for becoming Christian, a follower of Christ, these conditions should not be used as a condition for inclusion or exclusion or relating to one another. What makes for inclusion is "faith working through love" (Gal. 5:6) a "new creation" (Gal. 6:15) and "obeying the commandments of God" (1 Cor. 7:19).

"Listen! I, Paul am telling you that if you let yourselves be circumcised, Christ will be of no benefit to you" (Gal.5:2). The negation of Jew and Gentile in Christ implies that the distinction between circumcision and uncircumcision "counts for nothing" or "is nothing" (Gal. 5:6; 6:15; 1 Cor. &:19). Differences will always be there as an undifferentiated humanity does not exist. What is of importance is 'faith working through love' (Gal. 5:6), a 'new creation' (Gal . . . 6:15) and 'obeying the commandments of God' (1 Cor. 7:19). In fact Paul applies the issue concerning circumcision to both Greek and Jew in a transposed manner as expressed in 1 Cor. 7:18 where he says: "Was anyone at the time of his call already circumcised? Let him not seek to remove the marks of circumcision. Was anyone at the time of his call uncircumcised? Let him not seek circumcision". In Jesus Christ these categories that determine differences are irrelevant and of no avail. Paul, therefore, does not plead for the removal of differences between people, but he seeks to emphasize that these differences do not count within the Body of Christ. Paul appeals to the God characteristic of impartiality to be adopted as a characteristic of Christianity and this has implication as to how Christians are to behave to each other without distinction.

5.2.2. Neither slave or free

Slavery was an ignoble feature of the ancient world (Buckel 1993:13; Helmut Koester 1989: 59-62). It has been estimated that one in five persons in the Roman Empire was a slave. They became slaves in various ways: some were born into this state; others became enslaved through imprisonment by war, others became the property of their creditors. Regardless of how they assumed the condition of slavery their social inferiority was marked in Jewish society, and even more so in Mediterranean society; they had no legal rights, were subject to harsh conditions, and were not expected to live long.

Slaves, as well as women and Gentiles, were disqualified from several religious privileges within Judaism as these were safe-guarded only for free Jewish males. In fact similar formulas existed even among the Gentiles. The distinctions, important for Jewish life, are declared by Paul as invalid in Christ. For Paul a Christian slave, too, inherits the same promises as a free person, despite the fact that the slave is viewed as inferior to his master as evident in (Mt 10:24): "A student is not greater than the teacher. A slave is not greater than the master". Knowing the contradictory terms of social inequality of the time whereby the slave will always be inferior to his/her master even if the slave has better manners or deeper faith than the owner, the inclusivity of belonging to Christ has a universal touch to it and renders ineffective all classifications.

Paul in the context of the Galatian statement appeals that slavery and free should not be put forward as a categorization for exclusion or inclusion within the body of Christ. This is endorsed in 1 Cor. 7:22 where Paul claims that these categories are irrelevant because "a slave is a freed person belonging to the Lord, just as whoever was free when called is a slave of Christ". While it is difficult to discern whether early Christianity attributed equal worth and authority to masters and slaves (Eph. 5:5-9) this research does not wish to involve entailments that may be useful for this contemporary era, but which did not reflect the time of Paul as well as Christianity in antiquity. It appears that even the reality of inequality between masters and slaves which reflected a clear differentiation of authority did not count within Christianity, but demanded a new way of relating together. All, male or female, Jew or Gentile, slave or free, were Christians in equal measure and full members of the body of Christ. Such distinctions are negated. This principle is intricately woven into the fabric of early Christianity that was based on inclusion rather than the indefinable issue of equality.

New Testament writers did not call for the abolition of slavery; however, Paul called for Gospel transformation (2 Cor. 3:18; Rom 12:2). In this context he laid down the principle that the Gospel transforms all human relationships. The inferiority of slaves, so marked in ancient Roman, Hellenistic and Jewish societies, is not a deterrent to receive Abraham's promises on an equal basis as the freed counterpart. In the Epistle to Philemon Paul provided a convincing argument for the abolition of slavery in this instance, but emphasized at the same time the irrelevance of the institution of slavery for status and relationship with Christ (1 Cor. 7:17-24).

5.2.3. Neither male nor female

In the world of the first century (including Hellenism, Judaism and even early Christianity) misogyny and discrimination against women were the order of the day (1 Cor. 11:3. 7-8; Col 3:18; 1 Tim 2:11-14).

Before baptism people were polarized into Jews and Greeks, slaves and free, male and female, but in baptism all became equal. This antithesis: "there is not male and female", also stresses the fact that distinction in sex has no relevance to the fact that both are heirs of the promised blessing. If one belongs to Christ, then one is Abraham's seed and an heir according to the promise. Christ's people are God's children, baptized by the spirit in union with Him, the Son of God and Abraham's seed. However, the egalitarian impact of this statement may be somewhat mitigated by the one that immediately precedes, namely, "in Christ Jesus you are all sons (children) of God" (Gal. 3:36). Baptism makes you a "son" (child) of God whether one was male or female by the reception of the Holy Spirit (Gal. 4; 7cf) (Rom 6:1-11; Rom 10:9). Interestingly in using this male/female couplet does reflect some wording of Genesis 1:27: "*So God created humankind in his image, in the image of God he created them; male and female he created them.*" It may be important to explore this quotation in relation to a negation of the distinction expressed in the original sexual differentiation of humanity. It would be a possible misunderstanding to suppose that the negation of distinctions should be equated with the removal of differences, which then results in undifferentiated humanity. To the contrary Paul argues that the differences, and in particular the differences between Jews and Greeks, should not be erased, as in the case of circumcision, differences remain, but they should not become a source for exclusion. This statement of Paul was echoed later in Gnostic circles which held that in the new age the human person would no longer be separated into 'male and female, but would revert to the pristine androgynous state where Christ is recorded as foretelling the day 'when the two became one'.

Women in the Roman world of antiquity had a subsidiary role in society. The head male of the family had the power of life and death over his wife and children. He could accept or reject a child at birth. Women were denied the privilege of citizenship and their testimony in a court of law was inadmissible. She was expected to give up her religion for his, and never the other way round (Buckel 1993: 14) (This practice has not changed in current South African cultural groups). Adultery by a woman was punishable by death, while adultery committed by a man was almost presupposed. By and large the Roman women were under masculine authority for their entire lives. In such a male dominated world, it can be assumed that Paul's declaration to Galatians whereby he stated that there should be no distinction between male and female (Gal. 3:28), that such a statement would have been regarded as nothing less than revolutionary (Buckel 1993:14).

Inequality, in the Old Testament, commenced at birth. Every first-born male 'who opened his mother's womb had to be redeemed with a special sacrifice. A girl-child did not merit the same significance and worth (Ex 13, 11-16). All male children had to be circumcised on the eighth day after birth. This was an essential condition for belonging to the covenant, more or less parallel to Christian baptism for belonging to the Christian community. There was, however, no equivalent right for women (Gen 17, 9-14). This was tantamount to meaning that God had concluded his covenant with the men, the sons of Israel and women participated in the covenant, but women only indirectly, through their fathers and husbands. Paul showed deep awareness of the revolutionary changes brought about by Christ's baptism, and it is therefore significant that he subscribed to the fundamental equality between men and women to their equal participation in the sacrament of baptism. There was no exception as to both male and female "putting on Christ".

Paul operated by a divided consciousness in this sense that in other letters he lost the *ontic* gender implications and social implications of both men and women. While, according to Rom 16:3-5; Acts 18:24-26; 21:9; Rom 16:7; Phil 4:2-3, women seemed to have played a prominent role in Paul's churches, then again, 1 Cor. 11:3-16; 1 Cor. 14:33-36 give a conflicting impression. Women were not to speak in Church and had to cover their heads at all times. It appears, however, that Paul seems to contradict his sentiments in his letter to the 1 Corinthians 11:7: "For a man indeed ought not to cover his head, since he is the image and glory of God; but woman is the glory of man". Both Paul and James, reaffirm this basic, fundamental biblical teaching. It appears that this particular passage excludes women from sharing in the image of God, which, if true, would clearly contradict Genesis 1:26 and 5:2. However, just a few verses later Paul shows that this is not what he meant. "For as woman came from man, even so the man also comes through woman; but all things (including His image, reflecting His character) are from God" (1 Corinthians 11:12). Apparently Paul in discussing the Corinthian congregation's conduct seemingly disregards the culturally proper distinction between the roles of men and women.

Typical also in the Old Testament era was that a woman could not act as a full person, independently in her own right within religion. Everything she did was in the light of her father or her husband (Num.27:2-17). Women could not present sacrifices, while the men had to present themselves three times a year before the Lord. Going to the Temple was not obligatory for women (Ex 23:17). Arrangements in the Temple of Jerusalem even limited the access of women to an outside court, while men were allowed to proceed to the 'court of Israel).

Rosemary Radford Ruether (in her *Women and Redemption* (1998:31) claims that the emphasis on "no male and female" attempts to overcome sexual bimorphism through celibacy with women aspiring to be men. Paul, according to Reuther, took the baptismal formula, not because he was interested in an ontological return to pre-fallen wholeness or its implications of social equality of women with men, slaves with masters and would allow either women or slaves to throw off their subordination to the paterfamilias of the household. She maintains that what interested Paul was the religio-ethic pair Jew-Greek. In Corinth

Paul in his baptismal formula had to take note of gender implications. This then led him to reformulate the baptismal formula.

Equality in being and worth (ontological equality) is a clear biblical teaching, affirming that all human beings—male and female—have equal standing before God as created beings, in need of salvation through Christ and called to the same destiny. The scriptural evidence for this equality is that both 'male and female' were created in the 'image of God' (Gen 1:27; Matthew 19:4; Mark 10:6); both have been redeemed by Jesus Christ, so that "in Christ there is "neither male nor female" (Gal. 3:28) and both are joint heirs of the grace of life (1 Peter 3:7, RSV).

In Gal. 3:28 all believers have become one in Christ, sharing equally the redemption that Christ has won by the atoning sacrifice. "In Christ" the phrase refers to the mystical, the universal, the representative and covenantal union of all believers in the Lord. The question remains whether the phrase "neither male nor female" refers to equality of males and females and that all differences, even role differences are to be obliterated? Does this verse refer to full equality between male and female and what does 'full equality' really mean?

5.3. EGALITARIAN IDEOLOGY DESPITE DIFFERENCES

Radical egalitarianism or equalitarianism holds that all human beings are equal despite differences. It protests exploitation as a result of differences such as rich or poor, male or female, black and white, educated and uneducated. However, to define full equality without differences is almost an anomaly as it implies obliterating human variations. There is a perception that equality among humans of being and worth is only ontological as it is a biblical teaching that claims that all human beings—male and female—have equal standing before God as created beings in need of salvation. This understanding is borne out of the Genesis statement that both 'male and female' were created 'in the image of God (Gen 1:27; Mt 19:4; Mk 10:6). Both male and female were redeemed by Jesus Christ so that in Christ there is neither "male nor female" (Gal. 3:28) and both male and female are joint heirs of the grace of life (1 Pet. 3:7).

The question is whether Gal. 3:28 refers to equality and what is meant by full equality. Does equality mean equal in all respects? What are the standards of comparison whereby one measures equality as things and people in life are both equal and unequal. Aristotle said that the worst form of equality is to try and make unequal things equal. It is clear that Gal. 3:28 cannot be coerced into the ambiguousness of equality. Is there a difference between biblical equality and other equality such as social or political equality? What is the nature of the equality that is taught by the polar opposites or couplets of Gal. 3:28? Both Jews/Greek, male/ female, slave/free, circumcised/circumcised are "equally justified by faith" (v.24), equally free from bondage of legalism (v.25), equally children of God (v.26) equally clothed with Christ (v.27), equally possessed by Christ (v.28) and equally heirs of the promises to Abraham (v.29).

The couplet "neither Jew or Gentile" captures the totality of humanity from a salvation-historical perspective since Scripture describes the Gospel promise as coming first from the Jews and to the Gentiles. From the ancient Roman perspective all people were either "slave or free". This was a legal distinction for dividing all people. The "male or female" couplet divides humanity according to their basic sexual identity granted to them at creation. Regardless of how people are viewed, be it from a salvation-historical perspective, or a legal perspective, or from a creation perspective, they all share the same privilege of covenantal union with God in Christ and they do so in equal measure.

Contemporary feminist egalitarianism calls for Gospel transformation as was laid out by Paul in Gal. 3:28; 2 Cor. 3:18; Rom 12:2). Historically it can be argued that the barrier between Jew and Gentile has been broken down, between slave and master and, according to these feminists authors the time has come for the gender barrier to be eradicated. According to Schüssler Fiorenza (1983:217-18) contemporary feminist readings of Gal. 3:28 Christian self-understanding are doing away with all male privileges of religion, class, caste, and allows not only Gentiles and slaves, but also women to exercise leadership functions within the mission of the Church. Whatever reading is most preferred by contemporary theologians, there is no doubt that for Paul human distinctions of race, social rank, and sex are in some sense nullified in Christ and the means that brings this about is baptism in Christ.

The exegetical understanding and implication of Gal. 3:28-29 implies a new vertical relationship in God resulting in a new equal horizontal relationship with people, male, female, free, slave, Jew or Gentile. All inequalities, as stated by Hansen (1994:112), racial, economic and gender barriers are removed in Christ as equality and unity of all in Christ are part of the essence of the Gospel. Equality in Christ implies inclusiveness, unity and justness in Christ and in the life and ministry of Christ. Paul was of strong opinion that racial equality between Jews and Gentiles was to be an implemented and experienced reality within the early Christian community. The expression of racial superiority of one group over another was a violation of the essence of the Gospel of Jesus Christ. Any expression of racial superiority, gender superiority (men over women), social superiority (the slave over the free) articulated then and now violates the truth of the Gospel. All divisions and prejudices Paul is of opinion had been abolished in Christ (Hansen 1994:112).

Paul argues that Gentiles do not have to become Jews to be fully accepted by Jewish Christians and in so doing become fully part of the life of the followers of Christ. In the same vein today, black people do not have to become white or females do not have to become male for full participation on the life and ministry of Jesus Christ. By faith in Jesus Christ the Gentile, the slave and the woman have been included in the full realm and inheritance of Christ. No restriction is implied in Paul's equalizing of the status of all people regardless of racial, social or gender status. By virtue of the fact that all believers in Christ belong to Christ, and as such are directly related to Abraham and are recipients of the blessing and promises promised to Abraham, they are also sharing in the full membership of the covenant People of God. Faith in Christ obliterates the need of the law as a means to secure or maintain that status and Paul claims that for any Gentile to gain status or receive blessing by observing the Mosaic Law is foolish since they have already been included in the community of Christ.

5.4. EVALUATION AND CONCLUSIONS

The identity feature of Christianity in antiquity that emerged in this chapter is that according to Paul's writing to the Galatians, Christianity is "*inclusive*". Once a person has put on Christ, or had been baptized into Christ, all boundaries that existed up till now had been broken down. The most profound distinctions within the human society namely racial, cultural, social, economic, sexual and gender are no longer relevant and this inclusivity forms part of the 'kingdom-perspective" which informed Jesus' ministry on earth. As indicated by Dunn (1994:207) it was not Paul's intension to have all these distinctions removed as in early Christianity Jews in Christ were still Jews (Gal.2:15) and Christian slaves did not cease to be slaves (1 Cor. 5:21). Instead these social, racial and gender differentiations were relativized seeing that it was thought that they indicated relative worth or privileged status before God, but according to Paul's teaching they no longer carried that significance as all were equal before God in Christ. This was so as the Jews were of opinion that "under the law Jews were regarded more highly by God than the Greeks. By implication what Paul addresses here is the assumption that the slave and the woman are disadvantaged before God a view that was also common in Hellenistic Christianity (Dunn 1994:207). The character of unity/oneness would then be not so much the eradication of all racial, social or gender differences, but an integration of such differences into a common inclusiveness 'in Christ'. This type of inclusiveness enhances the unity of the Body of Christ and enhances interdependence and the diversity which includes differences is a visible display of God creation.

This research therefore proposes "inclusion" as a principal identity characteristic of nascent Christianity and that it should not be confined to equality or egalitarianistic ideological perspectives. While egalitarianism holds that all human beings are equal and rightly protests against the exploitation resulting from human differences based on male and female, rich and poor, black and white, slave and free, foreigner and resident, the philosophy of "inclusions", as related to the understanding that "in Christ there is neither male nor female, circumcised nor uncircumcised, Jew nor Gentile, slave nor free" solicits an inherent significance for equality and egalitarianism. It is, however, designed to surpass the obvious concerns related to current interpretations of egalitarianism, but not to ignore them as they also fall within the realm of inclusivity. It appears therefore that the fundamental Pauline theological basis for "inclusion theology" invites us to transcend the ideological teachings of equality and egalitarianism.

The call to human oneness says John Riches (2008:210) is a stirring call to equality, but at the same time constitutes a clear threat to Jewish and other differences. The intent was not to deprive continued Jewish of continued existence, but it had that effect in the Christian development of history. For Schüssler Fiorenza (1983:209-210), Gal.: 3:26-28 provides clear evidence for the emancipating outlook of early Christian communities, which saw themselves called to a 'discipleship of equals'".

The Jesus-Movement offered an alternative interpretation of the Torah that opened access to God for everyone, whether they are members of the elect people of Israel or those who had little chance of experiencing God's presence in the Temple and Torah because of their social, religious or economic situation. Women were included in the early Christian movement and also in the communities among which Paul moved. Schüssler Fiorenza (1983:209-210) maintains that Gal. 3:28 was written to uphold the 'abolition of the religious distinctions between Jew and Greek'. In Christ all were truly set free and included, and for Paul to advise women to remain unmarried was undeniably a severe infringement of the right of paterfamilias since according to Roman Law a woman remained under the tutorship of her father and family, even after she is married. Thus Paul's advice to widows, who were not necessarily 'old', offered a possibility for 'ordinary' women to become independent. Paul seemed to have objected to the notion that a woman must become first a male so as to undo Eve's fall. This sexist view of salvation is found in the tradition of the Hellenistic Jews manifested in 1 Corinthians 11:2-16. By opposing this anthropology with its misogyny and asceticism it seems, says Mac Donald (1987:131), that Paul affirmed human sexuality—both male and female.

Human equality in Christ, as expressed in Gal. 3:26-28, is an important teaching worth exploring, but the theology of inclusions works towards counter-acting all barriers against the process of inclusions. Gal. 3:28 is therefore not merely a statement on equal access to salvation, but refers also to the three relationships that had perverted God's original plan by making one group unequal to another: (1) Jew-Gentile, (2) slave-free, and (3) male-female.

Gal. 3:28 is much cited today to promote equality, gender equality, social equality, racial and political equality. But the question is: does Gal. 3:28 teach full equality of unity? To be one in Christ: does not necessarily amount equality, or unqualified equality. To be one in Christ, presupposes the inclusivity of differences, as well as equality in differences. Gal. 3:28 does not teach full equality by means of the obliteration of differences. Jew-Gentile, slave-free, circumcised-uncircumcised, male-female differences do not preclude equal justification by faith (v.24), equal freedom from the bondage of legalism (v. 25), equal status children of God (v. 26), equal clothed with Christ (v.27), equally possessed by Christ (v. 29) and equally heirs to the promises to Abraham (v. 29).

The notion of inclusivity taught by Gal. 3:28 contains a true notion of equality in this sense that while there is no negation of the existence of distinctions such as male or female, it does, however, emphasize universality in oneness, or collective totality or common wholeness.

In a conference paper on Gal. 3:28 Samuel Koranteng-Pipim proposes that the first couplet namely: "neither Jew nor Greek", captures or symbolizes the totality of humanity from a salvation-historical perspective. Since Scripture describes the Gospel promise as coming first to the Jews, then to the Gentiles, from the religious perspective of the Jew all the world can be divided into two parts, Jew and Gentile. The second couplet "neither slave nor free" was the primary legal distinction for dividing all people. From a Roman perspective, all men or women were either free or slaves. And the third couplet "neither male nor female," divides humanity according to their basic sexual identity given them at creation. Accordingly, from a Creation perspective, all humanity can be divided into two groups—male and female[5]. The interpretation here is that regardless of how people are viewed, be it from the salvation-historical perspective of the Jew, or from the legal

---

[5]   The article "Feminism's "New Light" on Galatians 3:28—Part 2 Feminism, Equality, and the Church" is taken from the author's book *Must We Be Silent?*—Samuel Koranteng-Pipim. Director, Public Campus Ministries, Michigan Conference).

perspective of the Roman, or from the Creation perspective of God, they share in the same privilege of union with Christ.

The key to understanding this text is the powerful tension between Paul's strong identification of himself as a Jew and his equally powerful identification of himself as a Christian. By using this ancient baptismal formula Paul asserts that by baptism the status of the one who believes in Christ is unity, oneness and inclusiveness as this constitutes a baptized person's status in Christ. For all that were baptized in Christ have gone through a unifying incorporation into Christ, thus the Galatians have put on Christ (Rom 6:3-5; 1 Cor. 12:13). As stated by MacDonald (1987:10) Paul's use of the baptismal beatitude reflects revolutionary changes caused by Paul's original preaching in Galatia. Paul quotes the baptismal formula to remind them of the radical egalitarianism expressed in the common rite of initiation. The baptism into Christ resulted in the emancipation from religious, social and sexual distinctions. Gal. 3:28 belongs to the baptismal ritual which symbolized the initiates return to the androgyny of the first human. As pointed out by MacDonald (1987:11), Jews, early Christians and Gnostics often assumed that Adam was originally "masculofeminine". To put off the old human—refers to the removal of the robes of skin (Gen 3:21), the body and to re-cloth in the image of God one puts on Christ, the new human (Meeks 1974:207). Paul insists on the equality of all and their inclusion into the community formed by the Spirit—the new order is the image of God. The pairs of opposites in Gal. 3:28 represent the building blocks of the old world, which is being replaced by God's action in establishing a new creation. Religious and ethic differences and what which underlies them, the Law, are identified as the 'old things' that have now passed away; they give place to the new creation (2 Cor. 5:17).

Inclusiveness as a prime identity feature of Christianity inherent in the all-encompassing nature of the baptismal formula had ontological, cosmological and social implications for Christianity in antiquity, and even for today. Hansen (1994:14) alleges that whatever ethnic rivalries are destroying societies, the letter to the Galatians calls Christians to express the truth of the Gospel of communities where there is no ethnic or social or gender divisions. For Paul makes it clear that in Christ Jesus there is neither circumcision nor uncircumcision, this had no value, only faith which expresses itself in love is of value (Gal. 5:6).

Paul uses the truth of the Gospel to obliterate all ethnic divisions and this counts as the new creation (Gal. 6:15). This new creation is a new community of all believers where the divisions and alienations of the world is overcome and healed in Christ. While there is freedom in Christ to maintain and respect ethnic, social and gender distinctions, these distinctions must not be allowed to cause divisions between believers in Christ.

The central focus on the letter to the Galatians is the equality and unity of all believers in Christ. As will be reflected upon in the next chapter, Paul demonstrates that faith in Christ and the consequent presence of the Spirit establish the identity and guide of the behaviour of those who call themselves believers in Jesus Christ. Life in the Spirit determines a new vertical relationship with God and this in turn results in a new horizontal relationship with other human beings. All inequalities: racial, economic, gender or religious barriers are removed in Christ. The equality and unity of all in Christ are part of the essence of the Gospel of Paul.

Equality in Christ is therefore the starting point of all racial, social, ecclesial, religious and economical ethics.

The Church today is especially guilty in not expressing the equality and unity in Christ and as such its life and ministry is not faithful to the Gospel. Paul's immediate concern in his letter to the Galatians was to ensure that the racial equality of the Jews and Gentiles is implemented within the Christian community. Gentiles were in danger of being demoted to second class status because they were not Jews. The expression of racial superiority was a violation of the essence of the Gospel. Similarly, any expression of social class (slaves and free, the free over the slaves) or gender superiority (men over women) contradicts the truth of the Gospel (Hansen 1994:112). When women are excluded from significant participation in the life and ministry of the Christian community the essence of the Gospel is negated. Inclusiveness implies that Gentiles do not have become Jews to the fully accepted by Jewish

Christians and thus fully part of the Body of Christ. In the same vein: blacks do not to become white nor do females have to become male for full participation in the life and ministry of the church, of society and in the economic and cultural world. As stated by Bruce (1982:190) no restriction is implied in Paul's equalizing of the status between Jew and Gentile, male and female, slave or free person in Christ. "If in ordinary life existence in Christ is manifested openly in Church fellowship, then if a Gentile may exercise spiritual leadership in the church as freely as a Jew, or a slave as freely as a citizen, why not a woman as freely as a man" (Bruce 1982:190).

CHAPTER SIX

6. Paul's Ethics As An Established Christian Identity Criterion

6.1. Introduction

The purpose of this chapter is to examine Paul's ethics as an additional established Christian identity criterion ordained and shaped by the content of his letter to the Galatians. Identity here refers to the self-understanding that Christians came to develop about themselves as a group of believers in Jesus Christ. The formation of the growing Christian identity was based on criteria which included the mode of conduct or ethic which became apparent from the circumstances between the Christian Jews and Christian Gentiles, a situation which Paul was obliged to address.

This section intends to ascertain how Paul's ethical instructions mapped out the moral conduct of the Galatian believers. The ethical identity features of Christianity, as outlined by Paul's writing to the Galatians, will be extrapolated from Paul instruction on Christian behaviour and how this served as a directive towards Christian identity formation. Paul's ethics, as a specific Christian identity feature, concretely express how rules (ethics) inform behavioural categories and thus functionally display the people's distinctiveness and in this instance the identity of Christians in Galatia. It appeared that the Galatian Christians experienced a double identity crisis as far as their relationship with Judaism was concerned and their new-found faith known as '*a Way*' within Judaism.

This chapter also endeavours to establish how Paul's ethical teaching resembles those of Greek and Roman philosophers in content, form and terminology. It is crucial to assess the origin, the shape, logic and the continuing relevance of Paul's ethics regardless whether it is Jewish or Hellenistic in essence. As it is a position of this research to appreciate the Graeco-Roman world as a basis to comprehend Paul teachings so too is it important to grasp Paul's ethical instructions in order to understand what he perceived as acceptable Christian behaviour. While the Graeco-Roman ethics, contemporary to Paul, would have had an influence on his ethics, the Roman ethics would also have been perceived as somewhat revolutionary in the world of Paul's converts. An example, in case, is the idea to "humble oneself" or the down-to-earth virtue of humility, which was *not* viewed positively in the Greek ethical environment, but would have been valued as a good ethical feature for Paul. The reason was because Jesus Christ humbled himself and took the form of a servant and became obedient until death (Phil. 2:6-11). The God of the Jewish Scriptures also humbles the proud and raises the humble (1 Sam: 2: 1-10) but this was atypical in the Roman-Greek world.

While this research has interest in determining the relevance of Paul's moral specifications for Christians in antiquity, it also holds the attraction as to what significance it holds for people today. The letter to the Galatians embraces a whole gamut of ethical questions, but for the purposes of this research specific attention would be given to Paul's ethical instructions according to Gal. 5:13-6.10 as well as to the role of ethics and the law within Paul's theology. It is well to know that in Galatians Paul does not address questions of ethics, instead he issues ethical exhortation. Paul's ethical exhortation reflects the influence of Hellenistic moral exhortation or *paraclesis,* (from the Greek *parainesis* meaning exhortation, recommendation, encouragement, beseeching or appeal). The attempted definition of *paraenesis* by Dibelius reads that it is a text which strings together admonitions of general ethical content; it contains sayings and groups of sayings very diverse in content, lacking only particular order, and contains no emphasis upon a special thought of pressing importance for a particular situation (A commentary on the Epistle James—H. Green Philadelphia 1976:3). In the words of Gerard Ebeling (1985:247) the vacillating Galatians at that time needed more than doctrinal instruction; they needed to be shaken up by exhortation and in this case ethical exhortations. The question of circumcision represented a danger to freedom and as such to the revolutionary newness of Christian life. For the exhortation to endure, Ebeling (1985:248) writes, it had to focus on the prerequisite of Christian ethical conduct, namely, on the virtue of freedom. Nowhere else in Paul's writings does one find such a systematic treatment of ethics from the ground up.

For the purposes of this research the term "ethics" is used to refer to the underlying theological substructure, particularly the principles or ethical pointers which serve as guidelines as to how a follower of Christ should conduct him or herself. To assess the nature and character of Paul's ethics as an identity characteristic of Christianity in antiquity, it is therefore essential to grasp what Paul had in mind for the Galatians and how they were to conduct themselves *after* he wrote the letter to them. The question was: as an end result would they have known what constitutes right from wrong behaviour? While the guidelines for right and wrong behaviour can be detected throughout the entire letter, for the purposes of this research, attention will be focused on ethical behaviour as specifically spelled out in Gal. 5:2-6:10.

6.2. SCRIPTURE AS THE FOUNDATIONAL PROFILE OF PAUL'S ETHICS

Paul's letter to the Galatians raises a whole range of questions concerning his ethics. While some relate specifically to Gal. 5:13-6.10, others arise out of the whole subject matter of the letter and the role of ethics and the law within Paul's theology (Barclay 1988: 27). Paul's *paraenesis* according to Gal. 5 appears not to be original, as the material of his contemporary Jewish and Hellenistic environment is evident within his moral instructions. There are similar citations on Lev. 19:18 as a summary of the law in Gal. 5:14. Paul's use of Hellenistic style *"sententiae"* in Gal. 6:1-10 also suggests that his *paraenesis* is not an entirely original creation (Barclay 1988:27). The Dibelius studies suggests that Paul's ethical teaching was adopted more or less wholesale from contemporary traditions and had no significant connections to his theological insights.

Various scholars would have different views with regard to the source of Paul's ethical content. While it appears that the Jewish origins of Paul's ethics is a somewhat neglected study there are prevailing views that much of his ethical material consisted of the modification of the Jewish catechism (Rosner 1995:15). This observation is based on the argument of Alfred Seeberg's *Der Katechismus der Urchristenheit* (1903) that Christian catechism in antiquity was based on the Jewish catechism and it contained a section that included catalogues of virtues and vices. It stands to reason, therefore, that scholars would claim that Paul's Jewish background would have made an enormous contribution to his ethical forms; this however does not rule out the idea that Paul would have appealed to his Hellenistic influences as well. The most recent scholarly research testifies that the ethical directives in Paul's letters are mostly from Hellenistic Judaism. All the same, as Brian Rosner (1995:17) points out, Paul's moral reflections cannot be separated from his own theological understandings as his moral imperatives customary rests on the basis of God's prior action on behalf of believers in Christ. For him the ethical injunctions and prohibitions are rooted in the redemptive acts of God. As a Hellenistic Pharisee it is also noticeable that Paul stood between the Jewish and the Gentile world. As again stated by Rosner (1994:24) there are relatively few quotations from Scripture in Paul's ethics, but despite this, the Scriptures do constitute a crucial and formative source for Paul's ethics. To endorse this claim the thesis uses Paul's own words when he said: Scripture was "written for our ethical instruction" (1 Cor. 10:11; Rom 15:4). This teaching in itself has considerable implications in determining Paul's ethical instruction specifically as an identity feature of Christianity in antiquity.

To ascertain the Jewish background to Paul's ethics implies obtaining evidences that his ethical instruction was definitely influenced by Jewish moral teaching. This can be done, as suggested by Rosner (1995:29), by dividing the study into four sections which cover:

- the early period
- household codes
- ethical lists and
- Paul's ethics in general.

The household codes, which are either Stoic, Jewish and Christian in origin, supply good evidence of the Jewish inspiration of Paul's ethics at the level of both form and content and this is particularly obvious in his traditional *paraenesis* found in Col 3:18-4:1 and Eph. 5:22-6:9. It appears, says Rosner's (1994:29), that the Hellenistic Jewish codes are significantly more similar to the Pauline codes than that of the Stoics. But what really interests this study is the *paraenesis* that engage the traditional catalogues of virtues and vices and examples thereof are found in 1 Cor. 5:9-11; 6;9-10; Rom 1:29-31;13;13; Gal. 5:19-23 and Phil. 4:8. It is an acknowledged idea that Paul would have been familiar with the ethics of Jewish literature and it is clear that some of Paul's ethics bear some similarity to extant rabbinic literature, sharing in the same ethical instruction tradition (Rosner 1994:35).

While it is a given that Scripture had significantly influenced Jewish moral teaching and to ascertain the Jewish mediation of Scripture to Paul's ethics implies examining each ethical pronouncement so as to determine to what extent Paul used the Old Testament in the ethical exposition of his instructions. According to the views of Rosner (1994:57) not only did Scripture influence Paul's ethics directly, but it also influenced his direct use of Scripture. Besides his familiarity with Jewish moral teaching, which in itself distilled and developed Scripture, it has also indirectly influenced his ethical perspectives. Rosner (1994:57) holds the opinion that Paul heard the moral demands of Scripture through his Jewish 'filter' particularly when he formulated the ethical instruction as recorded in his letters.

On the other hand to claim that Paul focused exclusively on, either the Scriptures or Jewish moral teaching, is to weaken the origin of Paul's ethics and runs the risk of impoverishing the exegesis of his paraenesis. Even in the case when the influence of Scripture does not appear apparent in Paul's ethics, Rosner (1994:58) is of opinion that on close study it will be revealed that the influence of Scripture is indirectly related via the mediation of Jewish moral teaching. It can thus be reliably concluded that the Jewish Scriptures are a crucial and formative source for Paul's ethics. The major lines of Paul's ethics in Galatians 5:20 can reliably be traced to the Scriptures as well as to Jewish or Hellenistic sources.

6.3. THE INDICATIVE AND CORRELATIVE ORIENTATION OF PAUL'S ETHICS

The overall orientation of Paul's ethics is the close correlation between the indicative (what God had done) to the imperatives (what believers must do). The imperative is integrated into the indicative and *vice versa* as each is part and parcel of the other. The imperative constitutes merely the ethical cutting edge of the indicative, as the indicative forms the fundamental and transformative basis of the imperative (du Toit 2006:172).

The unique feature of Pauline paraenesis is the direct influence of the word on the life of those whom he addressed in his letter. In Ebeling's (1985:250) view, to speak in the imperative can be useful only against the background of a strong indicative. Ebeling is therefore of opinion that the loss of the Christian paraenetic imperative is most likely due to the impoverishment of the confessional indicative. What follows is an illustration of the transformative nature of Paul's paraenetic imperative and the indicative. For example this can be seen with the compass of a single verse in the following three cases namely:

- 1 Cor. 5:7: So get rid of the old yeast (imperative) and make yourselves into a complete new batch of bread, unleavened as you are meant to be (Indicative).

- Gal. 5:1: when Christ freed us, he meant us to remain free. (indicative). Stand firm, therefore, and so not submit again to the yoke of slavery (Imperative).

- Gal. 5:25: "since the Spirit is our life, (indicative) let us be directed by the Spirit (imperative).

The understanding is that the behaviour of believers should inform their identity and the identity of believers ought to inform their behaviour, that is, they are to become what they already are in the eyes of God. In the light of this reasoning, the identity features of Paul's ethics would determine the identity features of the behaviour of those who call themselves believers in Christ. The logic of the indicative can be perceived as a distinguishing mark of Paul's ethics, but also of biblical ethics in general. Throughout the Bible, human behaviour is always considered in the context of the underlying and overarching relationship with God; what God's people have become is the basis of what they must do. This is evident in the following Old Testament examples and one could be certain that Paul would have been familiar with these verses and their implications.

The Decalogue . . . the first three commandments
Exodus 20:2
Numbers 15: 40-41
Deut 7:5-6; 14:1-2; 29:9-10

In the prophetic literature of the Old Testament, misconduct is uniformly concerned with unfaithfulness to the God of the covenant who redeemed the Chosen People. The same balance and reciprocity of the moods are evident in 1 Cor. 5:7; Gal. 5:1 and 5:25 and can be observed in the Old Testament in Leviticus 20:7-8. "Consecrate yourself therefore to be holy (imperative) . . . . who makes holy (indicative).

The indicatives above show that the imperatives of progressive sanctification are not optional. Christian conduct for Paul implies "appropriate, becoming, seemly conduct" as suggested by Col 3:5-14 where he says "take off your old clothes, put on something more suitable to your status as those chosen and loved by God". Paul, in Rosner's (1995:20) view, links theology to ethics so there is a connection between orthodoxy and orthopraxy, following the understanding that good doctrine leads to good behaviour. Good doctrine is thus supposed to support good behaviour or else could lead to empty and impotent moralism.

The identity of the ethics of Paul is based on the "truth of the Gospel" (Gal. 2: 5 and 2:15) and according to D.F. Tolmie (in J.G. Van Der Watt 2006:248) the three theological concepts that dominate the ethics in Galatians are *spiritual liberty, love and the Spirit*. This in itself, as instructed by Paul, is not a once for all achievement, but a gradual process. Tolmie (2006:250) explains further that the ethical behaviour of Christians reflects spiritual liberty and is generally restrained by love and guided by the Spirit. While the opposite is also possible, in this sense, that it reflects a return to spiritual slavery by succumbing to the flesh. The three concepts could never be isolated totally from one another as they are essentially inter-related. The best way perhaps to summarize the ethics in Galatians would be to link these concepts together as one, namely: *"Spiritual liberty, love and the Spirit"*. However, to pinpoint the characteristics of Paul's ethics as a specific identity characteristic of Christianity in antiquity, distinctive attention will need be given to *"Spiritual liberty, love and the Spirit"* so as to determine how these three concepts provide Christian ethics with a specific Christian substance.

6.4. THE NATURE OF PAUL'S ETHICS IN GAL. 5:19-23

The customary appreciation of ethics is that it deals with conduct that is acceptable and honourable; with behaviour that is good and just, and although it can be done by all and maybe not be automatically recognized by all, it can, however, be expected that everyone has the capacity to live out of it. In general it appears that Paul's ethics is open to what can be expected of most people, it is a fundamental standard of all human conduct and this is especially true of Paul's description of the fruit of the Spirit (Ebeling 1985:248). According to Tolmie (2006:251) the distinction between what Paul puts forward as right and wrong behaviour correlates with that which would have been considered by many people in antiquity as the norms for right or wrong conduct. The "vice and virtue lists" of Paul would not have fallen outside the realm of the common knowledge of believers in antiquity. There is thus a common agreement that Gal. 5:19-23 would have belonged to the form of "virtue and vice catalogues", which consisted of a dualistic or "two-way scheme" (Brinsmead 1982:165). The dualistic form or two-way scheme of the Gal. 5:19-23 "virtue and vice catalogue" is both paraenetic and propagandistic in intent. The vice list in Paul's letter to the Galatians is expressed in the following manner:

> 19 Now the works of the flesh are plain: fornication, impurity, licentiousness, 20 idolatry, sorcery, enmity, strife, jealousy, anger, selfishness, dissension, party spirit, 21 envy, drunkenness, carousing, and the like.

The virtue list is related to the Spirit and reads as follows:

> 22 But the fruit of the Spirit is love, joy, peace, patience, kindness, goodness, faithfulness, 23 gentleness, self-control; against such there is no law.

The so-called catalogue of virtues and vices, of which the above text contains an impressive example, in effect testifies to the type of shared or common knowledge that constituted right or wrong behaviour. What is dealt with here is traditional ethical material and there can be no claim that it was specifically Christian. Ebeling (1985: 248) claims that the catalogues above demonstrate in particular their dependence on popular Hellenistic philosophy and Jewish morality. The ethics of freedom which is an ethic of the Spirit, obviously does not lead to moral—or even immoral—extravagance, neither does it lead to elitist in-groups or heroic accomplishments, but to a surprisingly inconspicuous way of life that, for the most part, adapts to custom and the existing order. For this reason, as remarked by Ebeling (1985:248), it would be wrong to create an impression that ethics is merely an unspecific appendix to the Christian faith.

A good example to illustrate this idea is to peruse the list of the works of the flesh in contrast to the list of the fruit of the spirit, which for Betz (1979: 281-282) corresponds to a large degree to the vice and virtue lists that existed in antiquity. This, however, in Tolmie's (2006:251) view, is not altogether true regarding Paul's two lists in Galatians, as these lists reflected the notions present in the world in which he lived. In actual fact Paul's correlations resonate stronger with the Judaic ideas of his time, despite the fact that his letter to the Galatians is very much addressed to the rights and wrongs of both the Gentile and Jewish Christians of the time. Coupled with the contrast between the work and the fruit there exists a difference between a significant plural (works of the flesh) and a significantly singular (fruit of the Spirit). The difference is reflected in the structure of the catalogues (Ebeling 1985:256).

Relating to Tolmie's view, despite all the correlations that can be pointed out, "the 'total package' presented in Galatians was a unique combination of the ancient world in this sense that it differs from both Gentile and

Jewish views. In support of this perception Gal. 3:26 illustrates that Paul's views on right and wrong differ from the dominant views of the Gentile world since he echoes the baptismal tradition:

> 26 for in Christ Jesus you are all sons of God through faith. 27 For as many of you were baptized into Christ. 28 There is neither Jew nor Greek, there is neither slave nor free, there is neither male or female for you are one in Christ Jesus.

Gal. 3:26-28 makes it is clear that behaviour and attitudes based on all distinctions, distinctive of that time, are no longer acceptable and thus the presentation of Paul's ethics can be termed revolutionary. Martyn (1998:376) reasons that the distinctions, as outlined in Galatians 3:26, were nothing more than regulated behaviour in ancient society and in many cases such distinctions would have been regarded as the elements that gave the world a dependable structure. Be that as it may, with Paul this was no longer the case as in Christ such distinctions no longer have any meaning and value, in fact they served no purpose.

Reference to baptism here is the essential newness that becomes apparent in Paul's ethic. It lies not in the new forms of ethical behaviour, but in a decisive shift in the division of the ages. In Christ the new ages has already arrived, the spirit has come and the new person has already appeared. By virtue of their baptism into the community of believers namely the "Body of Christ", they have already become righteous and holy (Brinsmead 1982: 165). What is new here in Gal. 5:24) is that Christian ethics are eschatological ethics, the ethics of life are for the first time turned towards the future (1 Cor. 6:12-20). The catalogue of vices and virtues as cited by Paul is the indicative on which the imperative is based. The first five vices: fornication, impurity, licentiousness, idolatry, sorcery and the last two, drunkenness, carousing, belonging to a family environment and the other eight vices namely enmity, strife, jealousy, anger, selfishness, dissension, party spirit, envy, relate specifically to community life.

The list of virtues: love, joy, peace, patience, kindness, goodness, faithfulness, gentleness, self-control are the fruit of the spirit and not separate individual traits of character. Love embraces as well as includes all the other virtues that follow. As expressed by Brinsmead (1982:167), these virtues put into ethical terms the life of the community of the new age, which is the life of the Spirit. It is primarily with the subject of love in the community that the ethical topoi are concerned, hence the final part of the imperative inclusion is the call to love in the community and this is taken up immediately. The life of the new age, which is the life of freedom from the law and freedom in the Spirit, is a life of love in the community in concrete terms (Brinsmead 1982:168).

The lists of vices and virtues function both are indicative and as imperative. The virtue list climaxes in the declaration of the arrival of the new age. The list has become for Paul an indicative which lifts Christian ethics to an entirely new plane. The double catalogue and the ethical topoi are inseparable in function and content. The double catalogue takes up the well-known ethical values of the Jewish opponents and modifies them at most significant points, and proclaims these as the values of the new age into which the Galatians have already been established by faith and baptism. So the ethical topoi take up the traditional values which belong within the ethical propaganda of the opponents themselves (Brinsmead 1982:169).

Six of Paul's vices are enumerated in the Qumran catalogue and Paul's vices belong more to the common Greek ethical tradition than do his virtues. The virtue list are much more reflections of the self-understanding of the community. Paul raises to serious heights the failure to live out love in the community and this very ethic is also at the very heart of the Qumran catalogue. In Gal. 6:2 Paul came to characterize his ethics as the law of Christ. The fulfillment of the "whole law" became a real eschatological possibility only in the new freedom of the Spirit; the new creation is there the possibility of realizing the command's intention to bestow life (Brinsmead 1982:180).

The vice list climaxed with the threat of damnation whereas, the virtue list climaxed by salvation. In both, says Brinsmead (1982:171), there is a tension of indicative and imperative. In Galatians the time of salvation, the time of the Spirit, has already come: the flesh has been crucified and there is no need for someone to live under its domination.

There were definitely differences which Paul's ethics reflected from both the Gentiles as well as the Jews of his time. One such difference would be his rejection of idolatry as a religious practice among the Gentiles. In Gal. 4:8 Paul reminds the Gentiles that idolatry was a behaviour of theirs prior to them becoming Christians, but it is not congruent with Christian behaviour, as this falls among his list of vices cited in Gal. 5:20 (Tolmie 2006:252). Worshipping idols is another of these differences. It is a practice that can be traced back to the time when their lives were that of spiritual slaves (Gal. 4:8-9). Despite the fact that there are quite a bit of overlapping between Paul's list of the fruit of the Spirit and the virtues admired by the Gentiles of his time, there also existed distinctions between Paul's views of right and wrong conduct and those commonly accepted by Jews of his time. For example the Jews considered it wrong to eat with Gentiles, while Paul saw nothing wrong with Jewish Christians having table-fellowship with Gentile Christians. In Paul's estimation to have created this separation was unethical as well as hypocritical (Gal. 2:13).

As far as the Jews were concerned circumcision was a God-requirement and the Gentile Christians were thus under religious obligation to conform to this practice to ensure full participation in the Christ-community. Here too Paul was of different opinion and went that far to warn the Galatian Christians that if they adhere to this Jewish practice Christ would be of no benefit to them (Gal. 5:2). Paul objected vehemently to the Gentiles being subjected to the cultic celebrations unique to the Jewish calendar. Being a Jew himself, Paul had no problem with the practices *per se*, but to have it imposed on the Gentile Christians as a prerequisite towards full membership in the Christian community was, in his view, unethical and thus totally unacceptable.

Paul, as articulated by Tolmie (2006:252), presents a unique ethical package and this distinct combination of right and wrong behaviour cannot, according to his letter to the Galatians, be motivated by the law. For Paul the law does not articulate the will of God for humankind. Instead the fruit of the Spirit presents what is required to produce behaviour aligned with God's will. For Paul ethical behaviour is embodied by three notions: ***spiritual liberty, love***

and the guidance of the Spirit[6]. Unethical actions and behaviour are regarded as immoral because they do not embody these notions. According to Paul Christians who are unethical are enslaved by things of the flesh. According to Paul's teaching, ethical behaviour embodies "spiritual liberty restrained by love and the guidance of the Spirit" (5:14-15; 19:21). It is therefore unethical to force Gentile Christians to live like Jews (2:14). Coercion for Paul embodies spiritual slavery and this in his terms is immoral. In the words of Tolmie (2006:254): "the line of distinction between right and wrong behaviour is drawn by the contrast between *spiritual liberty/ love/ Spirit and spiritual slavery/ the flesh*".

6.4.1. The ethics of freedom (spiritual liberty)

The freedom of which Paul speaks in Gal. 4:31 and 5:1 is not freedom from commandments as such, but freedom from slavery "under sin". The fact that Paul equates being under the power of sin with existence "under the law", has, according to Cosgrave (1988:160), nothing to do with whether believers are obligated to conform to certain ethical norms, whether these norms happen to be found in the law or not. Freedom from the law in Galatians means redemption from the subjection of sin, not from the law and the commandments as such. The ethos of the law is ethically exclusive, but the Gospel of Christ offers liberation for both Jew and Gentile. Where Paul speaks of freedom from specific ethical norms he does not imply freedom as liberation, but always freedom as ethical obligation (Cosgrove 1988:161).

Verses 1, 13 and 25 of Gal. 5 give the paraenesis of the ethics of freedom its structure: it is an exhortation in three stages and a call to freedom based on freedom. Gal. 5:1 exhibits the typical structure of Paul paraenesis namely an imperative that develops out of an indicative. It reads: "For freedom Christ has set us free; stand fast therefore and do not submit again to a yoke of slavery". The dominant notion of Paul's ethics is that through the death of Christ the liberation of humanity from spiritual slavery is procured, which implies a movement away from spiritual slavery to the status of children of God. This freedom is not a passing event as it has made freedom the constitutive element of

---

[6]   These three notions are extensively dealt with later in the chapter.

the life in which we currently live (Ebeling 1985:241). To concentrate on the ethical aspects of spiritual liberty in Galatians Tolmie (2006:248) claims that it is something that needs to be maintained by love since the notion of spiritual liberty is balanced and restrained by love. The two are linked to such an extent that one could say that liberty without love ceases to be liberty.

The indicative statement about the gift of freedom is followed by the imperative to live in freedom, not to weaken, not to be fooled, not to give way, not to return to slavery under the law since Christ has redeemed humanity (Ebeling 1985: 241). In preserving freedom, Paul argues against the law as well as for the sufficiency of the Spirit in dealing with the flesh. "Christ was crucified to set us free from the curse of the law so that we might receive his Spirit" (Gal. 3:1-2, 13-14). The Spirit, and not the law, proved to be the identity characteristic of the followers of Christ as sons and daughters of God (Gal. 4:6). Believers were therefore obliged to defend their freedom in Christ particularly from social pressures that promote ethic divisions (Gal. 5:1-6) and by so doing they are also under obligation to preserve their freedom to serve one another in love (Gal. 5: 13-14). As claimed by Paul: once one is a follower of Christ there is no place for the law to direct one's actions, one is led by the Spirit that unites us (Gal. 5:18). Paul admonished the followers of Christ to stand firm in the freedom which Christ has given them (Gal. 5:1) and to resist the desires of the flesh, and instead work in the Spirit in which they have life (Gal. 5:25)

Gal. 5:13 the indicative states a call to freedom and according to Ebeling (1985: 242) this call does not mean a task that has just been set, or a goal that has been attained. The indicative is taken up without any limitation and leads to the ethical imperative to make right use of freedom, not to abuse it so that it turns into freedom of the flesh. The result will be a loss of freedom and an immediate reversal to slavery. In Gal. 5: 25 the ultimate representation of freedom is the Spirit and in this variation the Spirit, let us walk by the Spirit".

Reflecting on Paul's presentation of freedom, Ebeling (1985:242) is of opinion that one of the accomplishments of Pauline theology consists of its successful claiming of the concept of freedom. The use of Paul's freedom derives from Greek philosophy with unforeseen consequences for the Christian faith. He asserts that there is no immediate equivalent to the concept of freedom in the Old Testament of even in Jewish thought; hence it marks the point at which faith in Jesus Christ goes beyond the Old Testament and breaks its association with Judaism. Due to Paul's Hellenisitc background his understanding of freedom reveals certain points of contact with the "freedom" of the Greek *polis* which implies the right to say anything with truthfulness. But he goes even further by applying the Hellenistic notion of freedom which inherently holds the concepts of self-knowledge and self-control. It even includes the incipient Gnostic understanding of freedom which contains the notion of liberation from the power of elemental spirits of the universe (Ebeling 1985:242).

Paul's understanding of freedom is not primarily an idea, for him it is an experience. His understanding also stood in striking contrast to the understanding of freedom held in the contemporary world. Paul saw freedom as grounded in the crucified Christ and recognized it as an experience based on the gift of the Holy Spirit. The basis of his notion of freedom is a new reality in the Christ event, in Jesus' loving sacrifice of himself for humanity. Freedom is therefore not founded in the law, neither in the individual, not in an escape from the world, but in the love of Jesus Christ, which through faith in Him becomes the love we reveal to others (Ebeling 1985:243).

Significant of this progressive development in Paul's understanding of freedom is that it was not only an addition to the Torah, but this became the shifting ground between what would eventually complete the process of separation between Judaism and Christianity to Christianity itself.

Paul was of opinion that the Galatians needed more than just doctrinal instruction, but needed to be shaken up by exhortation. According to Ebeling's (1985:248) scholarly analysis, nowhere else in Paul does one find such a systematic treatment of ethics from the ground up as is found in Gal. 5:13-24. The ethics of freedom which is an ethics of the Spirit amounts to the Christian ethics to love as well as freedom to serve. This, for Paul, is the *Magna Charta* of Christian ethics as he claimed that freedom and service are identical (Ebeling 1985: 252). Freedom to give ourselves in love to others even when they seem to stand as far away as one's enemies is the direct derivative of the ethics of freedom, hence the focus of the ethics of love.

6.4.2. The ethics of Love

The idea of love and the idea of freedom are both ethical principles however, freedom is freedom only as love, and love is love only as freedom. To serve one another in love does not limit freedom. Instead it is the unfolding and fulfillment of freedom. Paul warns not to let freedom become an opportunity for self-emancipation of the flesh and it should not lead to a demand to rein in freedom and to limit it, but it should be an encouragement to live the freedom to the uttermost as was opened through Christ. Nevertheless the totality of Paul's teaching can be reduced to the love command: love of God and love of neighbour (Rosner 1995:21). This is not original to Paul as the love command was central to Jesus and is usually equated with the ethics of the Gospel. Jesus ethically guided the behaviour of his followers by giving a new commandment: "Love one another". This, in fact, is the only moral rule given by Jesus in John (13:34-35). Van Der Watt (2006:1160, in reflecting on the saying of Jesus in John's Gospel namely: " . . . that you love one another as I have loved you . . ." perceives it as an expression of egalitarianism. He claims that it implies common reciprocation within a particular group and it also implies social interdependence (2006:1116). Believers should love as Jesus has loved them (Jn 13:34) and this love is shown in actions.

If love was central to the message of Jesus, it should be expected that love will also be the essence of Pauline ethics. He takes the "Jesus quality" of this love further as it plays a pivotal role in his *paranaesis* in Gal. 5:13-6:10. In 5:13-14 loves qualifies the correct practicing of freedom. In 5:22 love is fore-grounded when Paul describes the fruit of the Spirit where he concludes his description with the proposition that "against such things there is no law". The commandment to love is radicalized as expressed in Gal. 5:14 this law to love is "redefined and radicalized in the Jesus tradition as the law of unconditional, universal, self-sacrificing love, and exemplified by Jesus in his life and death"

(Du Toit 2006: 175 in van Der Watt). For Paul the law continued to have ethical force, but only in the sense of the 'law of Christ'. Love concentrates primarily on the positive inner disposition of the believer towards God and neighbour which results in a specific style of living and doing. For this reason it is understandable that the work of the Spirit and love are inextricably interwoven as both deal with the innermost being which emanates into their outward behaviour and without love their outward actions would be meaningless (du Toit 2006:176). Love is the first on the list of the fruits produced by the Spirit. The love command has central meaning in Paul's ethics as according to him decision and action are both influenced by love and this determines Christian conduct.

While the idea of ethics and the idea of freedom are both ethical principles it is the unification of both into a single whole that is something novel to Paul. This, for Paul, was grounded in the experienced reality of Christ who gave himself in love and the Spirit sets us free for love.

6.4.2.1 The ethics of the law versus the ethics of freedom

The distinction between ethics of the law and ethics of freedom according to Ebeling (1985:254) is based on unfulfilment and seeks to attain life and righteousness. The law pays laborious heed to infinite detail, but never attains the whole. Ideally it is better to relate the ethics of freedom to the ethics of the law, and the ethics of the law is promoted by the ethics of freedom. The ethics of freedom is based on fulfillment, on the driving force of the Spirit and grows out of life and righteousness which gets granted by grace. It knows the spontaneity of the Spirit and the whole is grasped joyfully in the singular detail. This depends on the self-forgetfulness of those who enjoy freedom from themselves.

Paul does not speak of freedom from the law in the banal sense of abrogating the law. For him Christ freed humanity from the curse of the law (Gal. 3:13) as well as from the unfulfilled law whose dominion is hopeless slavery. Those in bondage of sin can never redeem themselves from the law and cannot be brought to true life by the law. He claims that if one is led by the Spirit one is not under the law (V 18). For Paul

the law is the law of love (Lev 19:18). If true love is present, there is
no requirement of the law; the law is redundant.

6.4.3. The Spirit

The importance of the Spirit on Galatians is clear from the way in
which Paul emphases its role in 5:16ff. Here he calls upon the Galatians
to walk according to the Spirit. Gal. 5:16 to 5:25-26 consists of at least
six statements about the Spirit: starting with: "Walk by the Spirit and
you will not satisfy the passion of the flesh" ending with: "Since we
live by the Spirit, let us also walk by the Spirit" (5:25). Earthly life is
both a gift and a responsibility, so is the life given us by the Spirit.

In Gal. 5:22 Paul provides a list of the fruits of the Spirit that functions
as a "word-picture" of the effects that the Spirit produces in the lives
of the believers with love significantly occupying the first place on the
list. In Gal. 5:25 he calls upon them to walk according to the Spirit.
According to Tolmie (2006: 249) the best way to summarize the ethics
that underlie Galatians would in fact be to link these three concepts
together as if they were one: spiritual liberty—love—Spirit (2006:249).
There is, however, the downside to this positive picture in this sense
that it is possible to start with the Spirit, but end in the opposite
direction namely the flesh (Gal. 3:3). Paul says that despite the fact
that the children of God had been liberated by Christ, they have the
ability to become enslaved again (Gal. 4:9). Despite their liberation in
Christ they may submit to spiritual slavery again (Gal. 5:1). This abuse
of spiritual liberty could even reach a situation in which Christ will be
of no benefit at all (Gal. 5:2) and this falling away from grace (Gal.
5:4) brings the person to the other side of the "word-picture", namely
the list of the works of the flesh. The presentation of this dualistic
ethical picture is what Tolmie (2006:250) calls a realistic picture of
what occurs in all Christian communities and in this particular case
the Galatian Christian community who behaved in ways that were,
according to him, morally wrong.

The theological significance of this opposing word-picture is that
despite being liberated, being justified, having Christ within, having
become children of God, having being crucified with Christ, having

received the Spirit, all may not guarantee change in ethical conduct, as behavioural change is gradual, it is as Paul said it is, a process whereby Christ "was formed among you" (Gal. 4:19). It is a lengthy process, a gradual process, which can sometimes go terribly wrong.

6.4.3.1. The struggle between flesh and Spirit (16-18)

Concerning the struggle between flesh and Spirit Paul is not referring to two elements of human nature, but to two powers whose battleground is the human self (Ebeling 1985:254). In Paul *flesh* suggests that which is unnatural and *Spirit* that which is natural. According to his reasoning there is something inherently chaotic about the works of the flesh. "Flesh" refers to everything that human beings are and accomplish by their own power. It is not limited to corporeality; it includes what is intellectual and spiritual to the extent that it is controlled by sinful human centeredness and misused for self-legitimation. The category of flesh includes religious striving for justification through the law. Spirit, on the contrary, is everything wherein God's presence rules in the human sphere and influences it (Ebeling 1985:255). The fruit of the Spirit is one and indivisible, a harmonious organization, and is meant to symbolize a perfect totality. Everything derives from love, including joy. Joy is the seat of the seal of the Holy Spirit. Paul includes his list with self-control, through which we forego that which is attractive not out of hatred and resignation, but, because and insofar that it is good to do so.

Paul does not base ethics on the desire for or confidence in an uncorrupt human nature. Neither does he base it on good will, which even if present turns out to be powerless. Neither does he base it on the requirements of the law, even though the law is to be taken seriously, precisely because of the power with which it holds us captive with its powerlessness to make us the people it requires us to be. Paul approaches this from our situation before God, the situation of sinners towards whom grace has been shown. This situation is seen correctly only when both are taken seriously, namely, sin and grace; the power of the flesh and the power of the Spirit, described by Paul, as the Spirit of the Son of God (Gal. 4:6).

The ethical realm as such is far from being a realm of triumphs; it is rather a realm of repeated defeats in which the Spirit cries out "Abba" making this clear: "those who belong to Christ Jesus have crucified the flesh with its passions and desires (v 24). To allow the fruit of the Spirit is to gain the upper hand over the works of the flesh (Ebeling 1985:256).

6.5. THE LEGAL FOUNDATION OF PAUL'S ETHICAL EXHORTATION (GAL. 5:1-6:10)

Paul's contrast between being led by the spirit and being under the law (5:18) has prompted many attempts to express the distinction between Pauline and legal ethics.

6.5.1. The Law and ethics

Paul's rejection of the Law, as a means of justification, did not mean that he rejected its moral demands (Gal. 3:10-14). He considered the moral demands of the law as summed up in the commandment "love your neighbour as yourself" also evident in his letter to the Roman community (13:8-10). In the Epistle to the Galatians Paul displayed a different attitude towards the law and the faith of Israel. While Judaic Christianity saw keeping the law as the path of life with God, Paul's view of the law differed radically; for Paul the law brought not life, but death. He claimed that no one was justified or made righteous in God's sight through the law. The basic problem according to Paul's insight was not the law itself, but the weakness of human nature. Human nature he refers to as "flesh" while God is "Spirit" and in this context flesh and Spirit oppose each other, because an evil power called "sin" dwells in the flesh, causing it to act against the will of God. Though the law in itself is good, it has an unfortunate effect on human beings who are "in the flesh" (Burkett 2002:294). Paul is of firm opinion that justification comes through faith in Jesus Christ. As a means of salvation Paul replaced the law with the death of Jesus, interpreted as a sacrifice. Paul believed that the death of Jesus, with him shedding blood, satisfied God or paid the penalty for the sins of humanity. One merely had to have faith in Jesus combined with baptism to receive the benefits of this sacrifice (Rom 3:21-26). Through faith in Jesus combined with baptism, the believer was justified, reconciled and redeemed. "No one is justified by works of the law, but only through faith (Gal. 2:16).

As explained by Dunn (2005:16): Israel's covenantal nomism, where separateness to God (holiness) was in fact understood to require separateness from the (other) nations as two sides of the same coin, and the law was perceived as a means to maintain both. The law and adherence to the law, according to Paul, did not make provision for inclusiveness, but instead for sectarianism against which Jesus protested. The law did not make provision for table-fellowship (food laws); (Matt. 11:19 / Mk 2:17). It was exclusive in the sense that the uncircumcised where not admitted into the Jewish community (social laws). The law had more of a boundary-making function than a unifying function. The Law of Moses, by preventing any mixing, intended to keep Jewish people pure in body and soul. This covenantal privilege, encouraged by the law of works, affirmed that God is God of the Jew only. Works of the law somehow functioned to reinforce Israel's exclusive claim on God. The covenant gave exclusive status to the Jewish people and this status was affirmed and maintained by works of the law. The works of law, which demonstrated and constituted Israel's set apartness. This attitude Paul came to perceive as a failure to grasp the all-inclusiveness of faith.

As mentioned previously the ethical exhortation or paraenesis of Paul, as expressed in Gal. 5: 1-6: 10, also forms a distinctive element of his argumentation and philosophical dialogues in the letter to the Galatians. It contains warnings against adherence to the Jewish Torah (Gal. 5:1-12) and corruption by the flesh (Gal. 5:13-24). All of the above are effective arguments for the sufficiency of the Galatians' spiritual experience without legalism. Paul's ethics is based on freedom and the legality thereof is summed up in the law to "love neighbour as oneself".

> For freedom Christ has set us free; stand fast therefore, and do
> not submit again to a yoke of slavery. Gal. 5:1.

Hansen (1994:26) maintains that it is not accurate to view Paul's letter to the Galatians as an attack on Jewish Christians for legalism in their own relationship with God. The common confession of Jewish Christians Paul expresses in Gal. 2:15-16: that justification is by faith in Jesus Christ and not by works of the law. He maintains that Jewish Christians did not have a legalistic view of their own relationship to God because they knew they had right standing with God not because of the law, but because of their faith in Christ. Hansen (1994:26) states that the problem was not so much legalism, but ethno-centrism. They were convinced that the blessing of God was only given to the Jewish people and that only the Jewish people were the People of God. So they insisted that all Gentile people should become part of the Jewish nation before they could enjoy the full blessing of God. Paul rejected this legalistic approach for the Gentile believers precisely because it contradicts what the Jewish Christians believe to be true for themselves namely: "We who are Jews by birth and not 'Gentile sinners' know that a man is not justified by observing the law, but by faith in Jesus Christ" (2:15-16).

6.5.2. The self-styled ethical functions of the Mosaic Law

Paul in Gal (5:1-6) proclaimed freedom from adherence to the Mosaic Law not only as the basis for beginning the Christian life, but also as the basis for continuing the Christian life (Hansen (1994:27). In Paul's view the Mosaic Law has a moral function, but only negatively. It largely points out transgressions and as such imprisons all people under sin (Gal. 3:10, 19, 22). In this sense he claims it cannot impart life nor produce righteousness (Gal. 3:21). In this sense a person cannot obtain moral rightness by trying to observe the Mosaic Law (Gal. 3:2-3) nor can a person obtain moral realization over one's immoral desires by simply submitting to the guidance of the Mosaic Law (Gal. 5:13-18). Paul is of firm opinion that what the law cannot do is done by Jesus Christ by grace as well as through the cross of Christ. Jesus had removed the so-called curse of the law (Gal. 3:13) and by means of the Spirit, God had reproduced the righteous character of his Son in all people (5:22-23) so that the ultimate moral standard of the law is fulfilled (Gal. 5: 14; 6:2). If the believer is open and controlled by the workings of the Spirit, then the slavery of the Mosaic Law (Gal. 5:18) will no longer be effective (Hansen 1994: 28).

Adherence to the Mosaic Law was used to separate the Jewish people and all other racial groups. The Galatian converts felt a loss of identity, social and religious, since the new faith in Christ excluded them from the Jewish synagogues as well as from their pagan temples. To solve this lack of identity, they sought identification with the Jewish people by adhering to the required marks of a Jewish identity, namely, circumcision (Gal. 2:12-14); Shabbat observance (Gal. 4:10) and to eat Kosher food (Gal. 5:2-3; 6:12-13). This implied observing the works of the law. They had a need to belong and this need convinced them that if they came under the discipline of the Mosaic Law, the law would empower them not only to overcome evil, but will provide the necessary identity measures for them to be recognized as believers in Jesus Christ. Hansen (1994:15) asserts that their focus shifted from union with Christ by faith and dependence on the Spirit to identification with the Jewish nation and observance of the law.

The developed system of Mosaic regulations held the Jewish people captive and enslaved to the law (Gal. 3:23). The identity of the Jewish people was inextricably linked to their observance of the Mosaic Law. The dilemma for Gentile Christians was to bow to the pressure of Jewish Christians to adhere to the Mosaic Laws and by so doing be identified with the Jewish people, who are the People of God.

For Paul it was not the adherence to the Law of Moses, but rather the presence of the Spirit that established the identity of Gentile Christians as sons and daughters of God (Hansen 1994:27). Since the Galatian believers were already identified as the People of God by the presence of the Spirit, Paul regarded it as "foolish" for them to find their Christian identity by first becoming Jews by means of observing the legal practices of the Mosaic Law.

Paul's understanding of the moral function of the law is based on his rejection on keeping the law as an appropriate response to God's blessing. As stated by Hansen, (1994:27) there was a general agreement that "observance to the Mosaic Law is not the way to *begin* the Christian life; many still maintained that observance of the Mosaic Law is the way to *continue* the Christian life. In Gal. 5:1-6 Paul proclaimed freedom from the obligation to observe the Mosaic Law not only as the basis for beginning the Christian life, but also as the basis for continuing the Christian life.

Paul is therefore of opinion that that while the Mosaic Law has a moral function, it does so in negative terms as it points out transgressions and keep adherents in prison (3:10, 19, 22): it cannot impart life nor produce righteousness (3:21). For this reason one cannot obtain moral realization by trying to observe the law (3:2-3), nor can we gain victory over our "sinful nature's desires" by submitting to the guidance of the Mosaic Law (5:13-18). Paul believed that when one is justified, one is no longer subject to God's wrath and, when reconciled, one is no longer at enmity with God, and, when redeemed, one is no longer subject to evil powers of the flesh. The law is in no position to do this, only God does this by God's grace and thus through the cross of Jesus Christ God removed the "curse of the law" (3:13). The ultimate moral standard of the law is fulfilled through the righteous character of Christ. Characteristic of the identity of Christianity is for Christians to be controlled by the Spirit and so to have freedom from the curse of the law as well as the supervision of the law (3:25) and thus to be liberated to live for God (2:19) and to serve each other in love (5:13).

While Paul was regarded as the real founder of Christianity he drew many ideas from the earlier Christian tradition. He was the first major influential figure to deny that the Jewish law provided the path of salvation. He states in Gal. 2:21 that if justification were through the law, then Christ died for no reason. This attitude towards the law may have been developed from the need to find reason for Jesus' death. Or as an Apostle to the Gentiles, he saw circumcision as an obstacle to the conversion of Gentiles and dietary regulations as an obstacle to full fellowship between Jews and Gentiles. By making the ritual unnecessary and placing salvation of Jews and Gentiles on the same basis, he made it easier for Gentiles to accept the message and removed the barriers that kept Jew and Gentile apart (Burkett 2002: 295).

This step of Paul decisively affected the future of the early Christian movement. It was Paul's perspective that was adopted by the Gentile Christian communities and that subsequently became the normal teaching of Christianity. Apart from the Jewish law, Christianity could no longer be considered a sect of Judaism. Consequently it became a distinct religion in its own right, according to Burkett (2002:295).

Since the Galatian Christians also belong to Christ, and since they are directly related to Christ, they also qualify as recipients of the blessing that was promised to Abraham. Since the full membership in the covenant People of God, "the seed of Abraham", is granted and maintained simply by union with Christ by faith, there is no longer any need for the ritual law as a means to secure and maintain that status. Any attempt by the Galatian Christians to gain status or receive blessing by observing the Mosaic ritual Law was regarded as foolish, since they had already been included within the realm of full inheritance, in which there is no racial, social or gender hierarchy (Hansen 1992: 114).

Purity of heart matters more than purifications of the Law, mercy more than the Sabbath. Religion consists in the infiltration of both the sacred and the profane by the gifts of internal grace, which transmits to people the very life of a God of love. The whole field of action and existence of the human person, in the domain of the profane and of the sacred, becomes the field of interior sanctification. The social function of the sacred is to serve as an instrument for this sanctification, this spiritualization. Love is the fullness of the Law and the human person is saved by faith. Paul's conversion took him from one extreme of belief to another concerning the Mosaic Law. First he wanted to reinforce that adherence to the Mosaic ritual Law was of vital importance in obtaining righteousness. His Christian proclamation is very radical in this sense that one is justified through faith in Christ apart from the Mosaic Law (2:16). Justification is now associated with Christ and not the Mosaic Law. He is therefore convinced that the precepts of the Torah concerning circumcision (5:2) and dietary regulations (2:12) had no role to play in obtaining righteousness.

It is apparent that emerging Pauline (or Gentile) Christianity shared many values with the surrounding cultures. Some of its ethical teachings resemble those of popular Greek philosophy, but on the whole the larger culture according to Paul was hopelessly corrupt. The present world was a place of moral and spiritual "darkness" in which the Christians were to shine as "lights" (Burkett 2002: 297). The rejection of the ritual Law by Paul as a means of justification did not mean that he rejected the moral demands of the law. He considered the moral demands of the Law to be summed up in the commandment "love your neighbour as yourself" (Rom 13:8-10).

The goal of Pauline ethics was to transform people's affections, perceptions, and emotions as well as their intellect. These are necessary to bring ethical theory and reasoning to the endpoint of committed action.

6. CONCLUSION

To explore Paul's ethics as the foundation of Christian identity formation is in reality an effort to concretize and apply the moral exhortations or *"paraclesis"* towards the instruction of behaviour or conduct as he perceived was based on the life and teachings of Christ. By so doing a whole range of extraordinary problems come to the fore. The concrete form of the Christian community brings humanity together in a special manner, from both earthly and eschatological perspectives. The acute human differences related to religious background, social class, gender and various cultural norms simply become irrelevant, even though they continue to exist. This holds true as well for the conflict between the flesh and the spirit which continues throughout the life time of each person. The central ethical focus on human life in community does not grow out of the nature of the individual personality nor out of the nature of the transpersonal situation. What is crucial is the relationship of one person to another. Those who would truly see and understand others must first truly see and understand themselves.

To constitute a moral ontology is to highlight the importance of an alternative moral identity. Identity, which gives a sense and a knowledge of who one is, is to be oriented in moral space, a space in which questions arise about what is good or bad, what is worth doing and what is trivial and secondary (Taylor 1989: 30).

Paul's emphasis on freedom, the Spirit of Christ, had led many to conclude that the roots of Paul's ethics lie not in his doctrine of justification by faith, but rather in experiencing the gift of the Spirit. Paul's ethics are rooted in a life that participates in Christ through the Spirit rather than in concepts such as 'justification' or 'covenant'. Paul's ethics in Galatians are an interchange between the divine and human activity; between the two dominant categories of 'Spirit' and 'Flesh'. While some parallels are found in Qumranic and Hellenistic literature, Paul's special use of these terms in an ethical context is particularly noteworthy.

To live according to the Spirit of Christ, received at baptism, the believer will produce a good character in the same way as the good tree produces good fruit. The fruits of the Spirit include traits such as love, joy, and peace (Gal. 5:16-26; Rom.12:9-14) and this links up directly with Paul's conception of the "mystical" life in Christ, a possible influence of Hellenistic mystery religions. Paul reinterprets a believer's entire existence in view of Jesus Christ and perceives life in view of the unfolding of the divine plan. The believer is no longer deemed as an enemy of the Church, but an apostle of the Risen Lord. In his personal life he claimed that his experience of Christ, the Risen Lord, had altered the way he viewed the sacred traditions of his Jewish ancestors. From henceforth it was Christ and not the Mosaic Law that played center stage in his life.

Nascent Christianity became conscious of the God-given mission in which liberty from the exclusive nature of Judaism makes provision for pure universality. It is based on the understanding that the Son of Man had not come only for the Jews, but for all humanity indeed for the human race in its whole entirety, for all nations of the earth. Both those who come out of circumcision and those who come out of non—circumcision were equally called to belong (Maritain 1964:2). Hence the idea of perceiving the "true Israelites" though in Spirit and in Truth, circumcised at the heart, not in the flesh.

What came into being was the spiritual body of Christ and Jacques Maritain (1964:3) says that it was necessary to understand that salvation is for all people. That is why in Christ there is no Jew or Gentile. The power that works for salvation is not the ritual Law of Moses, but faith in Jesus who was crucified in the name of the Law. It is precisely this great intuition that enflamed Paul's mind, the awareness for the universality of the Kingdom of God as well as the realization of salvation by faith and not by law. Another intuition inseparably bound to the former is the primacy of the internal over the external, the spirit over the letter, the life of grace over exterior observances; it is indeed this that amounts to the spirit of the Pauline Gospel. It is also in this sense that Paul understood the immense spiritual revolution that was carried out by Jesus. The new primary law is written in the heart of people and not the external fulfillment of rites and prescriptions. In Rom 3:21-31, Paul's attitude towards the law should be understood in relation to his doctrine of the inclusions of the Gentiles into the Kingdom of God. Within this framework Paul refutes the ritual Torah as a means of obtaining righteousness, because the ritual Law acts as a restrictive force that separates Jew from Gentile, and prevents the universal unity that was destined to come. Through the redemptive death of Jesus, the harsh exclusions derived from the Law came to an end, thereby allowing uncircumcised Gentiles to participate in the blessing of Abraham on equal terms with the Jews (Buckel 2002: 123-124). This equal access to salvation is what undergirds the ethical teachings of Paul and became a concrete identity characteristic of nascent Pauline Christianity.

CHAPTER SEVEN

7. Christian Unity Of Faith With Love And Freedom In The "Body Of Christ"

7.1. Introduction

"Christian unity of faith with love and freedom in the "Body of Christ" characterizes one, among many, of Paul's intentions for the early followers of Christ. Early Christian believers obtained their sense of oneness in the faith (Gal. 4:13) by means of their close identification with the Risen Lord. This identification was formed by baptism since baptism is the ritual that initiated the Christian followers into what Paul called the Body of Christ this ritual initiated the Christian follower into what Paul called the 'Body of Christ' (1 Cor. 12:27; Gal. 3:27-28; 1 Cor. 12; Rom 12:14-21). Thus the same faith and the same baptism, not only incorporated them into the one Lord who forms the head the Body, but also constitutes the source or basis of Christian unity. All who are baptized in Christ received the same Holy Spirit and is gifted with the divine attributes of the Holy Spirit (Gal. 4:4). By virtue of being baptized into the one Holy Spirit, the members of the Body of Christ are intimately bound to Christ and to one another (1 Cor. 12:13). Paul pictured the Body of Christ as a united whole consisting of many individual parts or members (Rom 12:4-5; 1 Cor. 12:12-31cf; Col 1:24, Eph. 5:23). He announced that for those who are in Christ, all previous barriers which had formerly divided them had been removed since the members of the early Christian community came from all levels of society; from all social, cultural and religious groups: the rich and the poor, the old and the young, the so-called free as well as slaves. The members of the Body of Christ had, therefore, to realize that all prior distinctions between Jewish and Gentiles Christians, slave and free, male and female, are a thing of the past (Gal. 3:28; 1 Cor. 12:13). Paul uses very strong and mystifying language to describe the tremendous change that takes place in the person who came to believe in Christ Jesus and had undergone the rite of initiation and the consequent unity is also eschatological in essence as Christians anticipates and communicates the final cosmic unity planned by the one God, through Jesus (Eph. 1:9).

This unity in diversity, reflected in the unity of Jews and Gentiles (Eph. 2:16) as well as in God's different gifts to each member of the Body of Christ, is the final goal of God's plan which is to bring everything in heaven and earth together in Christ. Through the unity of Jews and Gentiles, already accomplished in Christ's death and exultation, God's plan is made known and will culminate in a renewed cosmos where all is in harmony with Christ completely filling the universe with his rule of life (Eph. 1:10). This sense of unity portrayed by being part of the Body of Christ is viable since Christ, through the Cross, had reconciled both Jews and Gentiles to God. Paul is adamant when he writes that there is but one Spirit of God and both Jews and non-Jews alike have equal access to the Father (Eph. 2:18).

This characteristic of Christian unity of faith with love and freedom in the "Body of Christ", as depicted by Gal. 3:28 as the unity between slave and free, male and female, Jew and Gentile points not only to the "egalitarian ethos of oneness in Christ" according to Fiorenza (1983: 205), but to the identification of Christians with Christ, which is also a resolution of their differences into unity (Hogan 2008:3). This specific chapter attempts to analyze an understanding of this identity characteristic of early Christianity as well as its implications as portrayed by Paul in his letter to the Galatians (5:13-6:10) whereby all are called to freedom, led by the Spirit so as to be set free to love.

7.2. CHRISTIAN UNITY AS FAITH WORKING THROUGH LOVE

Since the very beginning of his ministry Paul championed unity within the Body of Christ as a prime characteristic of Christianity. The subject of unity was the point of controversy when he had to confront Peter at Antioch since it concerned the question of how this unity reflected the integrity of the Gospel. For Paul unity among the followers of Christ was not mere petty talk as unity had to be demonstrated in practical terms between the Jews and the Gentiles " . . . for in Christ Jesus you are all children of God, through faith" (Gal. 3:26). It is quite apparent that the symbol of identity had shifted from the Law to Christ, in whom there is no longer division and exclusiveness, but unity and inclusiveness (Gal. 3:26-29). This sentiment is illustrated repeatedly by Paul's expressions such as "in Christ Jesus" (3:26); "one in Christ Jesus" (3:28); "baptized in Christ" (3:27) "have put on Christ" (3:29). In view of the fact that God is one God and that God is God both of Jew and Gentile, slave and free, of male and female (Gal. 3:28) reiterates the belief that Christ's death had procured salvation for all God's people. Christ's death created *one* community and there can or should no longer be barriers separating disparate groups or individuals. It is for this reason that circumcision implied division between Jew and non-Jew and between male and female while on the other hand baptism into Christ implies unity (Cousar 1982:85). However, it is somewhat curious to determine what kind of unity Paul had in mind when he put forward that all divisions and distinctions are and had to be obliterated within the Body of Christ.

In the light of the above it appears that the kind of unity which Paul contemplated was supposed to discount ethnic, social and sexual distinctions. However, as pointed out by Cousar (1982:85) the three sets of polarities are not exactly parallel, given that one was either born male or female; and in Paul's time either Jew or not Jew and the status of slave and free was not inherently alterable as it depended on the economic condition or fate of each individual. Seemingly changes in status were not as uncommon as could be imagined, however, the three sets of polarities are not parallel and in Galatians Paul made no distinction between them. Nevertheless, if Paul is to be taken as a model then it could be said that the differences between the categories do remain for him throughout his writings. He continues to reflect a Jewish self-consciousness not only in his letter to the Galatians (2:15) but also in other writings such as in 2 Cor. 11:22; Phil. 3:5 and Rom. 11:14. The same goes for treating Jews and Gentiles as ethnic units (Rom. 9-11) and to address slaves, slave owners and men and women as distinct groups. In the light of this, as also pointed out by Cousar (1997:85-86), the unity that is declared by Paul is not the kind in which ethnic, social, and sexual differences vanish, but one in which barriers, hostility, chauvinism, and a sense of superiority and inferiority between the categories are destroyed. Being one in Christ does not do away with Jew and Greek, male or female, even slave or free, but it does make these apparent differences irrelevant before God. All the same this new unity given in Christ has tremendous social implications as on all levels of existence the Jew-Gentile distinctions are rendered irrelevant. Even on the question of slavery, Paul sets a direction whereby he sent the runaway slave Onesimus back to his owner Philemon as a "beloved brother", no longer as a "slave" because they are brothers both in the flesh and in the Lord (Philemon 16). In spite of this in 1 Cor. 7:20-22 Paul encourages slaves to accept their lot in life and not work to be freed. This ambiguity is ostensibly justified by the view that Paul expected the end of the world to be imminent, indeed within his life time. He urged the slave-masters to keep in mind that they have another Master, greater than themselves who is the Lord in heaven and with whom there is no partiality (Eph. 6-9; Col 4:1). Can it also be that that this ambiguity was circumstantial depending on the conditions he wished to address? Be as it may, it did not make the notion of establishing unity within the Body of Christ any easier.

What binds Gentiles and Jews together is not the Jewish way of life, but their common allegiance to Christ and hence not the Law (Gal. 5:3). In this regard circumcision and uncircumcision is of no relevance as both are of no consequence to being a follower of Christ. Whether one's identity is Jew or Gentile, whether one is circumcised or uncircumcised has nothing to do with one's standing with God. The only thing that matters according to Paul is 'faith working through love". For this reason Paul characterized the Christian life as "faith working through love" as iterated in (Gal. 5:6) (Williams 1997:139). In this context the one distinctive characteristic of being Christian is 'faith' and the other characteristic is "love" (agapē). Paul spoke of the Son of God that loved him and gave himself up for his people. The noun *agape* and the verb *agapan* in most cases denotes a disposition of a person towards other persons, and this disposition is often expressed in conduct or behaviour (Rom. 12:9; 13:8, 9, 10; 1 Cor. 4:21; 13:1-13; 14:1; Phil. 1:9).

The prime model of this love is Christ whose self-giving love would shape the Galatian believers and thus the summation of Christian life namely "faith working through love". Even though God's love or Christ's love is the source and paradigm of human agape, as explained by Williams (1997:143), it remains a term most frequently used to name the nature of creative human-human relationships. Faith is perceived as that disposition of the self which is the necessary element for human relationships with God. Paul's theological vocabulary demonstrates this point whereby he presents "faith" as a 'vertical' term and love, most frequently, as a 'horizontal' one. By this Paul means that love is the public evidence of faith given that faith is look upon as a "private" matter. *Agape* is therefore the public evidence of a right relationship with God because faith, the human disposition necessary for such a relationship, manifests itself and has effects through love. Faith that does not materialize as love cannot sustain a relationship with God, because it knows nothing of the One who, in the fullness of time, sent the Son who "loved me and gave himself for me" (Gal. 2:20; 4:45) (Williams 1997:143). In this context faith can thus be described as that response to God's initiative that opens the gates of the self to God's transforming power and this faith erupts into communal life and love.

"Faith works through love"

In Gal. 5:6 the expression goes that "faith works through love". This for Paul implies receptivity, though not passivism, since God has acted freely through Christ to save humanity and the only appropriate response is acceptance, trust in God and complete reliance on his faithfulness. Cousar (1997:117) says that faith in this context cannot remain quiescent and the one who believes becomes aware of a community of believers and faith is then characterized by a concern for others. For Paul a decisive element of faith is obedience, but obedience for him is marked with love precisely because it is grounded in God's own love. In this sense the Christian is summoned not only to love, but also to be a loving person and for this reason according to Furnish (1968:202) love and obedience are inseparable in Paul's theology. Because faith is an active component and it issues forth into deeds of love and love in turn functions as the hidden, but essential, requirement of salvation, hence the understanding that "faith works through love".

7.3. CHRISTIAN UNITY IN FREEDOM

7.3.1. Freedom as a Christian trait

Gal. 3 and 4 suggest that Paul associated the state of being free with the Spirit of Christ as well as with faith. Faith is here presented as the necessary condition of freedom and the power that creates freedom is the Spirit, since it is the Spirit that transforms people into members of the family of God. The children of the promise are free only because they are heirs begotten by the Spirit. In contrast, the identity of Christians is *not* to be found in the ceremonial rites as recorded in the Torah, but to be in union with Christ where the experience of true freedom is occurring. This freedom is sustained when it is active in love (Gal. 5:5). Paul also exhorts the Galatians to exercise their new-found freedom in a responsible manner since "freedom is not a commodity obtained and stored away for a rainy day; it is a gift which increases its value in the using and can be lost through misuse" (Cousar 1997:122). To this end Paul provides his ethical guidelines showing how to exercise this freedom which Christ's death initiated (Gal. 5:13-6:10).

According to Paul's ethical instructions:

- freedom means the loving service of neighbours (Gal. 5:13-15).

He regards:

- the Spirit as the mode and power for the life of freedom (Gal. 5:16-26).

He stresses:

- the responsibilities of the free and loving life of the Spirit (6:1-10)

It is appropriate at this stage just o elaborate briefly in the above ethical instructions of Paul:

7.3.1.1. *Freedom as loving service of neighbours (Gal. 5:13-15)*

As already established the command of love is the dominant theme of Paul's letter to the Galatians (5:13-6:10) and while love is not a replacement for the Law, it is an expression of true freedom. It comes as a fruit of the Spirit and is related to being in service as well as bearing the burdens of others. What is obvious here is the interrelation of freedom, love and the Spirit and as stated by Cousar (1997:123): "this interrelation of freedom, love and the Spirit is addressed in a way that is relevant to the situation of the Galatian readers". The Galatian situation causes Paul to stress love as the work of the Spirit, mutual help and the need to do good. In this sense Paul strongly affirms the ethical "value relevance" of the Spirit.

The Galatian Christians are defined by Paul as "children of the free woman". In his subversive rereading of the Sarah/Hagar story (Gal. 4:21-31), he exhorts the Galatians not to revert to their previous state of slavery (Williams 1997:135). Paul claims throughout his letter, but in particular in chapter 4:21-30, that Christians are free from the Law. In Paul's reading this freedom correspond to Isaac; and those who are enslaved to the Law correspond to Hagar and her slave son, Ishmael. Similarly Galatian converts are free persons and in a sense assumed freedom as they became hearers of Christ who had set them free. It is precisely this freedom in Christ, says Paul that he defended when he visited Jerusalem (Gal. 2:1-5). By him using the allegory of the two women i.e. the mother of Isaac, the so-called free woman, and the mother of Ishmael, the so-called slave woman, (Gal. 4: 21-30), that prepared the way for him to articulate the truth of the Gospel in terms of freedom. This resulted in his powerful statement: "it is for freedom that Christ had set us free". According to Williams' analysis this is about the most persuasive declaration in the letter to the Galatians and the central injunction namely: "stand firm, therefore, and do not submit again to a yoke of slavery" refers not only to slavery to the Mosaic Law, but also to the *stoichaia tou kosmou* to which the Gentiles had been enslaved (Williams 1997:132). So in a sense the statement had relevance to both Jewish and Gentile Christians pertaining to their respective contexts. Freedom is both a human and divine factor and while the idea shapes the earlier passages such as 4:1-7, it is, as emphasized by Williams (1997:133), the prominence thereof in Gal. 5.1 that elevated it to become the centerpiece of Galatians. It is however, well to note that Paul's ideals of freedom have little in common with the current Western ideals of individualism and self-determination. The opposite of freedom for Paul are issues such as:

- Sin as articulated in   —Gal. 3:22
- The Law   —Gal. 3:23
- Pedagogue and trustees   —Gal. 3:25
- Managers   —Gal. 4:2
- Elements of the world   —Gal. 4:3

The alternative to the above is a life in Christ since a life in Christ means a life of freedom and this life of freedom, as suggested by Paul, signifies belonging to Christ Gal. 3:29. This sense of belonging implies been designated to the Lordship of Christ, as well as being assigned to the community of believers who are responsible to and for each other. Freedom, in this sense also implies abandoning violence as a way to rid the world of values and beliefs that threaten one's own value and belief system (1:13-14). It means release from the religious and cultural prisons whose darkness breeds prejudice, suspicion and resentment (Gal. 3:26-28).

The all-encompassing question remains: what exactly does Paul mean by "freedom" as he makes it quite clear that it is certainly not a freedom that makes provision for the 'flesh' or for 'self-indulgence'. Paul presents the 'flesh' as a power that can take advantage of the freedom God and the "flesh" can use freedom for its own unloving purposes. 'Flesh', which is the opposite of the Spirit, says Paul, has its own desire (5:16), engages in the inevitable conflict with the Spirit (5:17) and as a result produces its own 'works' (5:19-21) that contrasts sharply with the 'fruit' of the Spirit (5:22-23). Paul, in William's (1997:145) view presented freedom as a divine gift and not as an inherent right. While God has called Christians to live freely, this freedom is not a good in itself, but rather a means to the great good of human relationship. Freedom is not untrammeled personal autonomy; it is rather opportunity and possibility. The possibility to love neighbour without hindrance, the possibility of creating human communities based on mutual self-giving rather than the quest for power and status (Williams 1997:145). The very key to the proper use of freedom is love as it is love that enables persons to give themselves as slaves to one another (Gal. 5:13-14).

This concept of reciprocal enslavement is one of the prominent themes of Paul's Galatian parenesis of mutuality. For those who are together 'in Christ' genuine mutuality nourishes the oneness of community and disallows attitudes of superiority and inferiority. In Christ all are recipients of grace and where love prevails all of such like attitudes disappear. For this reason Paul enjoins the Galatians to rather enslave themselves to one another and this is different from the institution of slavery in the Greco-Roman world. Paul's idea of a mutual enslavement is not a forced disposition, but is engendered by freedom and love. This un-coerced love, in Paul's view, creates community and Christian freedom and is experienced within community and nourished by love. This is done to the point of becoming slaves to each other. In this sense those who belong to Jesus do not love because the Law commands them to love, they love because the Spirit produces the fruit of love within them (Gal. 5:22). The Spirit which is the Spirit of God and simultaneously the Spirit of Christ, inspires one to live in Christ and when one lives in Christ one will do the right and loving thing, because the Spirit produces its fruit in a righteous person. It is in this context that Paul stressed the sufficiency of the Spirit for Christian living. For those who are led by the Spirit, the Law is not a requirement; in fact according to Paul it is not even a necessity. Since the Law is superfluous for one who lives in the Spirit of Christ, it is also not considered necessary as an analytical tool of unacceptable behaviour or to function as a moral guide. Therefore in this sense freedom is not a good in itself; it is rather a means to the greater good of human relationship (Williams 1997:145). The ability to love out of genuine freedom, and refusing for freedom to collapse into mere uncontrolledness, provides freedom with the unencumbered opportunity to serve another, even as slaves, because to be enslaved by love is in reality a means of freeing each other.

The freedom that comes from Christ is not a freedom through one's own effort, but a freedom that comes through the death of Christ who was free enough to love and give himself up for those who are still un-free hence the saying: "for freedom Christ has set us free". Freedom, as perceived by Paul, implies a healthy enslavement to Christ, which also means an indifference to please other people (Gal. 1:10).

7.4. SALVATION OF THE HUMAN PERSON UNDERSTOOD IN TERMS OF FREEDOM

When Paul uses the terms "slavery" and "freedom" to describe God's salvation in Jesus, he had in mind only secondarily the institution of slavery that was operative in the first century. What was more important for him was the pattern of God's action in the history of Israel at the time of the exodus from Egypt. "Christ has set us free" means that God's decisive salvation has been accomplished and a complete change of allegiances has been effected. The People of God are no longer bound to sin, to the law and consequently to death. Christians are now free in the service of God. Like Israel they are also God's possession, also a special people, set apart and whose identity derives from being in union with their liberator, Jesus Christ. The liberation experience is more than just being liberated from an external oppressive situation; it encompasses the experience of inner freedom that comes from being emancipated. While it can be argued that deliverance in Christ is marked by transference from one dominion to another, the new bondage in Christ is presented as "perfect freedom". As stated by Paul this freedom obtained by Christ both overlaps and sharply differs from many expressions of freedom found in common parlance and occasionally in theological discussions today (Cousar 1997:107).

Christian freedom for Paul was not a side issue, but at the heart of Christian living. He describes Christian freedom not just as freedom, but as *the freedom*. The principal nature of Christian freedom is not an abstract concept neither is it the kind of freedom the noble Romans enjoyed. Christian freedom is the freedom that Christ died to bring about and the importance is that this freedom is brought about specifically for salvation. Hence the notion that salvation is to be understood in terms of freedom. For this reason Paul's emphasis in Galatians that Christ freed us so that we should have, maintain, exercise and enjoy freedom (Morris 1996:153). Christ has set us free and this tremendous act of liberation has consequences; a great price had to be paid to bring about Christian freedom and Paul is of strong opinion that those who had been liberated are to live in freedom, since it is unreasonable for free people to seek bondage. However, while freedom in Christ is important, there exists for Paul a real danger that freedom can degenerate into an exercise of selfishness if it is not exercised in love. It is therefore believed that because it is the love of God that has brought salvation to humanity, it is also essential that believers should reflect on the idea of divine love and allow it to be manifested in their personal actions.

7.5. CHRISTOLOGICAL FREEDOM AND THE CONTEMPORARY REFERENCE TO FREEDOM

Freedom, the other pivotal characteristic of Christianity is the basis for love and love is the proper exercise of freedom. Christ freed us for freedom hence Christians have a high stake in defining Christological freedom. To compare Christological freedom with the contemporary reference to freedom implies that one has an appreciation of the average meaning of freedom as understood in daily living. A broad comprehension of freedom centers around the understanding that the individual has the option to choose among several alternatives and this includes *inter alia* the: *freedom to make choices; freedom as the absence of oppression; freedom as psychological liberation and freedom as liberation of the self.*

7.5.1. Freedom to make choices

On the whole people are free to make decisions in their life for example what religion they wish to adhere to; what professions they wish to follow and what commitments they would like to make. Such freedom can be valued and cherished. It is a positive to have the freedom to make choices, and not to be manipulated, controlled or even to be treated like puppets. While a believer would be of opinion that God also wants the human person to make free choices, this is not to be confused to what Paul had in mind. Choices and the privilege to make choices is never entirely a free decision as choices as well as the act of making choices are always conditioned by a multiple form of factors such as culture, immediate environments, education, publicity, subconscious drives and the like. In this sense choices are always determined in some measure by one factor or another. Cousar (1997:108) is of opinion that freedom comes not only in human choices, but also in divine choices. God's Chosen People in Christ have the responsible task to respond in faith and obedience to the One who had chosen them. With respect to the Galatians, Paul holds the view that the human person is not at liberty to choose circumcision because in so doing they lose their freedom, and by so doing they return to bondage (Gal. 4:8-11; 5:2-4). In this sense according to Cousar (1997:108) Paul's understanding of freedom is much more radical and realistic than the mere the possibility of choices.

7.5.2. Freedom as the absence of oppression

Another way of looking at freedom in the general sense would be when persons experience the absence of social, economic, or political oppression. Generally a nation would be considered free when a tyrannical leader or government is overthrown and citizens can determine their own form of government. People are liberated when economic or political exploitation, racism, or sexism and other related oppressions are destroyed. Freedom in this context is understood as independence, self-determination, and at least the opportunity to make significant decisions without the constraints of a coercive or patronizing person, group or authority. According to biblical teachings Christians are encouraged to identify with the poor, the oppressed and to take part in movements that aspire towards human freedom and the alleviation of injustice (Cousar 1997:108). However, the distinction between freedom as the removal of oppression and freedom as mentioned in Gal. 5:1 amounts to success in correcting a social wrong; it involves the establishment of a new regime of loyalty and dependency. While citizens are not free to determine their own destiny, they are "claimed for service by the living, loving God, who immediately sets them in the fight against all dehumanizing tyrannies" (Cousar 1997:109). Christological freedom, based on the saying: "for freedom Christ has set us free", takes into consideration the real danger of returning to the yoke of slavery which comes in various forms in modern living.

7.5.3. Freedom as psychological liberation

In contemporary reference freedom can also be referred to in a *psychological sense*, whereby the removal of emotional barriers, the healing of the past wounds, the coming to grips with internal forces form part of the process. The aim is not to be controlled by personal emotional impediments and this movement toward liberation entails the destruction of deterministic patterns of behaviour in which the individual is caught so that creative instincts can emerge and decisions can be more freely made. This is of special interest to Christians as psychological liberation assists individuals to become fully functioning human beings. Jesus, in this regard not only fed the hungry, but also healed the sick and cast out demons.

It is obvious that Christological freedom cannot be separated from emotional freedom. Unhealthy restraints and inhibitions have the ability to thwart personal growth, whereas genuine relationships give way to new openness and ease. Christian freedom goes even beyond that given the fact that individuals who form part of the body of Christ are linked with the historical figure of Jesus. Freedom comes to Christians as a reality into which they are called and in which they participate. It is not an innate quality or state of being which the individual discovers by sorting out past experiences and relationships. It is a gift bestowed on the believer as a result of Christ having liberated humanity on the cross, which in view of that involves the recipient in the concern for the total well-being of self and others.

7.5.4. Freedom as liberation of self

Freedom is sometimes defined as the quality of controlling one's own existence by a type of self-mastery. In the early Christian context the Stoics for example believed that if they could control and curb their human emotions and desires they can obtain freedom. Paul however, understood freedom not as a retreat into the self, but liberation of the self from without; drawing on the example of Jesus, who did not withdraw from life, but suffered the consequences of involvement. Jesus displayed total obedience to the will of his Father and it is precisely in this submission and obedience to God that Christian freedom lies. Submission and obedience may appear to be in contradiction to ordinary human freedom, but it is in surrendering to the will of God, the Father, that Christian freedom abides. To experience the liberation of Christ is hardly an occasion for arrogant boasting as with freedom comes responsibility, and free people have to give an account for their own life and conduct (Cousar 1997:111).

Christian freedom does not necessarily amount to independence; it is rather openness to connectedness and mutual dependence. Williams (1997:133) claims that freedom is liberation from the enervating effort to protect the ego from the hurt of other's judgment. He says the effort to protect and the desire for approval normally requires a goodly portion of self-deception and dissembling, freedom from these compulsions allow the vulnerable honesty that is conducive to genuine personal growth and in human relationships.

7.5.5. *Love as the proper exercise of freedom.*

Talking about freedom implies at the same time talking about the command to serve. However, this service is qualified by Paul when he counsels that through love we are to be servants of one another. This love, Paul claims, "rejoices in the right" (1 Cor. 13:6) and "does no wrong to another" (Rom. 13:10). This type of love which Paul advocates does not shy away from conflict lest it deteriorates to mere sentimentality. For the entire Law is fulfilled in one sentence: "You shall love your neighbour as yourself" (Gal. 5:14). The one who loves his or her neighbour has fulfilled the law (Rom. 13:8). Love puts the law in perspective and as such "frees people from misuse through the law and frees the law from misuse by people" (Cousar 1997:131).

Thus, according to the letter of Paul's instructions to the Galatian community, love is one of the prime characteristics of Christianity because it is the sum and substance of what it means to be a Christian. Faith is another identifiable and pivotal characteristic of Paul's teachings and faith for him means surrendering to this love (Gal. 2; 20; Rom. 5:5, 8). Love does not do away with the law, but provides it with correct interpretation, however love for Paul is not a sentimental experience, it is expressed in God's giving of God-self in Christ (Gal. 2.20; Rom.

5:6-8). This self-giving lies at the heart of the command to love and this command to serve one another in love carries broad implications for the Body of Christ where the members of this body are given the vocation to love one another.

7.6. Spiritual unity as articulated within the Body of Christ

It is within the Body of Christ that Christian unity, faith, love and freedom is articulated. This new creation, this new presentation of humanity cannot be understood apart from Christ (Eph. 2:15) since it is by means of baptism that humanity "puts on Christ" (Gal. 3:27). This unity of which Paul wrote Gal. (4:1-6) is not one which the Christian needs to create, because it is already in existence within the mystical Body of Christ. All that Christians have to do is to preserve it meticulously (vs. 3). This unity is also based upon the quality of sharing life within the one Body of Christ (vs. 5, cf. 2:15, 16). All members of the Body of Christ are sealed and by virtue of baptism the same Spirit dwells within each member and all look forward to the same hope (vs. 5, cf. 1:18).

In writing to the community in Corinth Paul also emphasizes this unity by stating that the members of the Body of Christ possess one Lord, is bound by one common faith and is one in baptism. The preservation of this unity is done by means of the spiritual gifts given to every Christian and despite the fact that members are differently gifted the possession of various spiritual gifts are not contradictory to Christian unity, in fact they are complimentary as together they form unity within this diversity (vs. 16). This unity is sustained and governed by the Holy Spirit that abides in each member (5:13-26).

The unity clause that is embedded in the equality clause of Gal. 3:38 gives foundation for the fundamental unity which exists between all believers in Jesus Christ. This unity that exists within the Body of Christ makes irrelevant all forms of separations such as male or female, slave or free, Jew or Gentile (Galatians 3:28). All factors that cause division such as circumcision, status, background are relativized within the Body of Christ since in Christ all are one. Love is the outcome of unity as proclaimed by John (13:34-35) and in this unity he counsels members to love one another as Christ loves us.

Within the Body of Christ all members are inseparably joined to one another. This phrase: "all are one in Christ" is what refers directly to unity in Christ and baptism provides the members of the Body of Christ with a new identity since they had 'put on Christ'. As members of the Jesus community the religio-cultural categories simply do not apply, only the expression "be baptized in Christ" (3:27) and as a result all members are on a par and their belonging together is expressed in their equal participation in this identity trait.

To be a member of the Body of Christ is not only a Christological exercise, but also an eschatological one. It implies allowing one life to be directed towards the Risen Lord, and not by the Law. When members are united to Christ there is a new world, a new creation taking shape where the Spirit of Christ is in charge. This is where the Christian wrestles with the vocation of freedom. Freedom "provides unencumbered opportunity for serving one another, even as slaves, in love" (Williams 1997: 163). For those who are together in the body of Christ genuine mutuality nourishes the oneness of community and disallows attitudes of superiority and interiority. Within the Body of Christ all are recipients of grace.

Each member of the Jesus Community has been crucified with Christ just like Paul and this new life in faith in Christ implies not desiring anything from the world. In this socio-spiritual community the Spirit is at work transforming people into brothers and sisters. Both Jews and Gentiles are heirs of the divine promise and the Body of Christ forms part of the new creation. The distinctions of whatever nature are not relevant; all that matters is the Body of Christ, the new creation which implies life in the family of God. The cross is the center of the identity and value of the Body of Christ and is of an inclusive nature within the Body of Christ. The Body of Christ is born of divine grace, sustained in freedom, nurtured by faith and it is within the Body of Christ that the new creation is a constant work in process.

7.7. CONCLUSION

The above chapter endeavoured to look at the Christian identity marker which specifies that to live in Christ implies possessing the Spirit of Christ and this implies abiding by faith that works through love. The definition of this particular Christian identity places a strong and active emphasis on faith that must work through love. Connected to this is that Christian unity of faith with love and freedom in the Body of Christ is a way of summing up what Paul presented as vital criteria to live as a follower of Christ. By taking on Christ is to take on a new life; a life lived in the Spirit of Christ. Being the exponent of a Law-free Gospel, Paul brings to the fore a new religious self-consciousness whereby union with God and others is mediated through conscious participation in the Body of Christ. This religious consciousness realized by Christian unity of faith, lived out with love and freedom introduces Christianity in a universal manner that was not experienced hitherto. By advocating unity within the Body of Christ was and is of utmost value as the apparent disunity between the Jews and Gentiles, the Law and the Spirit, had the propensity to cause division concerning their respective understandings and experiences of God.

"Faith informed by love" (Gal. 5:6) enlighten the bond between love and faith, which is the source of unity among the followers of Christ and it determines a new mode of existence which makes the believers righteous in virtue of the love of God and in virtue of obeying the law. The outpouring of love through the Spirit brings with it the assurance of salvation as well as a new consciousness of God in Christ. This new humanity in Christ, the new life of faith in Christ, inaugurated by the believer's baptism, makes all people equal as sons and daughters, brothers and sisters before God and each other. This spiritual unity in Christ is so valuable to the degree that all previous differences are no longer relevant or appropriate. Not only are the old distinctions abolished, but the descent from Abraham is also redefined. The offspring of Abraham is no longer confined to physical descent, because the promise made to Christ as Abraham's spiritual son implies that those who are united with Christ in faith also qualify as Abrahams' children (Riches 2008:189).

In addition this specific Christian identity trait is also characterized by the features of a new life of faith based on Paul's Law-free Gospel. Freedom from the Law implies that the slave under the Law has been set free and now qualifies as a rightful heir and enjoys a new life of freedom in the Spirit, participating in the life of the Son who died to the Law. Those who have experienced the new life in the Spirit can no longer embrace the confines of the Law since it brings only death and bondage. This new way of life flows from the new relationship with the Spirit, from the life of Christ, which for Paul meant freedom from old bondages particularly those associated with the Law. Paul presents the Christian way of life which is 'faith working through love' and love is the fulfillment of the law (Lev 19:18). Christians are led by the Spirit and thus are open to bear the fruit of the Spirit. Christian freedom comes with responsibility; ethical responsibility and freedom is not to be misused since the whole law is fulfilled in the command to love God and one's neighbour as oneself.

This new life, the life in the Spirit, is presented by Paul as a life that flows from participating in the Spirit, not in isolation, but in union with all believers in Christ and is supposed to bear the fruit of the Spirit. With this comes ethical ownership as the propagation of the fruit within the individual's life implies having no self-conceit and to bear one another's burdens. More important at this juncture is the movement of a life from enslavement to the Law to one that is characterized by the freedom of living in the Spirit of Christ. This transition has the potential to unite all people, all nations and tribes into one body, the all-inclusive Body of Christ.

CHAPTER EIGHT

8. A GALATIAN CONTRIBUTION TOWARDS SHAPING A DIASTRATICALLY VARIATED SOUTH AFRICA SOCIETY

8.1. INTRODUCTION

In one sense this final chapter is an attempt to recreate Paul's theological and ethical arguments and by so doing measure the theological, social and cultural impact they may exercise in creating a new emerging South African society. It wishes to appraise the innovative dynamism and the effect of the tenets of the letter against the major problems South Africa is currently experiencing in the process of reconstructing a nation that is integrated and civilly mature. South Africa is multi-cultural and multi-religious in social composition and the new advanced secular Constitution of South Africa, serves a population of seventy-nine percent Christian *inter alios*, and holds serious implications for the meaning of Gal. 6:2 *"to fulfill the law of Christ"* and *"to walk in the Spirit"* (5:25). This chapter wishes to explore whether the Christian characteristics, as identified in the research thus far, provide adequate license to enlighten the new established South African power elites in the government, society and church. To this end the research ascertains whether the identified characteristics of early Christianity, as selected by this study, possess the capacity to assist in shaping the process of creating a more credible and healthy social community free from corruption, violence and oppression. Since Christianity is the fastest growing religion in Africa and the Roman Catholic Church the fastest growing mainline church in South Africa, this study functions from the pretext that the distinctive tenets of beliefs and ethics of first century Christianity may still possess the authority of an eternal truth to enshrine both diversity and unity in a society of such great variety, since Paul's theology boasts unity in diversity, and not so much class analysis although in 1 Cor. 11:17-22 this claim testifies differently.

Both the first century Jewish Messianic movement and Paul's letter to the Galatians hold significantly similar traits that can assist in articulating specific truths for Christian participation in the formation of the new emerging South African society. By dialoguing with Paul's central theological utterances and the identifiable traits of the Jewish Messianic Movement, this research is of the opinion that beneficial extrapolations can be made for a Christian contribution towards creating an authentically inclusive and ethical society in the post—apartheid South Africa. While Paul's writing does not carry one single meaning and is often stacked with ambiguity, this study holds the view that the Christian identity characteristics of antiquity, and in particular those of Paul's letter to the Galatians, still contain significant resources towards articulating a credible Christian worldview in the new South African context.

The Christian identity characteristics of the Jewish Messianic movement in antiquity and the Galatian Christian identity characteristics pose interpretative challenges for the formation of an ethically sound post-apartheid society. Having considered the characteristics of the Jesus-Messianic-movement as well as those of Pauline Christianity as they were initially communicated to the Galatian readers and hearers, this research proposes to discern the relevance of the identifiable Christian characteristics for the self-understanding of the Christian Community in the emerging mass culture of contemporary South Africa. Given the cultural, religious and social circumstances of the Greco-Roman-Judaic world of Paul's time, his message was perceived as revolutionary in essence. That is the reason why this study ponders whether the eternal truths of his message still possess a defining quality for modern day South Africa? What bearing could the message of the letter to the Galatians have on the ethical, religious, cultural and socio-political situation of contemporary South Africa? Debate and engagement with the content will test the eternal truths of the message without having to piece out each argument sentence by sentence. The purpose is not to solve the ambiguities in the letter, but to draw on the characteristics, experiences and beliefs of the ancient Jesus-Movement and the Galatians Pauline teachings to decipher the relevant value thereof for post-apartheid South Africa that is undergoing a transition in every sector of life.

This study, however, wishes to employ the concept *diastratic*[7] in a hermeneutic fashion to examine how the *social variations* that cut across different strata's of the South African society in a very broad sense cause underlying stresses in the transition phase of working towards a unifying nation. It also wishes to employ the meaning of the term as the ingredient that can be utilized to create a perception of the *diastratically variated* elements that constitute the unique nature of the South African society. In this period of social transition a tolerant attitude of openness and respectful acceptance of all the social, cultural, religious, economical and linguistic dimensions of variations present in the South African social reality is a mental and emotional disposition that needs to be cultivated so as to embrace that which is ultimately different and new. It appears that the formation of a new South African society has to take cognizance and embrace the great variety of *diastratic variances* present in all the different features of the South African sociological, economical, political and cultural context.

---

[7]   The term "diatratic" is generally used in the architecture of language where there are dimensions of variations. "On a diastratic dimension", according to Peter Auer (2010:233), "a language can co-vary with many different social factors. Besides social class, the main social factors which intervene to determine diastratic variation are age, sex, or better, gender (the sex of a person as reflected in social position, status, and role and their attributes) ethnically and social network. In many societies membership in social and professional groups or religious faith can also be relevant factors of language differentiation."

In diastratic variation, social class is by no means a clear-cut and indisputable category. Social class is a plurifactual concept that includes various mixtures of ingredients such as education, occupation, income, attributes, life-style and social networks: namely a structured set of social relations connecting a person and people with whom this person interacts (Auer 2010:233). Diastratic variations are used across socio-economic classes of social groups in this sense that it is that ingredient that constitutes the feeling or awareness of belonging to that social class, or language group and so on.

8.2. UNIVERSALISM, INCLUSIVENESS AND EXCLUSIVENESS

Christianity in antiquity, like Judaism, was monotheistic in a polytheistic world. Both demanded a high degree of consistent conduct from their members and by so doing deviated from the social customs otherwise practiced. The early Christians broke through the restriction of Judaism since Jewish membership was largely based on ascriptive recruitment (i.e. recruited by birth) and as such were closed to the outer world because of their ritual barriers (Theissen 1992:204). Christianity developed the power of diffusion which allowed it to open doors to others. The divisive norms of Judaism, such as circumcision and dietary laws, created prevention or preclusion preconditions. In contrast Christianity employed the freedom to break away from exclusive practices. In fact, as asserted by Theissen (1992:204), early Christianity was a Judaism that was accessible to non-Jews by doing away with dividing norms and in turn Paul assisted by providing a theological foundation for the renunciation of these dividing norms and practices.

The ancient Jewish Messianic movement advocated universalism and inclusiveness and, as was noted previously, these sentiments were also prominent in Paul's letter to the Galatians. This new universal religious consciousness, which became evident in early Christian faith clamoured to transcend the ethnic particularism of the then contemporary religions such as Judaism. While, in Baur's (1971:43) view, Paulinism was the first to bring about the break in Christian consciousness with Judaism, it is, on the other hand, Jewish particularism that became distinguished from Christian universalism. This newly acquired God-consciousness fostered by Jesus Christ and furthered by Paul gave expression to a new universal consciousness.

For Paul it was essential to transcend the particular and exclusive nationalistic forms of Judaism since the universal nature of the message of Jesus was for him the most essential part of the Gospel of freedom that he preached so ardently (Gal. 3:28). This new universal consciousness emerged with clarity and strength as Paul went along dealing with belief difficulties advocated by conscientious Jewish Christians. For example the zealous Jewish Christians imposed on the Gentile Christians a common principle among them that there was no salvation apart from Judaism. This belief was vehemently renounced by Paul. In fact it was these kinds of sentiments that brought Jewish and Pauline Christianity into direct confrontation with each other. Paul's religious consciousness confirmed the universalism which was preached by Jesus in the Sermon on the Mount. Within the Galatian milieu, pertinent to Paul's letter, the Jewish observances such as circumcision, food laws and the observance of the Sabbath, served not only as strong Jewish identity markers, but also as the harsh boundaries between themselves and others. For Paul the Christian principle of inclusiveness was essentially identical with the person of Christ (Baur 1875:124) hence the urgency for Paul to move away from the restricted nature of the nationalistic forms of Judaism to a more open attitude so as to include those who were previously looked upon as 'outsiders'.

Similarly this principle of inclusion is a vital one for nation building in modern South Africa. Although the new democratic Constitution and the national Bill of Rights of 1996 make provision for equal opportunities for all her citizens, it did not provide the resources to address mental, spiritual and attitudinal divides. This research is of opinion that the new Democratic Constitution of South Africa, which claims to be a very advanced document, did not prepare the people for the reception and practical consequences thereof. In fact the document was received by the people ill prepared for its reception and the "social tremours" shook the mental and emotional equilibrium of the nation. The consequent social transition from rigid racial compartmentalization and exclusiveness to emancipated movement and integration resulted in a new form of distrusted interaction.

8.2.1. The inclusive principle pertinent to the South African Christian scenario

Harsh boundaries in every sphere of life in South Africa were created by a national policy that separated people in all spheres of social, religious, economic and political life. This study is convinced that renewed awareness and consciousness of Christian identity characteristics such as *inclusiveness and universal consciousness* possess the instrumental value to remove the long-established wedges that still form national and social boundaries between people in everyday life.

Paul was exceedingly conscious of the inclusive nature of *life in the Spirit; of freedom; of reconciling humanity with God and of God's union with humanity through Jesus Christ.*

The revelation of Christ, a gift for both Gentiles and Jews and the consequent religious self-consciousness, was a crucial sign of the then emerging universal Christian consciousness (Baur 1971:125-6). This type of new social and religious consciousness is also important in the emerging new South African society. The Law-free Gospel, preached by Paul, is at the heart of this religious self-consciousness where union with God is mediated through consciousness of participation of Jesus (Riches 2008: 112).

The revolutionary dynamism of Paul's letter to the Galatians contains simultaneously the potential to impact on the emerging integrated society of contemporary South Africa as well as to endanger the uneasy grip of the young emerging society. In the formation process, according to the injunction of Paul, developing societies have to be ethically guided and led by the Spirit (Gal. 5:8). In the face of a Constitution that promotes a so-called secular society in South Africa, a society of whom seventy-nine percent professes to be Christian in sentiment and practice, it is questioned as to what it means to "walk in the Spirit" (Gal. 5:25) or to "be led by the Spirit" (Gal. 5:18). In the face of intense worldly and humanistic sentiments, reference to God and religion are minimized and the question is asked as to what role religion, and specifically Christianity, still plays in the public domain and how is it supposed to influence opinion.

Christianity in antiquity, which was in fact "a Judaism", had been transformed in its inner structure simply because it has opened its spiritual doors to non-Jews. It was a transformative path that was national, ethical and universal. In the letter to the Galatians Jews and Christians were interpreted as 'brothers", even "hostile brothers", but nevertheless "brothers". Christianity, according to (Theissen 1992:208) was viewed as "de-stricted or open Judaism". Through faith in Christ, Gentiles too could enter into God's history with God's people without having to become Jews (Gal. 2:18). This inclusive mentality declared Abraham the father of all (Rom. 4:16); hence Gentile Christians also belonged to "the Israel of God (Gal. 6:16). They were the people who were once not God's people, but who have now become so (Rom. 9:25 = Hosea 2:25). This all-embracing inclusiveness formed the axis of Paul's Gospel of Freedom and for this reason the Jews (Sarah) and the Gentiles (Hagar) need to live peacefully together as indicated by the Sarah-Hagar typology. Paul universalized the idea of redemption by exchanging the roles of Jews and Gentiles. By so doing Paul relativized the differences between the Jews and the Gentiles and as a result opened the way to inclusivity and equality.

A recent perception had been created that since the advanced secular Constitution of South Africa makes provision for the essential human rights of each citizen, it has in actual fact rendered the theological, spiritual, biblical and cultural belief systems ineffectual. If this is an experienced reality, more than just a perceived reality, then religious educators and Church ministers and authorities have reason to be concerned. In the effort to foster environments that engender the natural theological pertinence for Christian theological, spiritual and human formation, this research advocates the application of deep reflective mindfulness. Unless the Christian theological, spiritual and ecclesial environments articulate Christian identity axioms, South Africans will always experience a sense of dual "Christian-ship": one side to appease the government and cultural authorities and the other to satisfy religious needs. During the years of oppression, Christianity in South Africa was not only challenged, but it served as a challenge that was rooted within an environment of great vitality. The lucrative utilization of biblical insights, which had become part of the heritage of Christianity, was meant to open South Africans up to what could contribute to healthy resolves to the diverse environments so as to create resonant, inclusive and just social, political and economic conditions. The prophetic voice in South Africa has gone dormant and the voice of the Church and the voice of indigenous theologians have aligned themselves with the majority sentiment. Since the basic human rights of all people in South Africa are enshrined in the country's refined constitution, the voice of biblical scholars and theologians in South Africa has gone quiet since they are of opinion that the said goals had been achieved and that the time had come to bow out gracefully and surrender any honourable grounds for further employment to government instruments. The rising black middle class in South Africa, among them first generation black theologians, has done extremely well and now shares a commonality with previous and contemporary oppressors. This study questions whether the glamour of this new-found release from oppression has blinded the first generation black theological and biblical scholars to the plight of those who are still living with the immorality of discrimination and exclusion on all levels of society. Church leaders, and in particular Black Church leaders, are maintaining an extremely low profile in the face of existing realities which oppress black and white communities such as the multiple forms of bondage related to social, economic, religious, gender, homophobic, cultural, xenophobic and ecological chains. As observed by Alistair Kee (2005:52) "after the passion and commitment of Black Theology, they (black theologians) now seem anaemic". Does the ardent voice of Paul have the ability to animate the prophetic courage of Christianity to address the still prevailing oppressive and discriminative situations in South Africa?

This research has identified inclusiveness as a primary Christian identity characteristic, celebrated by Paul and a most fitting quality required for the transformative process of nation building in South Africa. Taking into account its history whereby people of colour were excluded from basic rights, amenities, opportunities, and vital possibilities of living a full and free life, Paul's message of inclusivity could only carry positive conclusions for the people of South Africa. In antiquity Paul's message also occurred during a cultural, religious and social transition: a transition from the all-exclusive Jewish faith environment to an all-inclusive Jewish and Gentile faith amalgamation. Paul's view of inclusivity possesses the essential tenets for an all-encompassing nation building process in South Africa, a nation in transition by the promotion and implementation of humanistic principles.

Paul's letter to the Galatians redefines the concept "People of God' in the sense that before the coming of Christ the Jewish people took pride in the Law, the gift from God that set them apart as a special people and thus they regarded themselves as "unlike other nations and religions" (Cousar 1997:89). With the coming of Jesus the question of who really belongs to God is transformed as the principle of inclusiveness prevailed, non-Jews are included and the concept "People of God" took on an expanded meaning. The "People of God" no longer had to be determined by the Law, but by Christ, being joined to him by baptism. This redefinition of the "People of God" is in fact a revolutionary movement in the nature of the fellowship with Christ. In the previous South African regime the Afrikaner people also regarded themselves as the "Chosen People" of God and that people of colour could not aspire to such a privilege.

Despite the fact that inclusiveness and equality are the underlying guiding principle of building the new South African society, exclusivity still remains a very harsh reality and it is not only confined to tensions between black and white, rich and poor; it is also a harsh reality between black and black, between local and foreigner, between male and female. Despite the fact that much credit can be given to the new dispensation, old divisions had not been eradicated and regrettably new prejudices and divisions surface such as xenophobia, homophobia, materialism and criminal violence.

8.2.2. Xenophobia: South Africa's "new pathology"

"In Christ there is no Jew or Gentile . . ."

With the transfer of political power in South Africa there emerged a new range of discriminatory practices together with their victims. Despite the transition from authoritarianism to democracy, prejudice and violence mark contemporary South Africa and the brunt of the new prejudices and violence are also directed against foreigners and in particular black African foreigners. The axiom of Paul: *"In Christ there is no Jew or Gentile . . ."* can be utilized as a possible spiritual torch in addressing xenophobic tendencies and attitudes. The entire Letter of Paul to the Galatians is addressing the Gentile-Jewish divide and of course, while the word "xenophobia" was not part of the vocabulary of Paul's time, the prejudice and pressure to conform to Jewish religious and cultural requirements formed part of the Jewish *milieu*. Paul did not want the Christian group to turn into a cliquish sub-culture and a religiosity of a gathered elect and was insistent that to be a follower of Christ does not require any elaborate doctrinal or institutional structures, neither succumbing to all the practices of Judaism to provide them with a sense of identity and belonging.

In South Africa xenophobia has been dubbed the "new pathology" of the nation as "the foreigner stands at a site where identity, racism and violent practice are reproduced" (Harris: 2002:169). Harris portrays xenophobia "as negative, abnormal and the antithesis of a healthy, normally functioning individual or society (Harris 2002:169). She states that, currently, it forms an inherent part of the South African culture of violence. In addition, xenophobia is perceived as a socially located phenomenon, characterized by a negative attitude or mindset towards foreigners which is expressed in a deep dislike, a fear or even hatred towards them. Harris (2002:170) claims that xenophobia is often connected with violence and physical abuse and for this reason argues that it is more than an attitude—it is also a harmful activity. However, what is curious about xenophobia in South Africa is that it is not uniformly applied to all foreigners, since it is largely directed towards black foreigners, particularly those from other parts of Africa. Black hatred of other blacks, black-on-black violence, is a most fitting description of xenophobia in the South African context. Why black South Africans target their own African black brothers and sisters in such a violent and negative manner remains in itself a strange phenomenon.

Nonetheless, there are various explanations put forward to provide potential reasons for the violent form of xenophobia in South Africa. To provide explanations implies interrogating why it is present; identifying the people that are targeted and the manner in which they are confronted. It is suggested that much of the hostility towards foreign black Africans emerged from the unfulfilled promises of the new regime in South Africa. This deep sense of disconcertedness is strongly connected to problems related to housing, education, health care, employment, poverty and general deprivation. According to Tshitereke, also consulted by Bronwyn Harris (1998:171), in situations like these people create a "frustration-scapegoat" and in the South African context blacks foreigners are the scapegoats.

In addition to the "scapegoat hypothesis", Morris (1998:1125) explains that South Africa was isolated during the apartheid years and hardly ever allowed black foreigners into the country. This policy had limited South Africans' exposure to foreigners. This attitude of insularity created a space for South Africans to develop hostility and suspicion towards foreigners. As argued by Morris 1998:1125): " . . . the brutal environment created by apartheid with its enormous emphasis on boundary maintenance has also impacted on people's ability to be tolerant of differences". As a consequence, South Africans find differences threatening and dangerous and xenophobia exists because foreigners are different as well as unknown. In his letter to the Galatians Paul was hard at work to address the insignificance of differences before God and that by virtue of Christ and being baptized in Christ, differences should not exclude anyone from being treated as equals. While the differences between Jews and Gentiles were never referred to as "hatred of foreigners" by Paul, he did, however preach that within Christ there is "no Jew or Gentile" and that all are one and equal before God.

Social disorientation is a known experience all over the world, but in South Africa the violent and criminal component is an added factor. Curiously, this violent form of xenophobia, distinctive to South Africa, is not applied equally to all foreigners. It is a strange phenomenon, but it is a reality that African foreigners seem to be at greater risk than others. The social disorientation as experienced in South Africa is associated with criminality and illegality. Black foreigners are described as 'illegals', 'illegal aliens' and 'illegal immigrants' together with other derogatory terms. These terms entail both criminality and difference. A more disturbing factor is that xenophobia is not only negative for healthy nation building, but is also exacerbated by South Africa's culture of violence and in this sense it has assumed the sick characteristics of a national pathological condition. African foreigners are victimized with the same violence which was used during the apartheid years as a political vehicle for liberation. The only difference now is that the violence is in fact a tool for criminality. For this reason Harris (2002:180) claims that: "Xenophobia is a form of violence and violence is the norm in South Africa." Violence, she argues, was an integral part of the "old South Africa" and is still a dominant part of the social fabric of the 'new South Africa' although it is belied in certain quarters. Harris continues by suggesting that xenophobia as pathology is not only central to national discourse, but that it functions within the culture of violence to give definition to the 'new South Africa' and the forms of identity that accompany this discourse. To read xenophobia as a national pathology, because local black national identity seems under threat, is an area where Paul's theology is called upon to be seriously at work towards a national cure for a national disease.

8.2.3. Appealing to Paul's Christian ethics

An appeal can be made to Paul's ethics, values and norms as well as to the traditional values of African morality. Xenophobia, as a barefaced social illness, has infested South African society with dire consequences. This research holds the opinion that Black Theology is reneging on its task by not applying Paul's theology of liberation as an ethical principle in this context. If there is an impression among blacks that they had arrived at freedom square and they can now relax and concentrate on other things (Motlhabi 2008:15), then, considering the xenophobic violence and conflict experienced in South Africa, this is indeed a false impression. Since "the ultimate goal of African traditional morality, indeed of all morality, was seen as the promotion of human welfare" (Motlhabi 2008:56), Black Theology can appeal to the African values in a socially oriented manner. He explains that good moral principles, according to African traditional morality, are those which befit the welfare of the human being. Goodness, says Motlhabi (2008:56), was described in terms such as kindness, faithfulness, compassion, hospitality, and peace lovingness. These qualities in turn were to bring dignity, respect, contentment, posterity and joy to all people within the community. This was all done to promote human life and human life was the supreme good toward which morality was aimed in the traditional African context. These views are not unlike what Paul wished to drive home to the Christian Jews of his time.

As explained by Motlhabi (2008:56), traditionally in Africa the quest for human welfare was embraced by the value of good neighbourliness and this in turn was instrumental in the creation of good relations among people. Motlhabi (2008:56) continues stating that good neighbourliness was in effect the practical implementation of the value of *ubuntu*, which means humanness or personhood. The concept of *ubuntu* placed an emphasis on the person as the highest and most intrinsic value of Africanism. Traditionally, some of the manifestations of *ubuntu* were mutual respect, harmonious social and interpersonal relations, kindness, gentleness, cooperation and conformity to accepted communal customs. The fruits of the Spirit as related by Paul as love, joy, peace patience, kindness, goodness, faithfulness, gentleness and self-control are not out of harmony with *ubuntu* values. It was believed that the person who possessed all the above qualities not only possessed *ubuntu*, but is real *umuntu*, that is, *a person indeed* (Motlhabi 2008:56). On the other hand, the person who did not possess these human qualities, that person was not a human being, not a person. In addition, says Motlhabi (2008:56): "good interrelationships among people following from neighbourliness implied a good standing with God." It is understood that what generally promoted human welfare and social harmony is that which is ethical and morally good and that which was detrimental to a human being's welfare was regarded as evil.

Theologians and biblical scholars would have to be prepared to stick out their necks and become involved in addressing these oppressive and discriminative social ills as Paul did when he wrote to the Galatians. However, xenophobia is not the only social ill that needs to come under the spotlight of Paul's ethics in the effort towards healthy nation building in South Africa. Another disturbing social demise is gender violence and discrimination which can also not be ignored and overlooked. This remains an unresolved ethical concern despite the noble constitutional provisions.

8.3. GENDER VIOLENCE AND DISCRIMINATION:
AN UNRESOLVED ETHICAL CONCERN

"In Christ there is no male or female . . ."

The new democratic Constitution of 1996, not only guaranteed the rights of women, but also ensured that mechanisms be put in place to ensure gender equality. Despite the impressive mechanisms that were put in place to protect women, violence against women in South Africa remains an alarming statistic. There is no doubt that religion, sacred texts as well as cultural beliefs and practices had contributed to violence against women. Considering Paul's text that there is no difference between male and female can be a way of trying to establish an incisive view whereby Christians can overcome violence against women.

While recognition can be given to the new South African government in making theoretical justification for women rights and equality, Christians, on the other hand, need to interrogate their belief systems which are based to a large extent on their sacred texts and cultural systems (Nadar 2009:86) so as to renounce any theological, biblical and cultural justification of violence towards women. Violence against women is unethical as well as a crime. Since Paul teaching to the Galatians promotes equality between "male and female"; this Christian value requires serious deliberation in the effort to transform the injustices that still exist in South Africa. The deconstruction of "life-denying gender ideologies" (Nadar 2009:85) which are contained both in biblical texts, as well as in religious, cultural and social teachings and practices, needs serious scrutiny in the light of Paul's ancient Christian tenets. It is possible that the violence which occurred towards women in the Bible, in the history of the church and society could explain why the seventy-nine percent strong Christian population in South African remain mute in the face of violence against women

As suggested by Nadar (2009:87), a South African Indian biblical theologian, a genuine "wrestling" is needed with theological justifications of gender violence and the beginning is with Sacred Scripture. For this she proposes that a "feminist cultural hermeneutic" be applied. Nadar claims that while African theologies as a branch of feminist theology has attempted to engage with the issue of culture as a central concern of their work, it unfortunately met with the challenge of mindsets that claimed that feminism is a Western import (Nadar 2009:88) and thus needs to be rendered invasive. This mindset makes the task of African feminist theologians very difficult since feminists are aware that colonists and missionaries from Europe tended to demonize local cultures and in the light of this feminism is regarded as an alien invasion. Al the same modern feminists somehow need steering away from the intimidation of such mindsets and allow "feminist cultural hermeneutics" to enhance that which is good in local culture and to address those aspects that undermine and minimize the lives of women. It appears that some Christian denominations capitalize on cultural beliefs that deny women their rightful place in the church and society simply because culturally it was never a domain of women such as leadership in the Christian Church. Gender-sensitive cultural hermeneutics exacerbates the issue all the more. This research does not deny that much of Paul's teaching regarding women were also culturally bound and yet he took a very critical stance of religious practices that exclude Gentile men and women from the being full participants in the life of Christ; against practices and belief systems that proved harmful to women. The ethical principles which Paul preached to the Gentiles could be employed in feminist cultural hermeneutics as a means to counteract gender violence both in religion and culture. It is particularly difficult to separate culture from religion in Africa, just as it was difficult to separate Christianity from its Greco-Roman and Jewish roots. It is curious to realize that the rules of submission as well as silence for women in Greek philosophy found their way into the New Testament and today these rules are ardently considered as the "Word of God". This conflation of religion and culture form the foundation for justifications for men's superiority over women, to prescribe women's dress and behaviour codes, as did Paul in his letters, to determine women's place in the family, to condemn same-sex relationships and to judge the contraction of certain deceases such as HIV/AIDS as a punishment from God. Injustices and the denial of people's humanity had often been justified and motivated within the church and culture by taking recourse to so-called "biblical values" which render human rights worthless. This research inquires how Paul's teaching would deal with such a conflicting scenario and pave a way open to Christians who claim that they look to the Bible for their morals, values and guidance. The ambiguous link between human rights, religious and cultural beliefs are clearly illustrated in the conflict between human rights and the iniquitous nature and use of some "biblical values" as is illustrated in some of the human rights that the new South African constitution granted to her people such as the right to marriage to same-sex oriented people. Nadar (2009: 89) argues that if this human right, i.e. same-sex unions (Constitution of South Africa), is regarded as "unbiblical" then it can be argued that gender equality should also be regarded as "unbiblical". While the provision of human rights is a good thing, the provision of so-called "contentious human rights" has created a situation in the South African society that had enabled perpetrators to extend violence against women, foreigners and homosexual persons. An additional disturbing phenomenon is that gender violence against black homosexual women has intensified in vast proportions. As stated by Nadar (2009: 89) when religion and culture form a combination it can be perilous as was the case in apartheid years, but when another construction is added, it can prove to be more fatal for a woman's well-being. This is the distressing situation regarding gender violence in South Africa: it is experienced as even more lethal when the woman is *black* and *homosexual.*

8.3.1. Racial and engendered homophobic victimization

Despite the fact that post-apartheid South Africa was meant to replace legislated racism with equality, apartheid with democracy, segregation with unity, this is not a reality on the ground. Even though South Africa's 1996 Constitution is internationally recognized as one of the most progressive and inclusive in the world, and with the government showing exceptional commitment to acknowledge and uphold the human rights of all, this is not the situation for South Africa's lesbian, gay, bisexual and transgendered (LGBT) citizens, and in particularly for black LGBT persons. On 1 December 2006 South Africa became one of only five countries in the world to legalize homosexual unions, much to the abomination of other African states. Yet, based on the research done by J.A. Nel (from Unisa) and M. Judge (from Out-LGBT—Pretoria) (2008:19), the reality on the ground is in stark contrast to policy and legislative guarantees for fundamental human rights, since homophobic victimization is endemic in South Africa and in particular the engendered nature thereof. The research findings of Nel and Judge, based on self-reported data, indicate a disconcertingly high prevalence of homophobic discrimination in the black community. Exclusive and targeted victimization form part of the everyday realities accompanied by abusive criminal intimidation.

It is suggested that one of the interpretations of the historical dominical saying of Gal. 3:28 namely: "that in Christ there is no male or female" is that the meaning behind the most original version of the text was the social need of the female to become a male. It can be argued that for Paul the transformation was not into androgyny, but into social equality. However, in contrast, Lone Fatum (1991:50-133) claims that Paul called for an abolition of sexuality, not social distinction. She is of opinion that Gal. 3:38 "rests on a negative view of sexuality and of women as females, defining the annulment of sexuality in Christ as the eschatological affirmation of life i.e. as the eschatological re-establishment of Genesis 1:27". Women who remained in sexual relationships had to accept a subordinate status, not even being in the image of God, and only the woman who became an asexual Son of God had the possibility of equality (Hogan 2008:10). Nonetheless it is clear from Paul's use of the transformation formula in Galatians 3 that before God all men and women, regardless of legal status, ethnic origin and religious background are equal within the Christian community. There are definite indications that for Paul inclusiveness extended to the eradication of all distinctions. Paul's letter to the Galatians contains a dramatic challenge to South African ideas about social and sexual distinctions, oneness in Christ, equality and freedom. The question here is: to what extent has the equalitarian potential of Gal. 3:28 an impact on the new-found South African legislation that provides marital rights, freedom of sexual expression to all people across the colour divides, or across religious barriers or people of same-sex orientations. This comes in the context of an overridingly traditional and cultural population with Christian influences and definitely far from ready to alter customary mindsets regarding same-sex relationships and even marriage.

According to the findings of research conducted in the Gauteng province of South Africa, LGBT persons are not only targets of general violence, but are also stigmatized and discriminated against through criminal acts. The research purports that LGBT people from poor black communities and black lesbian women in particular, are disproportionately at risk of discrimination since they face violence twice as often as heterosexual women. The malicious phenomenon of "corrective rape" has in particular been documented among Gauteng township-dwelling black lesbian women. Violent intimidation is not experienced equally across class, race and gender lines since women from lower socio-economic levels are often more susceptible to gender-based crimes such as rape, domestic violence and child abuse. These experiences have been borne out in the SABC investigative journalism and documentary programme known as "Special Assignment"—2004 and updated with renewed evidence in February 2010. These programmes revealed the escalating incidences of homosexual and transgender prejudice in black townships. With empirical evidence they showed that, despite the post-apartheid shift from the prior criminalization of homosexuality to legislative and constitutional support for the equality of all people, LGBT people in South Africa remain the most vulnerable to hate crimes. This is significantly evident in many black communities where a disproportionate number of LGBT persons continue to face oppression, marginalization, discrimination and victimization.

While it is not the intention of this research to take a stand on the biblical, theological or ecclesial standing of LGBT persons, there are nonetheless some disturbing biblical texts that regard LGBT people to be perceived as sinners and moral deviants and inhuman. The classic Old Testament texts of Gen 19:1-19; Jg 19:16-29; Lev. 18:22; and the New Testament texts such as Rom. 1:26-27; 1 Cor. 6:9 and 1 Tim 1:10 provide the basis for a theology of exclusion and condemnation, which no other texts in the Bible can be compared in regard to blacks, slaves or women. As pointed out by Garner and Worsnip (in Speckman and Kaufmann 2001:225) "valiant attempts have and are been made to interpret these texts in a light, if not favourable, then at least ambiguous to the position of gay and lesbian people." They state that while this exploration is necessary and important it remains fairly unconvincing. However, this research deems it necessary to bring to notice the astoundingly submissive voicelessness and slow responses, if any, of African biblical scholars and theologians to the alarming and disturbing treatment of same-sex-oriented people. Very few talk about the systemic homophobic prejudice in its varying manifestations except maybe to single out one voice, that of Archbishop Desmond Tutu. This veteran theologian has added his name to the fight against homophobia, particularly in Africa. At the launching of the book *Sex, Love and Homophobia*" (Baird: 2004), for which he wrote the forward, Archbishop Tutu affirmed that homophobia is a "crime against humanity" and "every bit as unjust as apartheid". He stated that South Africans struggled against apartheid and were supported by people the world over because black people were being blamed and made to suffer for something they could do nothing about namely, their very skins. He maintains that it is the same with sexual orientation—it is a given—and discrimination against homosexual persons is nefarious.

Archbishop Tutu is of the opinion that he could not have fought against the discrimination of apartheid and not also fight against the discrimination that homosexuals endure. He states that he is proud that, in South Africa, when the black people won the chance to build their own new Constitution, the human rights of all were explicitly cared for in the revised laws. He reiterates that South Africa's Constitution guarantees equal rights notwithstanding sexual orientation, yet, he writes, as happens all over the world, lesbian, gay, bisexual and transgender people are being persecuted. "We treat them as pariahs and push them outside our communities. We make them doubt that they too are children of God and this must be nearly the ultimate blasphemy. We blame them for what they are." He in particular regrets the dominant negative views among his church colleagues, black theologians and ministers. They maintain that the expression of love in a heterosexual monogamous relationship includes the physical and that the totality of love makes each increasingly godlike and compassionate. The Archbishop asks: "If this is so for the heterosexual, what earthly reasons have we to say that it is not the case with the homosexual?" For him these "destructive forces" of "hatred and prejudice" are evil. He argues: "A parent who brings up a child to be a racist damages that child, damages the community in which they live, and damages humanity's hopes for a better world. A parent who teaches a child that there is only one sexual orientation and that anything else is evil denies our humanity and their own too" (Tutu in Baird 2004). Since Paul, in his Gospel of freedom, preached a message of equality, should his message have a similar interpretation for South Africans today?

From the above it appears obvious that all interventions crafted to address homophobic victimization require a strengthened partnership between scholars, the state, church and culture. Ongoing identity-based discrimination (on the basis of race, gender, sexual orientation, HIV/AIDS status and other characteristics) represents a fundamental challenge to biblical scholars. To realize lasting social transformation, theologians and biblical scholars ought to be bold enough to confront South Africa's enduring legacy of inequality, discrimination and prejudice. To achieve the Constitution's promise of gender equality and social justice, collaboration is required to develop an informed and unified strategy towards ensuring that all South Africans are able to enjoy human rights. Biblical ethicists need to build a collective morality that affirms human dignity and non-discrimination in a manner that is experienced in the lived reality of all those discriminated against in South Africa. The Christian churches in South Africa are not vocal enough in opposing the vicious injustices done towards LGBT persons; instead they pronounce condemnatory statements which in the name of Christianity encourage such persecution. This amounts to the same malicious practice whereby apartheid was substantiated by using a few unclear biblical references. Nonetheless, before black theologians embark on such a task they need to confront their own cultural, religious, social and personal homophobia since the victim mindset functions as a disincentive.

8.3.2. Appealing to Paul's ethics and teachings

While there are several texts in Scripture that attests to the subordination of women to men there is no evidence of blatant biblical justification for violence against women and violence because women displayed homosexual practices. To look at the realities of homosexuality in Paul's day, Victor Paul Furnish states that it was not a major biblical concern and to understand the two references (1 Cor. 6-7 and Rom. 1:26-27) in his writings to homosexuality one has to understand the place of homosexuality in Greco-Roman society. An awareness of the attitudes expressed in the moral teachings of Paul's contemporaries, Greco-Roman, rabbinic and Hellenistic Jewish, enables one to deal sensitively with the original meaning of the Pauline texts and the significance for modern Christians (Furnish: 1979:58). Apparently pederasty was a common practice among the Greeks. Plato described it as among the noblest of relationships; however, he did not refer to it as a physical relationship, but a "higher" from of love uniting two persons known as Platonic relationships. The same goes for the poetess, Sappho, who presided over the intimate community of young women on the island of Lesbos. In the Roman period of the first century homosexuality was still practiced by the upper classes, but moral philosophers started to question its merit, as it was compared with heterosexual relationships in marriage. The practice of homosexuality came to be associated with grosser forms of indulgence (Furnish 1979:60). Among the Jews, in contrast to the Greco-Roman world as a whole, homosexual behaviour was not common, as far as we know, in the sense of it being permitted. The rabbis regarded homosexual behaviour as a Gentile vice (Furnish 1979:64) and quoted Levitical prohibitions to avert the practice.

However, the terms "homosexual" and "homosexuality" were unknown in Paul's day. These terms were developed only with the advent of modern psychological and sociological studies. Homosexuality was not understood as "sexual orientation" since sex with one's own kind was associated with insatiable lust and avarice and regarded as exploitative. The Pauline texts on homosexuality would have been uttered with the same ethical views of his time and would have been related to his own theological convictions and social context. In both 1 Cor. 6-7 and Rom. 1:26-27 Paul supposes homosexual behaviour as something freely chosen by an individual, but, similar to Seneca, Dio Chrysostom and Philo, he also regarded homosexual activities as a violation of the created order (Furnish 1979:74). Furnish states that Paul shared common views with many "secular moralist of his time and was in accord with the teachings of Hellenistic Judaism and for this reason he condemns homosexual practices. He was not obsessively preoccupied with the matter and there is no evidence that Paul had to deal with a specific case of homosexual conduct. Furnish (1979:79) claims that his references to it are brief and formulated under the influence of traditional ideas about its causes and characteristics. In this sense Paul does not offer any direct teaching to his own churches on the subject of homosexual conduct and his letters cannot yield any specific answers to the questions being faced in modern Christianity. Furnish claims that it is therefore mistaken to invoke Paul's name in support of any specific position on matters related to the ill-treatment and exclusion of homosexual individuals. Since the modern behaviour sciences are still baffled by many aspects of this complex phenomenon and that many factors such as social, psychological and even biological play a role in the "gender identity" of an individual person, Furnish (1979:79) claims that it is not wise to speak of homosexuality as mutually exclusive categories. For this reason in the light of the present knowledge and lack thereof the issue of homosexuality cannot be significantly interpreted and evaluated by Paul's statement of the matter and neither can he be regarded as naïve and ignorant in the light of current information.

It can be concluded that Paul's teaching is therefore not sufficient to answer the intricacies about the ethically right or wrong on the matter. Paul's science and ethics and modern science and ethics cannot be coordinated into a forced synergy since Paul's ethical assumptions were related to Greco-Roman science. The biology that Paul learnt influenced his ethical assumptions and arguments and simply transposes the biblical attitude towards homosexual acts and modern scientific observations cannot be presumed univocal and sufficient unto the course. In this regard it is also suggested by Balch (2000:300) that it is necessary to ask how modern biology and psychology influence Christian ethics.

What is clear, however, is that when Paul referred to homosexual behaviour he was illustrating the wretchedness of the human condition when acting out of lust and thus debasing one's true identity and exploiting another person's; this amounts to violating a moral principle and doing harm to oneself and to another. Very important is the understanding that when homosexual or heterosexual relationships involve the dishonour of another person, they remain under the judgment of Scripture. For this reason, this research is in agreement with Furnish (1979:81), it is not appropriate to isolate Paul's remarks about homosexual behaviour from the wider theological context in which they stood. This implies remembering the function of Romans 1:18-32 as a whole and that in this instance homosexuality is mentioned as one among numerous vices. For Paul the most fundamental vice is idolatry whereby one worships the created order, an ideology, a religious system, a particular moral code rather than the Creator. As concluded by David L. Balch (2000:291), there is an important difference between Jewish and Christian readings of Scripture; unlike Leviticus 20:26, "the New Testament contains no passages that clearly articulate a rule against homosexual practices" (2000:291). Paul assumes gender differences, but he did not make an argument against homosexual acts similar to that in Leviticus 20:26. In the Christian debates about homosexuality and its appropriateness, it is well to appeal as well to the important commandment in Leviticus 19:18, "love your neighbour as yourself" which is surely more important that Leviticus 20:13, which instructs that Israel kill those who perform homosexual acts. Both Jesus and Paul appealed to the same Levitical command to love our neighbours, whether they are prostitutes, tax-collectors or noble citizens (Matt.5:43-44; 19:19; 22-39; Luke 6:27; 10:27; Rom.13:9; Gal. 5:14) as the greatest command.

Considering the proclamation of transformation stating that all believers in Christ have exactly the same status before God and in relation to fellow Christians, Paul in fact reinforces the message of equality with his use of the formula that declares not only Gentile and Jew, but slave and free, male and female to be all one in Christ. Paul considered the abolitions of such distinctions to apply to relationships in this world as well as before God. The question here is: how can Paul's ethics interrogate the alarming violence against women regardless of their status in society, their culture, colour and sexual orientation? This may require an exploration into the egalitarian potential of Galatians 3:28.

8.4. PAUL'S EGALITARIAN ETHICS GROUNDED IN THE ETHIC OF CHRISTIAN FREEDOM

8.4.1. "Christ has set us free for freedom"

Both equality and human freedom were not experienced realities for the majority of people in South Africa. The new-found civil freedom that came along with the new South African dispensation caught the nation off guard and it is argued that most South Africans were not equipped for the novelties and civil liberties offered by such a sophisticated constitution.

Paul's view of freedom definitely impacted upon his ethics. Wherever freedom was encouraged, trouble inevitably flowed as was the case in Galatia and Corinth. The conflicts over freedom were one of the crucial debates in Paul's life. His theology of freedom is real, pervasive and extremely important. If Jesus preached freedom and following him means freedom then Paul, says Richardson (1979:166), claimed that freedom. Not only did he claim it for himself, but he claimed it on behalf of the churches he founded.

According to Richardson (1979:166) Paul's freedom poses an enormous challenge to Christians today. We cannot afford to apply Paul's understanding of freedom in a one-sided manner. As Paul's view of freedom is a reinterpretation of the Old Testament in the light of Jesus and the Holy Spirit, so too should we today be the interpreters of Paul's freedom and apply it appropriately and intelligently to changing circumstances. Richardson (1979:168) calls this "hermeneutical freedom", which is the freedom to take development and change in Scripture as indicative of the freedom to apply the word of the Lord to specific circumstances in life. Hermeneutical freedom, interacting with Paul's view of freedom, allows Christians to transcend years of injustice and oppression for a completely liberated view of all who are oppressed. South Africa is experiencing the rise and fall of "situation ethics". In the light of this Christians are called to give serious attention to the notion that allows for genuine freedom expressed in concern for others, heed to the dominant principle of love in the building of a nation. A case in question is the abuse of freedom in South Africa that results in gross personal and corporate irresponsibility and corruption. How would South Africans' life style be shaped if they lived by the assurance that "Christ has set us free for freedom"? How can this tenet avert the harrowing abuse and disregard of the virtue of freedom in South Africa social and civil circles?

8.4.2. Civil freedom and corruption

Corruption and self-aggrandizement appears to be the rule of the day both in society and various government departments. The previous Apartheid regime set a high standard of living for the privileged section of society and many South Africans are of opinion that having obtained unconditional human rights implies living beyond one's personal income and means so as to come on par with affluent neighbours.

Though much contemporary corruption is inherited from the past, the simultaneous democratization and restructuring of the South African state is very vulnerable to new forms of abuse in different locations. Corruption is stimulated by new official practices and fresh demands imposed upon inexperienced bureaucrats including discriminatory political solidarity and the expansion of citizen entitlements. The extent of corruption had reached such alarming proportions in South Africa that the state called for the creation of a forum that would take responsibility for the *moral regeneration* of society. This call for the *moral regeneration of South Africa* seems to be intimately linked with former president Mandela's call for a 'reconstruction and development programme of the soul'. The rationale behind it was to put up a morally effective fight against corruption. However, the person that was placed at the head of this forum, the then vice-president of the country, Jacob Zuma, was himself guilty of gross immoral behaviour related to corruption and fraud. This rendered the forum a failure even before it could come into being. When it comes to individual moral failings such as greed and a proclivity to self-enrichment within a context of declining morals and values, the big question is: where and how should interventions be introduced, especially when measures to improve ethics are seen as the soft side of anti-corruption controls?

There are many reasons cited for the corruption in South Africa. Some claim that it can be attributed to the nature of the transition to democracy. In the changeover to democracy South Africa did not experience a true revolution, but a managed transition and by so doing the state with all its inequalities remained intact and the private sector was largely left untouched. During the transition period the so-called crony capitalists and the opportunists, who had exploited and benefited by the conditions created by apartheid to make vast amounts of money, just continued on their lucrative capitalist train and to justify their position, and to appease the country's sentiment of affirmative action, they went to work to capture and create a new black elite in order to protect their own financial interests. This all took place under the umbrella of "Black empowerment". While this benefited the privileged few it served as convincing window dressing, since the poor remained on the lower end of the social-economic strata.

In trying to determine the causes of corruption in South Africa the question was asked by an "Expert Panel Survey"[8] of 2001 whether South Africans are inherently corrupt, self-enriching, greedy and opportunistic. According to Johnson[9], quoted in the report, a society is generally corrupt when there are entrenched fraudulent features such as:

- low political competition;
- low and uneven economic growth;
- a weak civil society; and
- an absence of institutional mechanisms to deal with corruption.

He claims that the less developed political parties are, the more prevalent corruption appears to be. In contrast, those societies which are relatively free of corruption are premised on respect for civil liberties; they lay claim to an accountable government; a wide range of economic opportunities and structured political competition. These are mainly, but not exclusively, characteristics of developed western states.

However, corruption tends to increase in a period of rapid growth and modernization, because of changing values, new sources of wealth and power, and the expansion of government. Johnson (1996:321-335) continues by saying that there tends to be less corruption in countries with more social stratification, more class polarization and more feudal tendencies. These conditions provide a more articulated system of norms and sanctions, which reduces both the opportunity for and the attractions of corrupt behaviour. In addition he states that a country's ratio of political to economic opportunities affects the nature of corruption. If the former outweigh the latter, then people enter politics in order to make money, which will lead to a greater extent of corruption. If foreign business is prevalent, corruption also tends to be promoted.

---

8   A survey was conducted in 2001 to establish public opinion on the Causes of and Conditions for Corruption. The results of the Expert Panel Survey was published in Monograph No 65 September 2001

9   M Johnston, The search for definitions: The vitality of politics and the issue of corruption, International Social Science Journal 49, 1996, pp 321-335.

The respondents to the *Expert Panel Survey* provided a wealth of different answers as to the main causes of corruption in South Africa. According to the survey public opinion suggested convincingly that political and social corruption is entrenched in South Africa. The responses had been grouped into five categories for purposes of analysis. The most commonly cited reason for corruption in South African society was:

> a decline in morals and ethics accounting for nearly a third (31%) of responses. This was followed by greed and the desire for self-enrichment (25%); then the socio-economic conditions such as poverty and unemployment (18%). Institutional reasons such as weak checks and balances accounted for more than a tenth (14%) of the responses, followed by the apartheid legacy and the process of transformation (12%)

When asked about the causes of corruption in government, similar reasons were cited to those perceived in society. However, these were prioritized slightly differently by the experts.

> Weak checks and balances together with mismanagement were the most common reasons given (38%) as the main causes of corruption in government. Greed and self-enrichment were again ranked second, accounting for 28% of responses. The general decline in morals and ethics was the next most common cause (17%) followed by the legacy of apartheid (9%) and socio-economic conditions (8%).

In summary to the question as to what the causes are of corruption in South African society, experts cited: declining morals and ethics, greed, socio-economic conditions, weak checks and balances and political transformation; whereas corruption in government was seen to be more concerned with weak internal controls and systems, and mismanagement, followed by greed and a decline in morals and ethics.

These variations suggest a differentiated response to the control of corruption. They suggested that measures to address the causes of corruption in government therefore have to be aimed more at improving systems and controls rather than influencing individual or social morality. In addition they suggested that it would do no harm to improve the professional ethics of those working in government. However, it cannot be assumed that the ethicists approach to public service reform is sufficient in preventing corruption since more fundamental interventions are required from an early age to promote morals and values that uphold the values enshrined in the Constitution.

How, where and when these underlying causes of corruption be addressed was a task allotted to the then deputy-president and now president of the country. Jacob Zuma was tasked to bring the moral regeneration forum into being and invited Church leaders and various other social leaders of moral standing to assist in forming such a forum. The aim of this forum was to put measures in place that would assist the average South African to become a responsible and accountable citizen of South Africa. Thus there was appeal to be guided by religion, the law, the Bible and the Church. However, the deputy-president himself was guilty of gross corruption practices and it was suggested that before he heads such a forum he should lead by example and personally undergo moral rehabilitation programmes which would steer himself and citizens towards mutual respect, accountability and responsibility.

Accountability in the new dispensation of South Africa is an ethical challenge of enormous proportions and the evidence thereof is obvious among all sectors of society. Accountability, says Leander E. Keck (1996:2), implies living responsibly and taking commitment seriously and acts judiciously: "the accountable self is vulnerable to a verdict by someone authorized to render it". Keck continues by stating that accountability implies an "acknowledged authority structure in which the self knows that it owes an account and expects a response (1996:2). He states that accountability is usually reciprocal between equals and if the authority structures are accepted, then accountability is neither irrational nor onerous or intolerable. Somehow there is a difference towards accountability which is oriented toward an impersonal system, law, ideal or cause. It is precisely in this regard that this research questions whether the Christian ethics of Paul as presented to the Galatians can make any significant and substantial contribution towards the moral formation and regeneration of all South Africans.

According to Paul's letters the Gentiles were as accountable to God as the Jews despite the fact that they (the Gentiles) lacked Moses or the Law (Rom. 3:19). The Law for the Gentiles is written in their hearts confirmed by the phenomenon of conscience which will condemn and defend them until the day of God, the judge of secret thoughts and emotions will come (Rom. 2:14-16). Paul's persistent concern with the moral life of his readers is simply because he assumes that they are accountable to God for their behaviour. Paul's moral reasoning is not only oriented towards the Law, towards impersonal principles such as ideals, virtues, but towards the person of Christ and to the presence of the Spirit since for Paul to live ethically is to be "led by the Spirit" (Gal. 5:18) and this implies being accountable to the Spirit and the Giver of the Spirit, Jesus Christ. The one to whom Paul is accountable is the "Living God" who was revealed to him by the Son of God (Gal. 1:15); the one who lives in Paul and in whom Paul lives (Gal. 2:20). Since Paul sees himself as accountable to the Lord, this determines the quality of his discipleship and moral life. As Paul's understanding of what it means to be an accountable Christian transcends the limitations of his personal context, his ethics are still relevant and can be a means of instruction for the realization of accountability in all areas of life in South Africa. Keck (1996:11) claims that to be instructed by Paul's ethics is to appropriate into one's self-understanding those elements of his thinking that were not peculiar to his apostolic office but remain basic to Christian existence and its morality.

While there are various ways of developing an understanding of accountability and thus countering corruption, this research is of opinion that what is theologically implicit in Paul can be made explicit in South Africa today. We are still accountable to God, one's neighbour, self, the environment and in the secular sense to one's country. For Paul, however, loyalty to God is the non-negotiable starting point and guiding factor in developing an accountable moral self.

8.4.3. Deconstructing corrupt power-based leadership

Since 1996 the new political dispensation of South Africa has implemented a policy called "affirmative action" which functions as a "corrective action" whereby previously disadvantaged people are given first preference to occupy important positions in government, civil and business departments. This was supposed to serve as a transformative measure to redress the inequalities of the past. Unfortunately incompetence and uncertainty on behalf of those who have been placed in positions of authority and responsibility resulted in ineffective and unskilled services which proved destructive to the well-being of people and country. The so-called "affirmative action policy" set many people up for failure and corrupt practices. Instead of restoring the balance of equality, another form of oppression came into being whereby the poor and vulnerable are exploited and robbed of their human rights and essential services. Instead of empowering the previously disadvantaged, corrupt power-bases resulted in depriving people of basic civil services. Monies meant for municipal services, housing, fixing roads, hospitals, schools and public security are siphoned away into the pockets of dishonest and incompetent leaders.

The frantic clamour for high positions in leadership infiltrated all areas of life: social, economic, political, academic and church since this attraction provided the materialistic and self-serving leaders with a false sense of status and avaricious economic gain. The current president of South Africa, Mr Jacob Zuma, was prosecuted for fraud over a multimillion dollar 1999 arms deal. Regardless of the mountain of evidence that was hailed against him, he was still exonerated. This left him free to participate in the presidential election. While this was regarded by many as dishonourable and an abuse of democracy, very little was done about it since he is the president of the ruling party and their tolerance level for corruption appears to be very high. By the proverbial silence it appears that the electorate had become either active promoters or beneficiaries of the corrupt state of affairs or complacent and cooperative victims. Similarly the Black Economic Empowerment (BEE) strategy, charged with the objective of enhancing the participation of the previously disadvantaged black citizens in the economy, also succumb to objectionable abuse. They are frequently condemned for providing partisan treatment to wealthy black elites in connection with government people. Since corruption does not get solved by speeches at forums, another means has to be consulted to develop a sense of honest and accountable leadership in the life of South Africa.

Appealing to Christian principles for guidelines in the formation of responsible and accountable leaders, it is well to recognize that Paul and the other apostles did not live in an ideal world either, since Paul and his colleagues did not necessarily emerge as "ideal leaders". What Paul did emphasize was that when humans are called to a specific service they should try to accomplish it to the best of their abilities. Paul was fully aware that leaders can be ambiguous, deceitful and sometimes failed in their task hence stating in 1 Cor. 1:26-27, that they should consider their call . . . ; since "God choose the weak in the world to shame the strong . . ." However, in the effort to establish Paul's position regarding leadership and authority, let us say that it is clear from his works that to be a member of the Christ-movement implies exercising leadership not in solitary fashion, but within a team. To be a member of a Christ-movement implies being part of a corporate enterprise, since the image of a "lonely Christian hero" is a flawed image for Christian leadership. As alleged by Kathy Ehrensperger (2007:36) the image of leadership and authority that emerges in Paul is one that forms part of a network of people, closely related and in contact with others, interacting and communicating with them. Paul joined the original network of the Christ-movement (Gal. 1:18-19; 1:23). However, it was clear from the outset that Paul's activity as an apostle was not of a single man, but of a group of people who exercised leadership as a corporate activity.

In Paul's letter to the Galatians he refers to a situation of conflict between himself and other apostles over positions of power and authority. However, Paul makes it quite clear that he is not in competition with other apostles by virtue of the fact that "he is an apostle not from men nor through man, but through Jesus Christ (Gal. 1:1). In addition, he did not receive the Gospel from men but through a 'revelation from Jesus Christ' (Gal. 1:12). Paul does not claim to be superior to the other apostles, but calls for interdependence and for mutual recognition within the apostolic group. Ehrensperger (2007:43) argues that "the emphasis on his own divine call to proclaim the Gospel to the Gentiles seems to demonstrate that the leaders of both groups have come to the mutual recognition that their respective callings have rendered them equals". The need for mutual recognition as equals appears to be important for Paul and this mutual recognition is based on functioning in a community of equals. Despite the fact that Paul started off as a team member and co-worker within the early Christ-movement, he did emerge as one of the prominent members of this movement while having had others that worked in close proximity with him. These co-workers included both male and female members such as Timothy, Titus, Barnabas, Aquila and Prisca (1 Cor. 16:19 and Rom. 16:3). What remained evident in their interaction is that they constantly worked together in a team together with Paul. It is often difficult to establish the dynamic of power between them and Paul since in some respects they were subordinate to him as he sent them out and by so doing they either represented him or they operated as a substitute to him. Whatever the scenario they functioned as apostles equal to Paul.

It appears that within the network of co-workers within the Christ-movement hierarchies did exist, but they appeared not to be static nor "high', but rather fexible and flat (Ehrensperger (2007:54). There were no titles and offices in the Christ-movement. There seems to be no evidence that women were excluded from the group of team-workers in Christ and some were even mentioned as being in leadership, and in such cases there is no trace of any difference in their status due to their gender (Rom. 16:3; 12). Mary, Tryphaina and Persis (Rom. 16:12) were recognized as leaders within the early Christ-movement and Paul shared in this acceptance and appreciation without any reservations. "Thus there are no indications that leadership roles, that is, the exercise of power-over in asymmetrical relationships to communities by women was a cause of concern or problematic within the group of those commissioned, recognized and accepted as being entrusted with special tasks within the movement" (Ehrensperger (2007:55). Since the basis of the relationship between Paul and the communities was that of trust, the asymmetrical relationship was a transformative power, meaning that the purpose of the power exercised was to render it obsolete. In other words, even though Paul referred to himself to be listened to, it is actually Paul's particular aim to empower the Christ-following communities in such a manner that they learnt to live their lives according to the Gospel. In such a power-relationship the aim is to render the leader obsolete so as to remain a member of the community on equal terms. Leadership here amounts to mutual empowerment firmly rooted in Scripture.

To counter the corruption within the South African power-oriented-hierarchal leadership evident in government, religious and cultural circles, it is clear that it is necessary to appeal to a different value system. This appeal is in aid of promoting the transformative aspect of leadership and authority. Appealing to the values of the kingdom could assist in making leadership counter-cultural and trustworthy by challenging corruption and abuse. To employ the values of the kingdom in exercising authority implies deconstructing the dominance and avarice patterns of life. Paul, instead of constructing hierarchies of leadership in the communities that he established, called for the deconstruction of the hierarchies of this world. In Rom. (12:2) he says: "Do not be conformed to this world, but be transformed by the renewing of your minds, so you may discern the will of God . . ." (NRSV). Similarly, to exercise leadership in South Africa that is influenced by Christian values, a demand for the deconstruction of the value system of the new-found dominant materialistic streak has to take place. This implies adhering to the requirements of self-responsibility and the embodiment of the Gospel values. It is believed that trustworthy leadership infused with kingdom values should enhance interdependence, responsibility, accountability and is mutually empowering. To this end Ehrensperger (2007:186) declares that: "The anti-domination dimension of the Gospel is the overarching umbrella under which all the social interactions including those of authority and leadership stand". She argues that it would be contrary to the Gospel to claim authority and leadership according to patterns of domination and control, or any kind of absolute power. If leadership and authority are strictly limited by the characteristics of the message of the Gospel, it implies that hierarchies and leadership cannot be established on a permanent basis, they can only be functional in nature, serving limited purposes for a limited time. The Gospel understanding is that a position of authority is granted only to serve people. Yet numerous superiors today claim that they exercise their power-over subordinates to the best of the latter's interest, by either claiming to know these interests better than those dominated, or by blatantly disguised abusive behaviour as beneficial. This is often the case where people are most vulnerable and dependent on others says Ehrensperger (2007:186).

To be entrusted with leadership and authority according to the Gospel of Christ implies that leadership is only for the benefit and in support of others and in accordance to their needs and well-being (1Cor 12:22; Rom. 14, 15). If leadership of the Christ-movement and that of Paul be recognized as being entrusted with specific authority and exercised in accordance with these parameters, then a leader is not at liberty to exercise authority for personal gain in a dominating or controlling manner. Just as Paul and his contemporaries were not free to introduce leadership values of the elite into their ministry, so too leaders of today who claim to be Christian in ethos are not free to introduce corrupt values into their service. To be respected and accepted as leaders who are worthy of the trust that the community had placed in them means that they cannot lord it over them, cannot impose their own stance on the community, or force the communities into a way of life contrary to their own understanding of the call of the Gospel and the ability to raise their opinions in situations of conflict and debate. This was obvious in Paul's letter to the Galatians.

8.5. INFORMING THE HUMAN CONSCIENCE IN THE LIGHT OF GOSPEL OF FREEDOM

This study is of opinion that civic South Africa can effectively appropriate Paul's ethics to cultivate practical integrity by bringing moral values and norms to bear on policies, human conduct and social and political organization. The Constitution of South Africa, as a legal document, does not possess the power to bring the content thereof to value-based realization. This can be done by reflecting on ideal types of human conduct and social organization, and on the norms and values required to attain these ideals. This is also possible through deliberation on those aspects of social life which impacts negatively on accepted social, moral and religious norms and values, causing harm to, and conflict in, the community. To seek to arrive at social solutions that is in keeping with acceptable moral standards and thus conducive to harmonious and happy social life for all, implies working towards a truly responsible society by providing society with moral ideals and principles of decision-making which forms part of the responsible use of freedom and conscience formation.

Christian freedom was an identifiable and important factor that shaped the early Christian movement and a profitable means of building the Christian character. Paul himself was perceived as the apostle of 'free spirit'. Christianity retains the right to inform people's consciences in the light of Gospel freedom, the freedom for which Christ died. To foster an environment that is bolstered by an informed conscience and freedom, this research recommends that early Christian identity teachings be revisited, so as to provide moral guidance particularly when confronted with dissonant situations. Today *Gaudium et Spes* informs Christians to adhere to their own consciences, to be guided by their own belief systems, and to employ personal responsibility. Ethically it implies that if a person is taught to know right from wrong, that person is "responsible" in the sense of being "accountable". In the Catholic Christian tradition the concepts responsibility, freedom and conscience are inter-related and constituent components of human personhood. To this end *Gaudium et Spes* (16) teaches:

> In the depth of their consciences, human persons detect a law which they do not impose upon themselves, but which holds them to obedience, always summoning them to love the good and avoid evil . . . to obey it is the very dignity of the person . . .

Freedom of conscience is not a super-structure of the personality, but rather the person's essential dynamism towards wholeness. Bernard Häring (1978:224) describes conscience as the human's inner core where "one knows oneself in confrontation with God and with other human beings". In the depth of one's being conscience creates self-awareness, one's personal identity that one's true self is linked with Christ. The fundamental authority of freedom, as abiding by a good conscience, summons one to full humanity and human self-realization or salvation.

As freedom is a constituent factor of being human, the actual deliverances of conscience are profoundly influenced by time and circumstances. Responsibility presupposes freedom and a person can act responsibly only in so far as s/he is free. Karl Rahner, (1969:211) from a calculated theological perspective, defines freedom together with the exercise of freedom as the highest realization of the human person. When a person is deprived of the right to exercise his/her freedom, that person is no longer in a position to realize his or her full humanity. An informed conscience is the result of a disposition of mindfulness. For this reason freedom concerns the whole human person, and Rahner's transcendental theology views the human being as a personal being of transcendence and freedom. This is evident in that the human being is endowed with "infinite horizon", exercised in a spacio-temporal environment. By "infinite horizon" Rahner (1978:32) suggests that the human person has the ability to reach beyond human finiteness and to experience him/herself as transcendent. In describing an individual's transcendental make-up, Rahner refers to the person as spirit. However, he differentiates between human spirit and pure spirit. The human person is not pure spirit, but is transcendent in essence. Freedom is thus described as the concrete datum within the realm of human transcendentality and personhood. Transcendental freedom is the person's ultimate responsibility for his/her own self, not only as knowledge or self-consciousness, but also in an interior disposition (Rahner 1978:35).

Despite the human's corporeal nature in this world, freedom is always actualized in a multiplicity of concrete activities in time and space, history and society. In so far as the human experiences self as person and as subject, it is an experience of self as free in a freedom. The final and definite validity of a person's true self-realization in freedom before God is the fact that the individual accepts the self as it is disclosed in the choice of transcendence, interpreted in freedom. This takes place in the ambience of the human person who is mystery, and who is always in relationship with the ineffable mystery, God. The human person has the choice either to respond to, and turn towards God or to turn away. The totality of freedom is incorporated in what Rahner terms the "fundamental option" which implies the human choice towards the fullness of life. The proper exercising of this option orientates the person towards God and shapes the self towards the good. The human person cannot wish choices away, but will always be burdened with a decision to choose or not to choose God. This amounts to a radical self-realization or a self-refusal with regard to God.

In sum, freedom is always the self-realization of a person making his/her own choices with regard to his/her whole accomplishment before

God. This is brought about by the capacity of the heart for love. The love of God is the only total integration of human existence. It gives content to human dignity, to temporal eternity as well as to the eternity which is born from being present to God (Rahner 1969(a): 215). Human freedom is to be integrated into the sovereign freedom of God. As Rahner (1969(a):217) says "human freedom is free self-realization towards achieving finality". Real freedom must be present in our experience, and the experience of freedom is transcendental. It precedes, governs and is present in the whole of our ordinary experiences. This transcendental freedom is present precisely through the medium of everyday experience: "freedom and responsibility, like self-awareness and personhood, are realities of subjective experience" (O' Donovan 1981:24).

Freedom is who one is, as one creates oneself in time and relationships, the person one has already become and the person one proposes to be in the future. Freedom is therefore not the ability to do this or that, but the power to decide about ourselves and to actualize ourselves. The original freedom of the human person has to do with the whole person as whole person. All decisions about life, vocation, career, and family are only truly free if they mediate or concretize transcendent freedom. The purpose of transcendental freedom is the responsibility to create ourselves in the given circumstances of life and of this world. Only in eternity can human freedom exists as final, complete and fully actualized (O' Donovan 1981:26).

Rahner argues that God is ever present in enhancing freedom, uplifting, consciousness, provoking awe, unrest, questioning and movements of love that lead to a deepening of one's experience of both God and Self. In other words the correct use of freedom is always a choice and a response to grace. This implies that the choice for self-realization, to reach authentic human completeness, is also a human choice. It is never a forced issue and neither coerced by God nor humanity. South Africans on the whole need to strive to embrace the responsibility of civil and moral freedom in order to bring the individual to human self-realization. By embodying Paul's Gospel of Freedom, the "grace in transformative action" can transmit God's call to responsibility and accountability in human development.

8.6. TOWARDS DIASTRATIC UNITY AND EQUALITY: BONDING A DIVIDED PEOPLE

As was already determined, it was lack of unity that was at the heart of the problem in Galatia and in particular social unity. Social inequality together with social disunity is still a concern in South Africa. An original and significant factor of early Christianity was that it brought together men and women from different classes, cultures and races, something that was not part of the general practice of Hellenistic and Judaic societies of the time. As stated by Theissen (1992:214) the inclusive nature of Christianity formed the basis of "a diastratic unity spanning different social classes, but not a representative cross section of society as a whole". While it did not penetrate the imperial classes, nor was it equally distributed in town and country, it was drawn mostly from the lower classes. However, the diastratic cohesion in the early Christian congregations was something new in pagan society: free persons living and socializing side by side with slaves. Despite their different legal status, they were often socially on much the same level. The Christians and the Jewish congregations tried to influence the whole of everyday life with their norms and convictions. They shared meals every week, covered the whole of life, sickness, death, looking after orphans, old people, business transactions and travel arrangements. In this sense Christians of antiquity made a new "social offer" to pagan society namely "diastratic solidarity" (Theissen 1992:214). Christians followed Jewish traditions in this sense that the Jewish congregations also included people from various social ranks such as Roman citizens, resident aliens without civil rights, and foreigners. This diastratic structure of Jewish and Christian congregations in fact encouraged the relativization of status differences, economic social and sexual differences. It is precisely in this context that the earliest Christian congregations have lessons for South Africans on how to overcome Apartheid and establish a new social and political order that addresses divisions. In this sense it is able to make a positive contribution towards the development of solidarity in South Africa by establishing measures and inculcating attitudes that cut across class and race distinctions so as to establish environmentally diastratic unity.

Just as the ancient Christian *Sitz im Leben* has been freed from the situation which hitherto had excluded from it foreigners, slaves and women, this research is of opinion that with mindfulness of the elements of diastratic unity, the type that was envisioned by Jesus and preached by Paul, South African Christians would be in a position to make a contribution towards the creation of a Christianity based on diastratic unity. It is therefore not by mere chance that Paul in Galatians 3:28 named the three categories which were the underprivileged in social life, but who enjoyed equality in the Christian congregations that consisted of Jews and Greeks (foreigners to each other), slaves and free persons as well as women and men (Gal. 3:38). It is this self-definition of Christian equality that forms the basis of diastratic unity. As pointed out by Theissen (1992:218): even if the people of various differences had no place in the political community, they did have a place in the ecclesia of the Lord. Here they enjoyed the freedom of the heavenly Jerusalem (Gal. 4:1). The ethic of equality and freedom hitherto only accessible to the privileged was transformed by implementing the values and norms of Jesus Christ. The transformation was not merely into an internalized "spirituality of the heart" but into the social reality of the Christian congregation. Since the Christian indicative always brings the Christian imperative and since the indicative of the good news brought the imperative, of the Christian ethic, this principle has the potential to function as an operative ethic in establishing diastratic equality and unity in all spheres of life, physically and spiritually. Not only does division contradict the truth of the Gospel of Freedom, but as a distinctive identity characteristic of Christianity it has the potential to make a significant contribution towards transforming South African society into an egalitarian one.

While the Scriptures are replete with texts that appear to sanction violence, demean women, condone slavery, and discriminate against ethnic groups, Christians in South Africa cannot afford not to meet this challenge by using the "liberated hermeneutic" to speak about all divisions and inequalities. By so doing they are to break down the walls of divisions and distrust, to overcome obstacles and prejudices which thwart the proclamation of the Gospel of salvation in the cross of Jesus, the Redeemer of all people.

There is no doubt that unity is essential to the followers of Christ and they should give themselves completely to each other, just as Jesus did. It is more than just friendliness or togetherness, it amounts to perfect oneness: "that they may be one even as we are one" John 17:21. Hence the understanding that all people are to have the oneness of the Divine. Christians, who take their understanding of unity and equality from the Persons of the Trinity, so too should they embark on a diastratic unity and equality that reveal the love and unity of God for all people (I Cor. 12:13; Eph. 1:23).

Using the tenets of Christianity, as presented by Paul to the Galatians, is an attempt to make and keep Christianity authentic and relevant to South Africa; if this is not done the Christian faith will be stifled and killed instead of being relevant and operative. As has been observed, Christianity is not a culture nor a monolithic institution, but a personal message which encounters persons, not superficially but concretely in life situations (Magesa in Okure and Van Thiel 1990:113).

CHAPTER NINE

9. CONCLUSIONS

The early members of the New Jesus-Movement who became Christians discovered a new identity and along with it came new spiritual identity characteristics whereby they learnt to think of themselves as the "holy ones, children of God, slaves of Christ, brothers and sisters" members of the "Body of Christ" a person for whom Christ died. These followers of Christ were repeatedly urged to "exhort", "admonish" and "encourage" one another. Hence Paul's unashamed advice in 1 Thes 2:12 that they "should behave in a manner worthy of the God who calls them".

Having examined the origin of Christian identity characteristics and ethics through the content of Paul's letter to the Galatians, it is well to determine how formative and valuable the particular Christian tenets would be in the formation of the new South African nation. As previously mentioned, Paul's letter to the Galatian community was written during the cultural, religious and social transition of his world in antiquity. It was a transition from an all-exclusive Jewish and Gentile faith environment to an all-inclusive Jewish and Gentile amalgamation. Paul, in proclaiming the establishment of this "new creation", states that the meaning of the old order and its laws no longer "counted for anything" (Gal. 6:15). This research is of convinced opinion that the Christian tenets of Paul's message to the Galatians can be instrumental in constructing a new emerging South African social and religious order whereby constitutional principles, social and religious ethics need not force each other into compromising positions. South Africa is also in a transition phase from a political and social regime that excluded the people of colour towards a society that is all-inclusive, with equality and freedom for all people.

Paul's polemic against the Jewish-Christian opponents, a situation already identified, is a very powerful and attractive measure in support of shaping new communities in the making. The connection between Paul's Judaizing opponents in Galatia and the Christian communities in South Africa, in terms of love, honour and glory, and their carnal understanding of the law and their slavish desire for the rewards that it convey (Riches 2008:3), do indeed have some bearing on the insightful development of the modern South African Christian communities. Theoretically the Constitutional Law of South Africa makes provision to redress the atrocities of racial injustices and oppression, which had left both black and white victims of the system, but the same constitution, does not necessarily alleviate the wounded condition of the spiritual and emotional mutilation of the nation.

This research proposes that the already identifiable Christian characteristics possess the ability or potential to provide the crucial missing link to move from the pathological condition of self-hate to self-love, to religious, cultural and social stability as well as to probity in human relations. The Christian ethics and values need to move where the secular and benevolent ideals of the Democratic Constitution of South Africa cannot provide the solution. The identifiable Christian characteristics of Paul's letter to the Galatians do indeed possess the revolutionary and dynamic potential to undercut the uneasy grip of the secular over the religious values of the Christian communities. It possesses the ability to redress the social malady with theological overtones that caused black South Africans in particular to think of themselves as less than human and to restore their belief in the biblical truth that each person is an image of God and as such possesses infinite and inherent worth regardless of race, colour, creed, gender, orientation and persuasion. The wounded soul of the nation needs assistance to come to the spiritual realization that being created in the divine image is an intrinsic human worth, it is a universal truth and a grace.

By proclaiming the creation of a new order, implying that the old order and its laws no longer 'counted for anything' (Gal. 6:15), is most instrumental in the formation process of the emerging new world-order in South Africa. In this sense, Paul's polemic against the Jewish-Christian opponents serves as a very powerful and attractive measure in support of shaping the new inclusive communities in the making. Reconstructing Paul's arguments and addressing the theological social and cultural questions that arise in the contemporary emerging South African society of today may just be the way forward towards merging traditional cultural and religious values and identity markers with new emerging scenarios.

The primary aim of Paul's writings was to shape the life of Christian communities (Meeks 1986:12). Participants of the Jesus-Movement who subsequently became known as Christians had to discover their identity as Christians by behaving in a certain manner that provided some recognition of what it meant to be a Christian or a follower of Jesus Christ. Paul several times admonished the Christians to behave in a specific manner and in 1 Thess. 2:12 he states that:" . . . you should behave in a manner worthy of the God who calls you". "The history of the early Christian movement can thus be written as the development of "communities of moral discourse" (Meeks 1986:12). Stanley Hauer termed them "communities of character" since they shaped behaviour and character and identity, and in this instance moral character. The moral character of the Christian community in Galatia was addressed by Paul in relation to the circumstances in which they found themselves.

The letter to the Galatians was written in a cultural epoch that is indeed far removed from the present culture of South Africa. Many of the texts cannot just be observed as a repository of established theological conclusions and unquestionable rules for behaviour. This approach, warns Boys (2000:191), will make Bible texts progressively less applicable to many present day situations and people. When texts are irrelevant they are deemed "dead texts" and when texts are used to legitimate activity that goes counter to the Gospel, such as "slavery, homophobia, holy wars, patriarchal domination, anti-Semitism, the conclusion will be reached that Scripture is "dead," and will be laid aside as "unredeemably immoral".

Embracing Christianity implied re-socialization by taking on new values and perceptions of reality. Paul wrote in Romans (12:2), "Do not be conformed to this world, but be transformed by the renewal of your mind". Roman Christians lived in the world of the Roman Empire as well as in their own cultural and religious domains, and these scenarios formed part of their make-up, their mindsets, languages and ways of life. This deep re-socialization was the norm in the Pauline mission circle as well as of the early Christian movement, and this took place within the ambience of the moral admonitions of Paul. This re-socialized moral righteousness was characterized by the Law and religious righteousness characterized by Jesus Christ (Harnack 1996:109).

The world of the early Christians was befuddled with various forms of dualisms and of negativities. Similarly, a substantial part of the mainstream of South Africa is entrenched in various negative forms of dualism and is at the heart of all kinds of national bifurcations which exacerbates the already existing Christian dualisms. Demographics in South Africa are still dualistically designed, e.g., male and female, black or white, rich and poor, local or foreign, indigenous and alien, etc. Very little provision is made for anomalies so as to bring all people into the equation of just being human such as consideration for the multiple shades of skin colours as well as gender variations. As much as the national Constitution claims to make provision for all conventional and societal norms and criteria, it cannot make provision for all variances and thus exclude large number of minorities from the existing demographic criteria. It is imperative that the status quo of dualistic formations may have to be challenged. While the Democratic Constitution of South Africa makes provision for the human rights of all people and rightly so, this very concession of rights is also perpetuating dualistic trends and biases in church, society and cultural circles.

Human rights, alternatively also known as natural rights, carry the understanding that human rights belong to people simply because they are human beings. All human rights are supposed to be protected by Constitutional Law as it guards people's freedom of belief, religion, freedom of expression and association. All diversity and ethical values are supposed to be respected whether it is of race, culture, gender, sexual orientation, ability, geography and or socio-economic status. While these are all noble in themselves there are also other controversial human rights that seem to be contentious feeders for ambivalent social, moral and religious environments and many of these appear to be litigious simply because they are predominantly influenced and controlled by church and cultural norms and principle some of the most contentious human rights are related to gender equality, which includes the entire proliferation of genders; homosexual rights, conferring equal marital privileges on them as on their heterosexual counterparts; termination of pregnancy rights which enable young girls to exercise their reproductive rights from the age of fourteen by choosing to undergo abortion without parental permission, yet at the same time it is against the law in South Africa for a person younger that sixteen to entertain sexual relations since sex before sixteen is regarded as statutory rape and hence a crime. These human rights and many other related ones carry much constitutional and legal weight, but they appear to be situated in direct contrast with some traditional African values, religious, ethical and cultural belief systems. Consequently many people who live in the South African pluralist society find themselves living in a state of ideological, ethical, religious and cultural confusion as their sentiments vacillate from loyalties to family, state and church; from conservatism/liberalism to respectful adherence to cultural and religious norms. This research is of opinion that distinctive Christian identity characteristics should still be able to influence public order and policy precisely because the people of South Africa still claim to be extraordinarily religious in sentiment and outlook. There exists a suspicious sentiment among traditional South Africans that Christian values and norms are under severe threat and do not have a chance of survival in the face of an overarching secular constitution that create ambivalent social and religious scenarios, unless Christian leaders take it upon themselves to dialogue wisely with the underlying benevolent meaning of the Bill of Rights and the statutes of the Democratic Constitution of South Africa.

The ambivalent environments wherein human rights are acknowledged by law and at the same time denied by religious, cultural and social systems, have confused many and have shifted the underlying cultural, religious, political and social certainties and rhythms of South Africans in general. In addition the implementation of the constitution has in many respects weakened and exposed the sometimes ignominious power of the church and culture. This is not necessarily a bad thing as these force Church leaders to reassess the essentials of Christian teachings. Despite the fact that non-racism and non-sexism form the cornerstone of the South African Constitution, church, society and culture are still seriously culpable of using and abusing women and children and hereby perpetuating their inequality, their disadvantage, oppression and suffering. The primary task of Christian tenets is to enable the individual to pave a spiritual and moral route within ambivalent environments and provide guidelines where ambiguous and conflicting systems pull the individual in opposite directions. It is precisely in such obscure scenarios that Christians are required to call upon Christian characteristics to provide guidelines similar to the exactness of Paul in his writings to the Galatians so as to enter into the lives of people in South Africa.

While this research challenges South African Christians to utilize Christian identity marks to assist Christians to become and remain resonant and critical, it also advises biblical scholars and theologians to practice mindfulness by keeping abreast of contemporary environments and developments. This implies keeping the pulse on secular issues that irrupt intensely into religious, moral and cultural domains, thus urging Christianity to act responsibly when engaging with these ambiguous environments and scenarios. The perturbing problem here is: how do responsible biblical and religious scholars engage with dissonant social and political circumstances that comes as the result of providing people basic human rights? What instruments do they use to remain receptive and honest in probing the truth; where are human rights in conflict with natural rights and Christian values or rights? How do they abide by Christian characteristics within an apparent environment fostered by ambivalence and dualism whereby the Church that embraces Christianity teaches one thing and the government makes provision for the total opposite? What is the Christian to do: submit and be persuaded by the status quo and by so doing render biblical and theological discourse irrelevant and obsolete in the face of modern concerns? Would it be a matter of choosing the lesser of two evils or the lesser of two goods? The Church, together with its educators, are also confronted with the uncomfortable challenge to remain either spiritual partners to the implementation of the constitutional human rights or to become an irrelevant, negative presence operating on the sidelines.

This research is of opinion that Christian tenets contain the energy to be a driving force of the principles of Paul and the Jesus-Movement, but to the contrary questions whether theology, religion and the Church can exercise the custody of people's current spiritual and moral development. The Church in South Africa may have to revisit the most basic Christian characteristics and evaluate how relevant they are in modern expressions of life. While this research acknowledges the complexities of such religious and secular predicaments, it nonetheless proposes possible approaches towards conducting biblical-theological discourse in such environments.

This research proposes that South African theologians revise and employ the skillfulness of Paul's ethics and to apply it with close correlation between the indicative and imperative. As has been discussed in chapter six, the imperative constitutes the ethical cutting edge of the indicative and the indicative forms the fundamental and transformative basis of the imperative (du Toit 2006:172). This feature of Paul's paraenesis makes evident how the Word has direct influence on the life of those to whom it is addressed. The Word has the responsibility not only to bolster but, also to inform consciences. To revisit traditional Christian mindsets like that of Paul could help capture the enthusiastic spirit of Paul in reworking ancient Christian identity tenets into relevant theological discourses on contemporary ambivalent environments and developments. If taken seriously the identity features of Paul's ethics should influence the behaviour of those who regard themselves as followers of Christ. Since the identity of Paul's ethics is based on the "truth of the Gospel" (Gal. 2:5) it is that truth that will guide the life style, behaviour and belief systems of Christians.

Using Gal 3:28 as a "Christian self-definition" implies that when one takes on Christianity one must be prepared to be transformed. When according to Fiorenza (1983:217-218) the axiom "no longer male and female" is read and imbibed, it means an end to "structures of dominance" within the Christian community. This verse suggested a new-found understanding of an "egalitarian Christian self-understanding which does away with all male privileges of religion, class and caste, it allows not only Gentiles and slaves, but also women to exercise leadership functions within the missionary movement". It also implies equality in all senses of the term and this implies transformation. In the instance of the equality of female and male in Christ, it corresponds to the fundamental message of the Bible about the relation of the sexes, and in the light of this correspondence the passage about an interior role for women must be interpreted, says Jewett (1975:134), as accommodations to the cultural patterns of the first century. He states:

> To put matters theologically or perhaps we should say hermeneutically, the problem with the concept of female subordination is that it *breaks the analogy of faith*. The basic creation narratives imply the equality of male and female as a human relationship reflecting the fellowship of the Godhead; and Jesus as the perfect man who is truly in the image of God, taught such equality in his fellowship with women so that one may say—must say—that "in Christ there is no male and female." Any view which subordinates the woman to the man and is not analogous to but incongruous with the fundamental teaching of both Old and New Testaments. To affirm that woman, by definition, is subordinate to man, does not correspond to the fundamental radicals of revelation; rather it breaks the analogy of faith (1975:134):

Too often South African Christians had a share in the practices of injustice or totalitarianism which contributed to intolerable situations such as concentration camps, apartheid regimes, starvation and other forms of oppression. In this regard the potential of Paul's egalitarian ethics in the process of building the new South African nation needs to be probed further. The South African cultural and social attitude is in need of formation towards the healing of divisions based on differences by appealing to the egalitarian potential of Gal. 3:28. While people today would be conscious of the contemporary debate concerning the equal rights of both male and female, it may not be all that self-evident in the words of Paul in Galatians 3:28, since as pointed out by Elizabeth Schüssler Fiorenza (1983:205-41), the early Christians may not have had the same issues in mind when they heard the words of Galatians 3:26-29. However, while the social and historical context of Christian exegesis of biblical texts are important when dealing with texts of this nature, it is also of value to examine how this text would be interpreted in modern contexts and shaping the role of women in the Christian community, the church and society.

The Scripture text as the "Word of God" has a deeper and richer meaning than is often ascribed to it (Boys 2000:192). For each Christian the Sacred Scripture is a call to discipleship as well as deepening the sense of Gospel values, but Christians also develop a clearer vision of the moral unacceptability of texts that presume the legitimacy of slavery, sexism, gender violence, homophobia, patriarchy as legitimate. Profound involvement with the truth of the text claims the development of Christian consciousness within the contemporary community of faith which sometimes may require the rejection of biblical subject matter as untrue or immoral. It is however, the ongoing life of the Church which helps us to interpret Scripture.

BIBLIOGRAPHY

Armstrong, A. H.	1980	*The self-definition of Christianity in relation to later Platonism in The problem of self-definition (in Jewish and Christian self-definition. Volume One: The Shaping of Christianity in the Second and Third Centuries.* Edited by E. P. Sanders. Philadelphia: Fortress Press.
Altman, D	1993	*Homosexual oppression and liberation.* New York: New York University Press.
Balch, D.L.	2000	*Homosexuality, Science and the "Plain Sense" of Scripture.* Cambridge, William B. Eerdmans Publishing Company.
Baird, V.	2004	*Sex, Love and Homophobia: Lesbian, Gay, Bisexual and Transgender Lives (A-Z). Amnesty International, U.K.* (Forward: Archbishop D. Tutu).
Bishop, S.	1991	*Green theology and deep ecology: New Age or new creation? Themilios* 16(3):8-14.
Bradley, A B	2010	*Liberating Black Theology: The Bible and the Black experience.* Wheaton, Illinois: Crossway.

Barclay J.M.G.   1988   *Obeying the truth: A study of Paul's ethics in Galatians.* Edinburgh, T & T Clark.

Barclay, W.   The Letters to the Galatians and Ephesians.

Barnett, P.W   1999   *Jesus and the rise of early Christianity: A history of New Testament times.* Illinois: Intervarsity Press.

Barrett C.K.   1999   *Jesus and the rise of early Christianity: A history of New Testament times.* Illinois: Intervarsity Press.

Bauer, W   1971   *Orthodoxy and Heresy in Earliest Christianity.* Mifflintown: Sigter Press.

Betz H.D.   1979   *Galatians: A Commentary on Paul's letter to the churches in Galatia.* Philadelphia: Fortress Press.

Bligh, J.   1970   *Galatians. A discussion of St Paul's Epistle.* London: St Paul's Publications.

Bockmuehl, M   1990   *Revelation and Mystery in ancient Judaism and Pauline Christianity.* Eerdmans Publishing Company.

Bornkamm, G.   1975   *Paul.* London: Hodder and Stoughton.

Boswell, J.   1980   *Christianity, Social tolerance and homosexuality: Gay people in Western Europe from the beginning of the Christian era to the 14th century.* London: University of Chicago Press.

Boyarin, D. 1994 *Body politic among the brides of Christ: Paul and the origins of Christian sexual renunciation. In Asceticism.* New York: Oxford University Press.

Boys, M.C. 2000 Has God only one Blessing? Judaism as a source of Christian self-understanding. New York: Paulist Press.

Bright, L (ed) 1972 *Scripture Discussion Commentary 10 Paul 1: Galatians by Lionel Swain.* London: Sheed and Ward.

Brown, R.E 1997 *An Introduction to the New Testament.* New York: Double Day.

Bruce, C. 1997 Pure Kingdom: Jesus' Vision of God. SPCK Publishing.

Bruce F.F 1982 *The Epistle of Paul to the Galatians: a commentary on the Greek Text.* Exeter: Paternoster Press.

Bruce, F.F. 1983 *The Epistle to the Galatians: New International Greek Testament Commentary.* Michigan: William B. Eerdmans Publishing Company.

Bruce, L.M. 1989 *Christ and the Law in Paul.* New York: E.J. Brill.

Brinsmead, B.H 1982 *Galatians: Dialogical response to opponents.* Chico: Andrews University Scholars Press.

Buckel, J.   1993   *Free to Love. Paul's defense of Christian liberty in Galatians.* Louvain: Peeter's Press.

Buckley, T.W.   1981   *Apostle to the nations: The life and letters of St Paul. A biblical Course.* Boston: Daughters of St Paul.

Burkett, D.   2002   *An Introduction to the New Testament and the origins of Christianity.* Cambridge, University Press.

Caputo, J.D.   1997   *Deconstruction in a nutshell: a conversation with Jacques Derrida.* Fordham University Press.

Cameron, A   1994   Christianity and the Rhetoric of the Empire: the development of Christian discourse. Los Angeles: University of California.

Cock, J.   2004   *Engendering gay and lesbian rights: the equality clause in the South African Constitution.* Johannesburg: University of Witwatersrand, Department of Sociology.

Cameron, A.   1994   Christianity and the Rhetoric of the Empire: the development of Christian discourse. Los Angeles: University of California Press.

Cone, J H   2010   *Looking Back, Going Forward; Black Theology: in Black Faith and Public Talk, Critical essays in James H. Cone's Black Theology and Black Power.* Ed. Dwight N. Hopkins.

Cone, J H   1970   *A Black Theology of Liberation.* New York: Orbis Books. Maryknoll.

Cone, J H   2002   *Heart and Head, Black Theology: Past, Present, Future.* New York: Palgrave.

Cosgrove, C.H.   1988   *The Cross and the Spirit: A study in the argument and theology of Galatians.* Belgium, Louvain: Macon, Georgia.

Danton, D L   1998   *Freeing South Africa: The "Modernization" Male-Male Sexuality in Soweto (pp 3-21) in Cultural Anthropology: American Anthropological Association Vol 13, No 1. Blackwell Publishing, Emory University.*

Davis, C.M.   1995   *The structure of Paul's theology: the truth which is the Gospel.* Lewiston: Mellen Biblical Press.

de Gruchy, J   2006   *Confessions of a Christian Humanist.* London: SCM Press.

De Long, A   2000   *The Loyal Opposition: Struggling with the Church on Homosexuality.* Nashville: Abingdon Press.

de Villiers, PGR   1998   *The New Testament Milieu. In Guide to the New Testament. Vol II.* A.B. du Toit (Editor) Halfway House: Orion Publishers.

De Witt, C B   1998   *Caring for Creation: Responsible Stewardship of God's handiwork.* Michigan:

Den Heyer, C.J.	1993	*Paul, a man of two worlds.* London: SCM Press.
Du Toit, A.B. (ed)	1998	*Guide to the New Testament Vol II: The New Testament Milieu.* Halfway House: Orian Publishers.
Dunn, D.G.	1993	*Theology of Paul's letter to the Galatians.* Cambridge: Cambridge University Press.
Dunn, J. D.G.	2005	*The new perspective of Paul.* Michigan: William B. Eerdmans Publishing Company.
Dunn, J. D.G.		*Jesus, Paul and the Law.* Studies in Mark and Galatians. London: SPCK.
Dunn, J. D.G.	1993	*The Epistle to the Galatians.* London: A & C Black.
Dupuis, J.	1997	*Toward a Christian Theology of Religious Pluralism.* New York, Maryknoll: Orbis Books.
Ebeling, G.	1985	*The truth of the Gospel: An exposition of Galatians.* Philadelphia: Fortress Press
Edwards, D.	2001	*Earth Revealing, Earth Healing: Ecology and Christian Theology.* Maryknoll, New York: Orbis Books.

Ehrensperger, K. 2007 *Paul and the Dynamics of Power: Communication and interaction in the Early Christ-movement.* London: T & T Clark.

Ellis, E.E. 1999 *The making of the New Testament Documents.* Leiden: E.J. Brill Academic Publishers.

Fallon, M. 1989 *The Letters of Paul. A Commentary by M. Fallon.* Eastwood, NSW. Parish Ministry Publications.

Fallon, M. 2004 *New Testament Letters: St Paul, an introductory commentary.* Kensington NSW: Chevalier Press.

Fatum, L. 1991 *Image of God and Glory of Man. Women in the Pauline Congregation in the Image of God. Gender models in Judaeo-Christian Tradition.* Minneapolis: Fortress Press.

Ferguson, E. Scholer, 1993 *Studies in early Christianity. A of*
D.M. Finney, P.C. *scholarly Essays.* New York: Garland Publishing House.

Fiorenza-Schüssler, E. 1983 *In Memory of Her: a feminist theological reconstruction of Christian origins.* London: SCM Press.

Furnish, V.P. 1968 *Inside looking out: Some Pauline views of the Unbelieving public. In Pauline conversations in context: essays in honour of Calvin J. Roetzel.* Ed Janice Capel Anderson / Philip Sellew Claudia Setzer. London: Sheffield Academic Press.

Furnish, V.P.	1979	*The Moral Teaching of Paul.* Nashville, Abingdon.
Furnish, V.P.	2000	*Theology and Ethics in Paul.* Nashville: Abingdon.
Gager, J.G.	2000	*Reinventing Paul.* Oxford: University Press
Gager, J.G	2000	*Kingdom and Community: the social world of early Christianity.* New Jersey: Englewood Cliffs: Prentice Hall 1975.
Garner H and M Worsnip	2001	*Oil and water: The impossibility of Gay and Lesbian Identity in the Church in "Towards an Agenda for Contextual theology"* Ed. Speckman McGlory T. Kaufmann Larry T. Pietermaritsburg: Cluster Publications.
Goppelt, L. & Block, Adam and Charles	1970	*A history of the Christian Church. Apostolic and Post-Apostolic times.* London: SCM Press.
Graves-Brown, P. Jones, S. Gamble, C. (eds)	1996	*Cultural Identity and Archaeology. The construction of European Communities.* London: Routledge.
Hansen, G.W	1994	*Galatians.* Illinois: Intervarsity Press.
	1996	*What is Christianity?*
Haring, B	1978	*Free and Faithful in Christ.* Vol 1. Middelgreen, Slough: St Paul Publications.

Harris, B.   2002   *Xenophobia—A new pathology for a*
                                new South Africa in Psychology and
                                Social Prejudice. Hook, D and Eagle,
                                G (ends) p 169-184. Cape Town:
                                University of Cape Town Press.

Hengel, M.   1974   *Judaism and Hellenism: Studies in*
                                their encounter in Palestine during the
                                Early Hellenistic Period. Vol 1 Vol 2.
                                London: SCM Press.

Hengel, M.   1980   *Jews and Greeks and Barbarians.*
                                Aspects of the Hellenization of Judaism
                                in the pre-Christian period. London:
                                SCM Press.

Hengel, M.   1995   *Studies in early Christianity. A of*
                                scholarly Essays. Edinburgh: T and
                                T Clark.

Hengel, M. & Barrett   1999   *Conflicts and challenges in early*
C.K (Editor D.A   *Christianity.*   Harrisburg,
Hagner)   Pennsylvania: Trinity Press.

Hessel, D T   1996   *Theology for Earth Community. A field*
                                Guide. Maryknoll: Orbis Books.

Hessel, D.T and   2001   *Earth Habitat; eco-injustice and the*
Rasmussen, L,   *Church's response.* Minneapolis:
                                Fortress Press.

Hogan, P.N.   2008   *No Longer male and Female. Interpreting*
                                Gal. 3:28 in early Christianity. London:
                                T & T. Clark.

Janowitz, N.   2000   *Rethinking Jewish Identity in Late*
                                Antiquity. London: Duckworth.

Jewett, R. 1971 *Paul's Anthropological Terms.* AGAJU 10: Leiden: Brill. E.J.

Johnson, E. 1996 *She who is: the mystery of God in a feminist theological discourse.* New York: Crossroad. (1992).

Jones, S. 1996 *Discourses of Identity in the interpretation of the Past* (in *Cultural Identity and Archaeology. The construction of European Communities.* London: Routledge).

Keck, L. 1996 *Accountable Self: Theology and ethics in Paul. Essays in honour of Victor Paul Furnish.* Nashville, Abingdon Press.

Kee, A 2006 *The rise and demise of Black Theology.* Ashgate: Publishing Ltd, Burlington.

Kee, A 2005 *"The criticism of (Black) Theology is transformed into the Criticism of Politics"—Karl Marx in The Quest for Liberation and Reconciliation.* Editor: M. Battle. Louisville, Westminster John Knox Press: Oxford University Press.

Koester, C. R 1989 *God's purposes and Christ's saving work according to Hebrews in Salvation in the New Testament: perspectives in Soteriology.* Ed. J.G. van der Watt. Leiden: Boston Brill 2005.

Kummel, W.G. 1973 *The New Testament: The History of the investigation of its problems.* London: SCM Press.

Lambrecht, J.   2001   *Collected Studies in Pauline Literature and on the book of Revelation.* (Editrice Pontifico Istituto Biblico) Roma: Analecta Biblica.

Lieu, J.M.   2004   *Christian Identity in Jewish and Graeco-Roman World.* Oxford: University Press.

Lovering, E.H. &   1996   *Theological ethics in Paul and his interpreters.* Nashville: Abingdon Press.
Sumney, J.L.

Lightfoot, J.B.   1962   *The Epistle to the Galatians.* Michigan: Grand Rapids; Zondervan Publishing House.

Mac Donald, D.R.   1987   *There is no male or female.* Philadelphia: Fortress Press.

Magesa, L. (in Okure   1990   *Articles evaluating Inculturation of Christianity in Africa.* Kenya: Amecea Gaba Publications.
T and Van Thiel, P)

Malan, F.S.   2006   *Unity of love in the Body of Christ* in *Identity, Ethics and Ethos in the New Testament* (Ed. Jan G. van der Watt; assisted by F.S. Malan. Berlin; New York: Walter de Gruyter.
Malina, B.J.   2001

                               The New Testament world: insights from cultural Anthropology. Louisville, Kentucky: John Knox Press.

Maritain, J.   1964   *Saint Paul: Selections of his writings.* New York: McGraw-Hill Book Company.

Martin, B.L.   1989   *Christ and the Law.* Leiden: E.J. Brill.

Martyn, J.L.   1997   *Crucial event in the History of the Law (Gal 5:4) in Theology and ethics in Paul and his interpreters: essays in honour of V. P. Furnish.* Nashville: Abingdon Press.

Matera, F.J.   1989   *Galatians: Sacra Pagina Vol 9.* Collegeville, Minnesota: The Liturgical Press.

Markus, R.A.   1980   *The problem of self-definition (in Jewish and Christian self-definition. Volume One: The Shaping of Christianity in the Second and Third Centuries.* Edited by E. P. Sanders. Philadelphia: Fortress Press.

Meeks, W.A.   1973   *"The Image of the Androgyne: some uses of the symbol in earliest Christianity".* HR 13 (1974) 165-208. New Haven: Yale University Press.

Meeks, W.A.   1986   *The Origins Christian Morality: The first two centuries.* New Haven: Yale University Press.

Meeks, W.A.   1987   *The moral world of the First Christians.* London: SPCK

Montague, G.T.   1966   *The living thought of Saint Paul; an introduction into Pauline theology through intensive study of key texts. Contemporary College Theological Series.* San Francisco: Bancroft—Whitney.

Morland, K.A.   1995   *The Rhetoric of curse in Galatians: Paul confronts another Gospel.* Atlanta Georgia: University Press.

Morris, L.   1996   *Galatians: Paul's charter of Christian Freedom.* Leicester Intervarsity Press.

Morris, A.   1998   *"Our fellow Africans make our lives hell".* *The lives of Congolese and Nigerians living in Johannesburg, Ethnic and Racial studie*s, 21 (6) 1116-1136.

Motlhabi, M   2008   *African Theology/Black Theology in South Africa: Looking Back, Moving On.* Pretoria: Unisa Press.

Motlhabi, M   1973   *"Black theology and Authority" in Black Theology: The South Africa voice.* (Ed. Basil Moore). London: C Hurst and Co.

Murphy O Connor, J.   1996   Paul, A Critical Life. Oxford: Clarendon Press.

Nadar, S   2009   *Towards a feminist missiological agenda: a case study of Jacob Zuma rape trial. In Missionalia:* Southern African Journal of Missiology. Vol 37 No 1 April 2009.

Nanos M.D.   2001   *The irony of Galatians: Paul's letter in first century context.* Minneapolis: Fortress Press

Neill, S.   1964   *The interpretation of the New Testament 1861-1961.* London: Oxford University Press

Nel, J.A. and Judge, M	2008	*Exploring homophobic victimization in Gauteng, South Africa: issues, impacts and Responses in Acta Criminologica 21* (3) p 19-36.
Nel, J. A. and Kruger, D J	1999	*From policy to practice; exploring victim empowerment initiatives in South Africa.* Pretoria: Council of Scientific and Industrial research.
Newsome, J.D.	1992	*Greeks, Romans and Jews: Currents of Culture in the New Testament World.* Philadelphia: Trinity Press.
Neyrey, J.H.	1990	*Paul, in other words, a Cultural Reading of his letter.* Westminster: John Knox Press.
O Neill, J.C.	1972	*The recovery of Paul's letter to the Galatians:* London:
Price, J.L.	1987	*The New Testament: Its History and Theology.* New York: Macmillan Publishing Company: London Collier Macmillan.
Puskas, C.B.	1993	*The Letters of Paul. An introduction.* Minnesota, Collegeville: Liturgical Press.
Ramsey, W.M.	1965	A Historical Commentary on St Paul's Epistle to the Galatians. Michigan: Grand Rapids.
Radford-Reuther, R.	1998	*Religion and Sexism: Images of women in the Jewish and Christian traditions.* Simon and Schuster.

Rahner, K. 1969 *Grace and freedom.* New York: Herder and Herder.

Richards, H. 1979 *St Paul and his epistles: A new introduction.* London: Darton, Longman and Todd.

Richardson, P 1979 *Paul's Ethic of Freedom.* Philadelphia: The Westminster Press.

Riches, J. 2008 *Galatians throughout the Centuries: Blackwell Bible Commentaries.* Blackwell Publishing.

Ridderbos, H. 1977 *Paul: An outline of his theology.* London: SPCK.

Robertson, J 2005 *Same-sex cultures and sexuality: an anthropological reader.* Blackwell Publishing.

Robinson, J.M. & Koester, H. 1971 *Trajectories through early Christianity.* Philadelphia: Fortress Press.

Robinson, T.A. 1988 *The Bauer thesis examined: the geography of heresy in the early Christian Church.* Lewiston, New York: E. Mellen Press.

Rosner B.S. 1994 *Paul, Scripture and Ethics: A study of 1 Cor. 5:7.* Leiden, New York: E.J. Brill.

Rossano-Cazelles, P. 1981 *Commission Biblical Pontifical: On "inculturation" in the New Testament.*

| Sanders, C J | 1995 | *Empowerment ethics for a liberated people. A path to African American Social Transformation.* New York: Fortress Press. |

Sanders, E.P.(Editor) — 1980 — *Jewish and Christian Self-definition.* London: SCM Press.

1980 — *Vol 1: The shaping of Christianity in the second and third centuries.* London: SCM Press.

Sanders E.P. & Baumgarten, M (Editors) — 1981 — *Vol 2: Aspects of Judaism in the Graeco-Roman World.* London: SCM Press.

Sanders E.P. & Meyer E. F (ed) — 1982 — *Vol 3: Self-definition of the Graeco-Roman World.* London: SCM Press.

Sanders, E.P. — 1987 — *Paul, the Law and the Jewish people.* Philadelphia:Fortress Press.

Sanders, E.P. — 1992 — *Judaism: Practice and Belief 63 BCE-66 CE.* London: SCM Press.

Santmire, H P, — 1976 — *Ecology, Justice and Theology: Beyond the Preliminary Skirmishes in Christian Century. May 12, 1976, p 460-464.—Religion on line—*Ted and Winnie Brook.

Schiffman, L Seeberg, A — 1903 — *At the Crossroads: Tannaitic perspectives on the Jewish-Christian schism. Vol 2.*

Schwartz, R.　　　　1997　　*The Curse of Cain: The violent legacy of Monotheism.* Chicago: University Press.

Smiles, V.M　　　　1991　　*The Gospel and the Law in Galatia: Paul's response to Jewish-Christian separatism and the threat of Galatian Apostasy.* Michigan: University Microfilms International

Smith, D.　　　　2004　　*The rose has thorns. Presentation at the Annual General Meeting of Out-LGBT. Well-Being, June 18.*

Sparks, K.L.　　　　1998　　*Ethnicity and Identity in Ancient Israel Prolegomena to the study of Ethnic Sentiments and their expression in the Hebrew Bible.* Winona Lake, Indiana: Eisenbrauns.

Stacey, W.D.　　　　1956　　*The Pauline View of Man: In relation to its Judaic-Hellenistic background.* London: Macmillan and Co Ltd.

Stegemann, E.W. &　　1999　　*The Jesus-Movement: A Social history of its first century.* Minneapolis: Fortress Press.
Stegemann W.

Taylor, C.　　　　1989　　*Sources of the Self. The making of modern identity.* Minneapolis: Fortress Press.

Teeple, H.M.　　　　1992　　*How did Christianity really begin? A Historical Anthropological Approach.* Evanston: Religion and Ethics Institute Publication.

Theissen, G. 1982 *The Social Setting of Pauline Christianity.* Philadelphia: Fortress Press.

Theissen, G. 1992 *Social Reality and the early Christians: Theology, Ethics and the world of the New Testament.* Minneapolis: Fortress Press.

Tolmie, D.F. 2006 *Exploring the rhetorical approaches to Galatians* (In Van Der Watt).

Tshitereke, C 1999 *Xenophobia and relative deprivation. Crossings, 3 (2), 4-5.*

Tshitereke, C 2008 *"South Africa's Xenophobic attacks".* Editorial City Press: May 19, 2008.

Tshitereke, C 2009 *Protests scattered across South Africa in 2008 began as demonstration.* In Mail and Guardian on line. July 25, 2009.

Van Der Watt, J 2006 *Identity, Ethics and Ethos in the New Testament* (Ed. Jan G. van der Watt; assisted by F.S. Malan. Berlin; New York: Walter de Gruyter.

Viviano, B. T. 1988 The Kingdom of God in History, Good News Studies. Wilmington, Delaware: Michael Glazier.

Von Harnack, A 1996 What is Christianity? Nabu Press

Weiss, J 1959 *Earliest Christianity: A history of the period AD 30-150 Vol 1&2.* New York: Harper and Brothers.

Williams, Sam.K   1997   *New Testament Commentaries: Galatians.*
                                  Nashville: Abingdon Press.

Wills, L.M.   1977   *The Quest of the Historical Gospel: Mark,*
                                  John and the origins of the Gospel Genre.
                                  New York: Routledge.

Witherington, B.   1998   *The Paul Quest: The renewed search for*
                                  the Jew of Tarsus. Illinois: Intervarsity
                                  Press.